Silenced

ALSO BY ROSIE LEWIS

ROSIE LEWIS

Silenced

**The shocking true story of a
young girl too afraid to speak**

HarperElement
An imprint of HarperCollins*Publishers*
1 London Bridge Street
London SE1 9GF

www.harpercollins.co.uk

HarperCollins*Publishers*
1st Floor, Watermarque Building, Ringsend Road
Dublin 4, Ireland

First published by HarperElement 2022

3 5 7 9 10 8 6 4

A catalogue record of this book is
available from the British Library

ISBN 978-0-00-853842-2

Printed and bound in the UK using 100%
renewable electricity at CPI Group (UK) Ltd

MIX
Paper from
responsible sources
FSC™ C007454

To my children;
I love you to the moon and back.

Confidentiality

My main consideration when sharing my experience of fostering is to protect the identity of the children I care for. That's why some details in the following case have been changed, as well as names and locations. The rest is a true account of my time with the Powell family.

I shy away from using the word 'evil' because we're all a product of many factors over which we have little or no control. The abuse in this case, however, was so calculated and sadistic that it's hard to think of any other way to describe it, or to find empathy in my heart for the perpetrator.

One of the lessons I've learned in the last two decades of fostering is that abused children are often highly skilled at masking their pain. I hope that by shining a light into dark places we'll get better at recognising the tell-tale signs of a child in crisis. It's nice to think that this insight might also inspire some readers to embark on their own fostering journey.

Fostering has its challenges but the wonderful young people who have come through our door over the years have changed our lives immeasurably for the better.

Chapter One

The book flies through the air, seemingly out of nowhere.

I dodge out of the way, thinking for one disorientating moment that I'm the intended target. Shrinking behind the straggly bush growing over the Powells' front gate, I tighten my coat around myself and squint up at the small terraced house in front of me. A curtain shivers at the open first-floor window. Another book shoots through the gap. It hits the slush-covered pavement with a thud, quickly followed by a yellow plastic truck.

Raised voices reach my ears. My heart quickens as a tall figure flits into view. A series of low thumps follows.

The scant details in the profile I've been given about the family on the other side of the walls come to mind as my eyes run over the rusted guttering and peeling paintwork.

Two-year-old Louis is first to my thoughts. I hope he's nowhere near the gaping window. He and his siblings, Bartley, ten, nine-year-old Caitlin and Ethan, six, had been identified as children in need (CIN) a couple of years ago, after Bartley lashed out at his sister so violently that she needed treatment in A&E.

A child 'in need' is a replacement of the old 'at risk' term that was seen by many as pejorative. Children are classified as CIN if a family assessment reveals that their development is likely to be impaired without targeted intervention. Social services have a duty to safeguard and promote the welfare of CIN with the external provision of services.

It doesn't always work, and in the Powells' case a recent crisis brought everything to a head. Two nights ago, police received an anonymous tip-off that the children had been left home alone. Their mother, Bonnie Powell, was sectioned under the Mental Health Act after being found wandering the icy late-February streets half-dressed and stoned in the early hours.

Julie and Ryan Chambers, Bonnie's mother and stepfather, quickly stepped into the breach, but supervision has been deemed necessary while they are assessed as kinship carers.

Cue a specialist foster carer from the recently implemented Mockingbird scheme. Besides offering social workers a window into how well the Powells function as a family, my task is to offer non-judgemental support to Julie and Ryan while they adjust to their new responsibilities. Signposting them to services that might help them negotiate the tricky weeks ahead and acting as a single point of contact with social services will hopefully aid communication. By reducing pressure on the family, we're mitigating the risk of the children coming into full-time care. That's the idea anyway, provided I can make it safely into the house, that is.

When I've reassured myself that there are no further missiles in-flight, I pick my way cautiously over the books and toys littering the front path. I'm about to knock on the door when a scowling, ferrety-looking man yanks it open. He slams it to a close just as he registers my presence. 'Fuck!' he says. We blink at each other in surprise, then he mutters an apology and stamps off down the path.

I ring the doorbell, wondering whether I've just met Ryan Chambers. Whoever it was, they've left a pungent smell of cannabis behind. My heart flutters as I smooth down my unruly blonde and grey curls and blink a few stray flakes of snow out of my eyes.

Ever since I began task-based fostering almost two decades ago, I've felt a mixture of anxiety and excitement at the prospect of taking on a new placement. It's 2019 and just one week into my new role on the special scheme designed to keep struggling families together, I'm wary of what might be awaiting me on the other side of the door. I feel vulnerable, and my stomach twists at the clatter of approaching footsteps. It's a valuable insight into the minds of the children I foster, waiting on the doorstep to meet their temporary guardian for the first time, when all that's familiar has been stripped away.

As soon as the door opens and I catch sight of Julie Chambers, however, my nerves fall away.

Almost a foot taller than me and slim in a fitted blouse and black jeans, the children's grandmother smiles warmly as she invites me into the narrow hall. There's no outward sign of the strain she must be under with her daughter in hospital and four extra children to care for.

'Carnage,' she says, when I glance over my shoulder at the pock-marked lawn. 'You've taken your life in your hands coming to this place, Rosie.' Her kohl-lined, big blue eyes shine with amusement.

I laugh, already warming to her. I make a guess that she's around my age, but she's far less 'mumsy' than me, with her glowing tan, rows of bangles on each wrist and long, remarkably straight brown hair. 'Lively morning?'

'Oh, a hundred per cent.' She raises a hand to her forehead, bangles tinkling. 'They've just had a scuffle over – you know what? I don't even remember now.' She booms a laugh. 'Can I get you a drink? Oh, this is my youngest, by the way,' she says, as a girl with long, sandy-coloured hair breezes down the stairs. 'Linzi, babe, this is Rosie.'

'Hi,' Linzi says brightly, raising her hand in a casual half-wave. I read about the Powell children's young auntie on the family profile, born just a few months after Julie's eldest daughter, Bonnie, had her first child. 'I'll make it, Mum.' Almost my height in the fluffy pink-heeled slippers she's wearing, she gives me a confident smile. 'Tea, coffee?'

'Oh, tea with milk would be lovely.'

'Sure.' Slightly overweight, Linzi clops heavily down the hall.

'What a treasure!' Julie calls after her. She bustles me down the hall and into a very messy living room. 'She's still at the keen-to-help stage,' she mouths, although her attempt at a whisper still sounds quite loud. 'Long may it last,' she adds with another peal of laughter. She flaps a hand at the room and groans. 'It's like something out of *Trainspotting* in here. Don't go thinking I didn't try to help Bon keep on top of it. She just wasn't in a fit state, bless her heart.

'We're taking the kids back to ours in a couple of days, God help us. I wanted to get on top of the mess first, though. That was the plan anyway, but I've had *that* much to do!' She slaps her hands on her thighs, creating another cheery jingle of her bangles. 'Right, I'd best go and supervise the tea-making.' Whipping away the coat I've just shrugged off, she leaves the room in a cloud of heavy perfume.

My nose wrinkles as the stench of something sharply unpleasant overtakes Julie's musky scent.

'It's shit,' says a young voice behind me. I turn, noticing for the first time the track-suited figure stretched out on the sofa.

'Oh, hello!' I blink in surprise, trying not to gag on the rotting, fishy rue assaulting my nostrils. 'You must be Bartley.'

He nods, accentuating his double chin. 'Careful where you step,' he says, his dark brown eyes remaining on the iPad clutched in his hands. 'Dead bodies and cat shit everywhere.'

'Well, how about that,' I say after a brief pause, my standard response when I'm temporarily lost for words. Delicately described as 'a bit of a handful' in the report, I'd already primed myself to meet Bartley, so I'm pleasantly surprised by the sedate introduction.

It's only as I move further into the room that I notice a girl with mid-length, wavy dark hair and extraordinarily pale skin. Squashed on the floor between the end of the sofa and the bay window, she's sketching in the notepad on her lap with such concentration that I'm not even sure she's noticed me yet.

'Hi, Caitlin,' I say gently. She meets my gaze for a brief second, then quickly drops her own. The tabby cat spread over her thin ankles shows more interest, glancing up at me then stretching, turning a couple of circles and settling back down.

Another voice pipes up behind me.

'I'm Ethan. I'm six and I love football!' Slightly podgy, with dark hair like his siblings and pale brown eyes, Ethan bounces on his feet in the doorway like a boxer warming up before a match.

I crouch down to his level, taking in the long scratch down one of his cheeks that's still glistening with spots of fresh blood. 'Pleased to meet you, Ethan,' I say with a smile, also noticing his threadbare, overly tight pyjamas. 'I'm Rosie, I'm fifty-one and I love Tom Hardy.'

Bartley snorts an amused side-glance before returning his attention to his game. Ethan smiles back shyly, revealing deep dimples. Then his face turns serious. 'Don't look behind you, Rosie,' he warns. Reflexively, I swivel round.

'Oh dear!' I say, getting to my feet. My stomach churns as I take in the source of the rotten eggy smell – five dead fish floating on the top of an open-lidded tank in the corner of the room.

Ethan clamps a hand over his eyes and then drags it down his face. With a high-pitched screech that sounds animal-like, he runs a couple of manic circles round the room then disappears out the door.

'What did I tell you?' Bartley says from the sofa, with a heavy sigh of resignation. 'S'like *Night of the Living Dead* round here.'

'And whose fault's that?' Linzi says as she returns with a mug of weak tea. Her face is round with small features but her liberally applied powdered eyebrows and mascara give her a harsh appearance.

'Well, it weren't mine,' Bartley mutters.

Linzi hands me the drink, gives her older-by-a-few-months nephew a chastising glance, then focuses her gaze on me. "No, *course* it wasn't, Bart-ley.'

'Whatever,' he grunts, rolling over on the sofa so that he's facing the wall. 'Na-an!' he yells, without taking his eyes from the screen. 'I want food!'

I glance around the rubbish-strewn room, reining in the urge to roll up my sleeves and get stuck into cleaning up. If you weren't careful, you could be roped into doing all sorts in this new role. One of my fostering friends on the Mockingbird scheme was greeted last week with the words, 'Hi, Lucy, I've saved the washing up for you!' The next day she was urged to race post-haste to the chemist for the morning-after pill.

'No school today then, guys?' I lift the mug of insipid tea to my lips, trying not to inhale too deeply. Linzi, who's watching me eagerly, smiles broadly when I take a few sips.

'Actually, you can dunk one of the biscuits we made yesterday!' she cries, taking off with glee.

'Grab me a couple,' Bartley shouts with a slight turn of his head. It's lovely of Linzi, but my stomach plummets. The smell really is bad and the marmite toast my seven-year-old daughter Megan prepared for me this morning is churning vengefully in my stomach.

'There's an INSET day tomorrow so I thought, after the week they've had, there was no harm giving them a few days off,' says Julie, who's appeared in the doorway. There's a defensive edge to her tone and I mentally kick myself for making what might have come across as a judgy observation within minutes of meeting her. I always try to bear in mind that people who come into contact with foster carers are usually at a low ebb. I intend to make Julie and Ryan's lives easier, not make them feel that they're being assessed.

'Yes, yes of course,' I say, my stomach flipping at the sight of two large chocolate cookies in Linzi's hand. She slips one on the edge of the sofa for Bartley and gives the other to me.

I thank her and have a nibble, making fake noises of appreciation.

Julie smiles. 'They're really easy to –'

'Too dry,' Bartley interrupts his grandmother rudely. Somehow, he sits himself up and hands her the biscuit without taking his eyes off his screen. 'Put some Nutella on it.'

Still smiling, Julie rolls her eyes and leaves the room. She returns with the biscuit and a small pot of chocolate sauce. Bartley accepts both regally. Without a thank you, he starts dunking. 'He's never off that screen,' she says fondly, with a shake of her head in her grandson's direction. 'Anyway, as I was saying, the cookies are really easy for kids to make.' She tugs her phone from the pocket of her jeans. 'What's your surname? I'll friend you on Facebook and send you the recipe.'

'I don't really use it,' I lie, my gaze dropping to the dark-haired toddler charging into the room. Little Louis. He's wearing cute corduroy dungarees but they're faded and stained, and clearly too small from him. I crouch down again, smiling. He hands me a car with a word that sounds suspiciously rude.

It's important to maintain boundaries when fostering, something that's easier to do when interactions with birth parents are limited to supervised looked-after children, LAC reviews, or the two-minute handovers before and after arranged contact sessions. This is a whole different ball game, and one I need to hastily construct new rules for.

'Give us your mobile number then and I'll WhatsApp it over.'

There's a moment's silence as I weigh up my options. Julie doesn't pick up on my hesitation. At least, she shows no sign of it. She waits with a friendly smile, her fingers hovering over the keypad of her phone.

'I'm not sure I'm allowed to share it,' I say vaguely, although I'm simultaneously wondering what the harm could be. It's not as if the couple are going through care proceedings, and they certainly aren't under suspicion of causing harm to the children, so there aren't any of the usual safety or privacy issues to worry about. On the face of it, they are just an ordinary family doing the best they can in difficult circumstances.

'Okay,' Julie says flatly. She sounds disappointed, and slightly offended. A knock at the door offers a distraction from the moment of awkwardness. There's a pause in which the grandmother eyes the tall, thickset man, who wouldn't look out of place in a gangster film, coming down the stairs. 'Oh, Ry, this is Rosie,' she says, her cheery tone already recovered.

Uninterested, he lifts his brow wordlessly in my direction and then saunters down the hall towards the kitchen.

'What a charmer,' Julie laughs. 'I'll get the door then, shall I?' She shoots her eyes up at the ceiling and widens her eyes at me as if to say, '*Men!*'

Still wailing like a foghorn, Ethan appears and follows his grandmother to the door. Seconds later he cries, 'Miss Woods! It's Miss Woods!' From the living-room door, I watch as he throws his arms around the smiling young woman on the doorstep.

Miss Woods, who appears to be in her mid-20s, with long brown plaits hanging over each shoulder, pats Ethan affectionately on the back and then eases herself out of his clutches. 'I'm so sorry to disturb you, Mrs Chambers. It's just that Ethan was supposed to return Humphrey after half-term. I promised Bethany she could have him over the long week –'

'Well good luck with that.' Julie withdraws into the room nearest the front door. She emerges a few seconds later with a large blue hamster cage and plonks it into Miss Woods' grasp.

'Ah,' the teacher says, her smile fading. Even from where I'm standing, I can see that the lifeless ball of fur blocking one of the curly Perspex tubes has been dead for some time. The teacher blinks at Julie. 'Poor Humphrey.'

'I'll get the blame, I expect,' Julie mutters. 'Always the way.'

Ethan bursts into tears and looks up at his grandmother. Clearly, she hadn't thought to share the news of the animal's condition with the children. Then again, the poor woman has more than enough to cope with at the moment.

After a pause, Julie seems to come to. Crouching, she gives her grandson a hug. Over his shoulder I can see that her expression is pained. There's some exasperated annoyance there too; Humphrey yet another victim of her daughter's neglect, and her left to pick up the pieces.

My heart goes out to her. I make up my mind to go the extra mile to help her through the next few weeks, as her daughter recovers.

Silenced

'What did I tell you?' Bartley gabbles through a mouthful of biscuit. 'Corpses and crap all over the place.' I frown at him. Ethan might have been surprised by Humphrey's fate, but it seems that Bartley was already party to it.

'Cwap, cwap, cwap,' Louis says cheerfully as he toddles over and clutches a handful of my skirt.

Linzi laughs and shakes her head. 'What are they *like*?' she says, meeting my gaze with a rueful grin.

I raise my eyebrows at her, marvelling at the difference that 'good enough' parenting can make. Linzi isn't much older than Caitlin and yet is capable of holding a sophisticated, almost grown-up conversation. And yet her niece barely has the confidence to lift her head.

A couple of hours later, after assuring Julie that I'll return in the morning, I remove myself to my Fiat and work out how much time I can dedicate to the family over the next few weeks. I block out alternate days in my diary, although I suspect they won't need such intensive support. Some difficulties in families are so entrenched that it takes months to see any improvement, even after significant interventions are put in place. Sadly, there are some who, despite extensive outside help, still need to be escalated to the statutory route, with the children coming into care.

Julie's loving attention and the steadying certainties of regular mealtimes, clean beds and a firm but fair hand will work their magic on the Powell children in a few short weeks, however.

I'm sure of it.

Chapter Two

Rain gushes over my shoes as I hurry towards the Powells' house the next day. I ring the doorbell and huddle inside the small open porch, smiling as I recall Megan's reaction yesterday afternoon when I told her that we'd been 'matched' with a new family.

After breaking into a spontaneous dance outside the school gates, topped off with a cartwheel over the pavement, she leaped into my arms and gave me a brief, strangulating hug. 'Woo-hoo! Can I help get the room ready?! When are they coming? Boy, girl? Tell me, tell me!' Her disappointment on hearing that the Powell children wouldn't be moving in with us matched her momentary joy and she scowled all the way home.

My description of the children at teatime went some way towards satisfying her curiosity, but she was still pleading with me to give her the day off when we reached her school this morning. The arrival of her headteacher at the gates was all it took to change her mind. Charging over to Mrs Mundy, she bestowed a 'Megan' hug.

'Way too friendly,' hissed one of her classmates, pulling gently on Megan's hood.

Silenced

'Bye, Mummy, love you!' she called over her shoulder as she skipped towards her classroom. 'Love you too, Mrs Mundy!' she added, much to her friend's disgust. Mrs Mundy met my gaze and chuckled, shaking her head.

Fostered as a newborn and adopted into our family at the age of three, Megan is our little ray of sunshine. A marvellous pocket rocket who regularly reminds us how wonderful life can be.

Despite all the challenges she wrestles with daily – sensory processing and attention deficit disorders resulting from exposure to alcohol and drugs in-utero, hearing difficulties and a deep-seated fear of abandonment that developed after her initial adoption was disrupted – she embraces each new day with an enthusiasm that's both inspiring and contagious.

The broken attachments in her past have left their mark on her, however. Even now, years after her adoption, she has to constantly touch one of us to make sure we're nearby. How brave she is, I always think, to cheerfully get ready for school each morning, knowing how difficult the day ahead is likely to be.

Thankfully her bubbly, loving nature is a glorious counterweight to the merry mayhem she puts her teachers through, and the staff absolutely love her. The children in Megan's class adore her as well. They also sense her vulnerability. When she clung onto me one morning during her first year at school, a little boy from her class offered to carry her book bag and then shyly took her by the hand and led her away. Comically, she still holds out her bag to him each morning. He rather chivalrously obliges, carrying it into school and hanging it on her peg. It's sweet to see how protective her class-mates are of her.

My smile fades at the memory of my mother's less effu-sive reaction when I told her about our new Mockingbird family. Mum has been my back-up carer ever since I began fostering and usually can't wait to meet the children I look after. This morning, however, when I'd picked her up to give her a lift to Sainsbury's after dropping Megs off at school, she'd asked very little about the family.

'You take on too much,' was all she'd said when I relayed the flying books and toys incident. Her usual spritely step was absent as she made her way towards the supermarket.

Stamping from foot to foot in the icy wind, I wonder for a moment whether the Mockingbird process has left her feeling distanced, a little left out. But then I remind myself that she's still adjusting to the blow of losing her much-loved sister. Besides, she'll be eighty next year. It's normal to slow down at her age.

I'm so deep in thought that when an elderly woman calls out to me from the garden next door, I whirl around with a start. 'You won't get any joy there!' she yells over the squally wind. 'Gone away.'

'Away?' Reluctantly leaving the haven of the porch, I take a few steps towards her. I'm supposed to be meeting the children's social worker, Robert Jackson, here for a ten o'clock meeting to explore the children's wishes, and it's gone five to already.

'Yep, thank the Lord.' Her thin lips twist in disdain. 'All that screaming morning, noon and night. It's too much at my time of life. I shan't miss 'em, tell you that for nothing. S'her I feel sorry for.'

'Her?'

'Julie,' she says, shaking her head in dismay. 'Fancy having to put up with that lot, and old what's his face into the bargain. Miserable sod. I've tried passing the time of day with him. Waste of time. He'd knock you out soon as look at you, that one.'

'I'm sorry, do you know where they've gone?' I say, noting the disappointment on her face. I get the impression she'd like me to join in with my own choice anecdotes about the family.

'Took 'em back to their place, didn't they,' she huffs, as if it's obvious. 'Long may it last. Hear everything through these walls, you do. I've barely slept since they moved in.'

I thank her and jog back to my car to call the fostering team. Robert had emailed the Mockingbird paperwork defining the parameters of my involvement with the family early this morning, but hadn't mentioned anything about the change of venue.

Shivering as droplets of freezing rain trickle down the back of my neck, I can't help but feel a wisp of irritation at the social worker's failure to keep me informed. As the call connects, my thoughts drift to Julie. If the neighbour's testimony is anything to go by, the children's grandmother is the only responsible person in the family.

'Don't tell me you went to Bon's?' Julie says when she opens the door and takes in my sodden appearance. She groans when I nod. 'Oh, you poor thing, I can't believe they didn't let you know! I wish I'd had your number. Come on, let's get you a nice hot drink.'

She's wearing a long-sleeved top that's clingy across her

chest and slightly short, so that an inch of her tanned midriff is visible above the waistband of her jeans. Her strappy white sandals click over the white marble floor as she sweeps through the roomy hallway, leaving a trail of potent perfume behind her.

After removing my shoes, I follow behind, suddenly aware of my shapeless coat, long non-iron skirt and sopping wet tights that leave little puddles in my wake. The floor is hard beneath my feet, but presumably there's underfloor heating because it's surprisingly warm. My feet start to steam. A weird sensation, but at least it won't take long for me to dry out.

'I had planned on staying at Bon's today to carry on the clear-up, as you know,' Julie says as she shows me into a large living area with the same highly polished flooring. 'But the kids desperately needed some decent clothes so we went shopping instead.' She looks at me. 'To be honest, I couldn't bear it there any longer.'

Immaculately modern and almost entirely cream and white, her house is about as different from her daughter's place as it's possible to get. It's not surprising she chose not to hang around.

My eye is immediately drawn to the bi-fold doors stretching across the far wall and offering an impressive view of a 100-foot pristine lawn. There's a huge flat-screen television on the wall where I imagine a fireplace once stood, huge rugs with thick pile dotted here and there, and a glass-fronted, walnut drinks cabinet that's extremely well stocked. 'I presume you two are acquainted,' Julie says, as my eyes settle on an overweight man somewhere in his early 40s, seated on one of two plush sofas.

With a slight wheeze, he puts down the mug he's holding and comes towards me. 'Not in the flesh, no,' he says, his accent suggesting a private education. Most social workers stick to casual clothes unless they're attending court, but Robert is dressed flamboyantly in a purple velvet jacket, with a colourful cravat tucked into his shirt. 'But I've heard a lot about you, Rosie. All good, all good,' he says, holding up his hands with a smile.

I pat a hand on my coat to dry it before shaking his. 'Sorry I'm late. I went to Bonnie's house.'

Robert glances at Julie with a frown. 'But I thought –'

'I know, it's a shame I couldn't text you, Rosie,' she cuts in as she helps me out of my coat.

The social worker glances down at her midriff, flushes, then shakes his head. 'Sorry, my fault. I should've let you know, Rosie.'

I wave his apology away. Mix-ups are common when fostering, what with hefty caseloads, competing priorities and budgets too tight to allow social workers adequate administrative support.

Feeling complicit in turning children into dividends for hedge-fund managers, I left Bright Heights, the private agency I'd fostered with for well over a decade, and became an in-house foster carer at my local authority. I was initially a little wary of making the move, especially having been warned to expect poorer-quality training and less support from my supervising social worker, SSW. It's worked out well, however. The biggest negative has been the high turnover of staff in the fostering team. I've been through six SSWs in the last three years, and am currently without one.

'Rob, do you have any objection to Rosie and I exchanging numbers?' Julie asks, after hanging my coat in the hall. She hands me a towel to pat myself down and then pulls her mobile from her pocket. 'Poor lady, look at her, all bedraggled. And I don't suppose it's easy for you, Rob, being a go-between.'

'Fine by me,' Robert says, returning her warm smile without so much as a glance in my direction.

They both turn to me expectantly. Refusing seems churlish, especially as what Julie said makes sense. It will be easier to make arrangements for visiting without having to trouble Robert, who's undoubtedly up against it. Julie's manicured nails fly over the screen of her phone as I relay my number. She slips the handset back into the pocket of her jeans and then takes the towel. 'Right, I'll get you some tea,' she says, leaving the room just as little Louis makes an entrance.

Crawling on hands and knees, he's so intent on pushing along a large yellow digger that he doesn't even look up. He rams it into the side of the sofa and one of the wheels becomes lodged underneath. 'Bugger,' he curses, sitting back on his padded bottom and pulling on it hard. When it finally comes free it almost hits him in the face. 'Fuck's sake,' he curses again. I don't like bad language as a rule but it's an effort not to chuckle as I kneel down and say hello.

'Boof,' he says, thrusting the digger again, this time into me. He looks well cared-for today in a cute pair of baby chinos that fit and a jumper with an elephant on the front.

'I know a little girl who's very excited to meet you, Louis,' I say after giving my sore knees a rub. The two-year-old's boisterousness might serve him well when on the receiving end of one of my daughter's ebullient hugs. Slightly pudgy like all his siblings except Caitlin, his blue eyes shine as he grins and hands me the toy. For the first time, I notice a long silvery scar running from his right temple to his ear.

'Would you look at that?' I say, admiring the digger. He climbs onto my lap and takes back possession of the toy, twisting it around in front of my face so I can appreciate its glory from every angle. Sometimes making a connection is as easy as that. When I tell Robert, over Louis's head, about Megan's desperation to meet the children, the two-year-old presses the digger closer to my nose for me to admire again.

Robert smiles. 'Well, tell her I'm still trying to get my head around the Mockingbird system myself. Up to two nights a week at yours, isn't it?'

Louis slips off my lap when Julie returns from the kitchen. I rise to my feet, taking the drink she offers with a grateful nod. 'In an emergency, yes. I think there's plenty of flexibility, depending on what's needed.'

I first heard about the Mockingbird scheme from Des, my ex-supervising social worker and now close friend, who'd spent some time in the US a few years earlier.

Having proved successful over there, The Fostering Network launched a pilot scheme in the UK in 2015, with the roll-out continuing since then to all parts of the UK.

Besides providing support to families in need, the pioneering programme is designed to support foster carers, adopters, special guardians and kinship carers who are struggling with the children they've taken under their wing. The stress of 'giving from an empty cup' day after day can lead to burn-out, or empathy fatigue, as it's sometimes known. By wrapping our metaphorical arms around the parents and carers, effectively becoming their surrogate extended family, their chances of staying together are greatly improved.

Apart from the financial burden of taking children into care, there's the emotional impact of severing attachments with their birth family, plus the significant risk that siblings will be split up in the absence of a foster carer with a home big enough to accommodate them all. Most of the foster carers I know go out of their way to keep children together, but most only have one bedroom to dedicate to fostering, so it's not unusual for sibling groups to be scattered around.

Robert nods and turns to Julie. 'Right, I'm ready to get on with things, if the others are around?'

Julie yells the children's names at the top of her voice, leaning back slightly as if the extra few inches will make all the difference in projecting her voice up the stairs.

Caitlin appears barely 30 seconds later. The long-sleeved jumper dress she's wearing looks expensive and is clearly new, fold lines still visible across the wool. 'Here she is,' Julie says warmly. She opens her arms. 'Come here, my little smasher.'

The nine-year-old bursts into tears and falls into her grandmother's arms. 'Aw, there, come on now,' Julie says softly, wrapping her in a tight embrace. She cups her face in her hands and leans close. 'It's all been a bit too much lately, hasn't it?'

Tears streaming down her cheeks, Caitlin nods. Seconds later she staggers sideways as Ethan and Bartley explode into the room, straight into her.

Silenced

'You okay, sweetheart,' I say gently, reaching out to steady her. She reels away as if she's been struck. The elderly neighbour's words rush back to me as Julie gives her another hug – *all that screaming morning, noon and night*. My heart lurches as I do a quick mental calculation. The children were categorised as 'in need' two years ago, so there was no outside monitoring for the first seven years of Caitlin's life, apart from that which normally takes place in school.

I know from the family profile that all four children have different birth fathers. It's a worry when lots of men drift in and out of children's lives. Apart from the damage from broken attachments, a mother's ability to safeguard her children can be compromised by addiction issues. Unscrupulous people often use this fact to their advantage.

At least they're in safe hands now, I reassure myself, and Bonnie is finally getting the intensive help she needs.

Chapter Three

It takes a moment to realise that everyone's attention is focused on me. I glance at Robert, who seems to be waiting for me to take the lead. Wringing his hands, there's a slightly panicked air about him as he looks between me and the two boys, who have broken into a play fight in the middle of the room.

'Did you bring any "Voice of the Child" packs with you, Robert?' I say, taking pity on him. The number of social workers who demonstrate unease around children never fails to surprise me. Then again, a deep desire to help youngsters doesn't automatically endow individuals with the skills to go with it.

When Robert shakes his head and backs away from the scuffle, I clap my hands. 'Right, who wants to help me build some islands?' In the absence of any official resources, I'll have to use what's available.

Bartley looks up and loosens his grip on Ethan. The six-year-old scrambles away, but not before delivering a sneaky kick to his brother's stomach. 'What the actual fuck, Ethan?!' Bartley shouts, staring at him open-mouthed.

'I like building!' Ethan grins, his brown eyes gazing up at me.

'Great. I'll need some building blocks, or Lego, or books.'

Ethan returns a blank look and Julie shakes her head. 'We don't have much here yet.'

I think for a moment. 'Okay to use the cushions?'

'Of course,' Julie says, settling herself on one of the plush leather sofas. I look at Robert, hoping he'll ask her to leave us to it for a while. Formal question and answer interviews tend to make children clam up. 'Voice of the Child' techniques are visual games designed to help children communicate wishes they might struggle to express verbally. They only work, however, if the child can speak freely. Since most children have a deep-seated yearning to please, the presence of a relative can render it a pointless exercise.

Robert joins Julie on the sofa. They exchange warm smiles, looking for all the world like a couple settling themselves down to enjoy some morning TV.

'O-kay,' I say slowly, looking at them askance. They're oblivious, a lively conversation striking up between them. Deciding it might not be such a bad thing, I deliberately move to the other side of the room.

Bartley and Ethan help me to stack cushions into three piles. Caitlin hangs back. Sitting on the floor beside her grandmother, she rests her head on Julie's knee and watches us from a distance.

Another tussle breaks out over the largest cushion but I know that admonishing the boys before I've managed to establish some sort of relationship with them is futile. Children who struggle to regulate their behaviour are so used to being nagged that when a stranger piles in their criticism barely registers.

Foster carers are encouraged to consider the 'bank of goodwill' early on in a placement. A metaphorical trust account that needs building up before any withdrawals can be made. Every time a carer shows respect, consideration and loving care to a child, the account is credited. Demands can only be made once the account boasts a healthy balance. In other words, only once a connection is in place can the power of a child's innate desire to please be leveraged.

'So, this is your home, the Island of Always,' I say, ignoring the sideshow and flattening the top of the nearest island ready for its first inhabitants. The boys pause mid-tussle and watch as I move to the middle pile. 'This is the Island of Sometimes, and over there we have the Island of Far Away.

'Now, we need a bridge, something big and flat,' I say, scratching my head theatrically.

'This?!' the boys chorus, holding up the floor cushion and then playing tug-of-war with it.

'Perfect! Now drop it here,' I tell them, indicating the gap between the first two islands. 'This is our bridge to visit the Island of Sometimes. You each get to choose who you'd like to live with you on the Island of Always,' I tell them, explaining that there's a gate halfway along the 'bridge', and that they must put people on the second island that they'd like to see sometimes, but only when they choose to. 'And that one over there,' I say, pointing at the far pile, 'is a place for people you would prefer never to see again.'

Ethan charges over to the Island of Far Away with a roar and lands face down on top of it. 'He can bloody stay there,' Bartley mutters, demonstrating that these games are simply a mechanism to get children talking rather than a way of mining deep psychological insights that should be taken literally. A child who banishes one of their parents to the Island of Far Away, for example, might simply be feeling resentful after a recent telling off, rather than hinting at something sinister.

After getting them to draw everyone they know on a piece of paper, we cut the figures out, an activity Caitlin quietly joins in with. Then I ask them who wants to play the game first. Another scuffle breaks out between the boys, and with Louis engrossed with target practice – bashing his truck into the legs of the drinks cabinet – I nominate Caitlin.

'But that's not fair!' Bartley complains, as Caitlin gathers together the figures she's carefully drawn and gets to her feet. 'Why should *she* go first?'

'Because she's been waiting patiently instead of fighting,' I say evenly. I smile encouragingly at Caitlin, so I'm astonished when she walks to the door and stays there.

'Best leave her,' Julie calls out from across the room. 'She's a bit touchy at the moment.' There's a pause, but then Robert engages her in conversation again. I suddenly wonder if his lavish attentions are simply a canny way of distracting her so that I can get on with the job. If that's the case, I'm grateful for his ingenuity.

'That's okay, Caitlin,' I say lightly, 'you don't have to join in. This is just a bit of fun. A way of you letting the grown-ups know what your wishes are.'

'I want to win the World Cup!' Ethan shouts, punching a fist in the air.

'If you're granting wishes, I wouldn't mind a trip to Disney World,' Bartley pipes up.

Caitlin returns a few seconds later and hands me a folded note. *I wish for Mum to come back.*

Her eyes are filled with tears. Her expression is so earnest, and so beseeching, that my heart flies out to her. 'Ah, sweetheart, I know. But while Mum's getting better, it would be helpful to know who you'd like to take care of you.'

'Get on with it, ratface,' Bartley says nastily.

'Let's play the game without any name-calling,' I suggest gently.

'I can name-call as much as I want,' he snaps. 'She pisses me off.'

Without a word, Caitlin puts the figure of herself on the nearest pile of cushions. Ethan and Bartley have begun rolling on top of each other again, and this time I'm grateful for it. I watch as Caitlin sorts through the figures, placing her three brothers with her, as well as her mum and her cat. Her eyes flick momentarily over to Julie, who's still deep in conversation with Robert, then she places her grandparents on the middle island.

All she's done is re-create the living arrangements that existed a few days ago, but what's enlightening is the angle of her shoulders as she glances over her shoulder to the doorway, where Ryan now stands. I suddenly become uncomfortably aware of the heat rising up through my feet. My stomach rolls slightly.

The two boys re-create an almost identical set-up when it's their turn. Interestingly, however, they maroon their grandfather alone on the middle island and keep their grandmother with them, on the Island of Always.

A resounding vote for Julie then. At least we know that, in the absence of their mother, the children are where they want to be.

Then something occurs to me. 'You forgot to draw the cat, boys. Where –'

'Six Dinner Sid, we call him,' Julie says with a smile. Clearly, she's been half-listening. 'He belongs to the neighbour but Bonnie used to feed him sometimes.'

As I tidy up the cushions, Louis pads across the room and climbs onto Julie's lap. Bartley and Ethan join him, both competing with each other to wrap their arms around their grandmother's neck. Julie does her best to manage all of them, but I can't help noticing her frown as she looks towards the door.

I follow her gaze, curious to know how Ryan feels about being cast away to the middle island. He's nowhere to be seen, and Caitlin has disappeared as well.

Chapter Four

'I've packed their stuff,' Ryan mutters in the hallway a couple of hours later.

I blink at him, puzzled. It's the first time we've spoken and I haven't a clue what he means. He nods towards a small suitcase on its end near the front door, and hands me a pink rucksack, which I grasp automatically.

'Their stuff?'

'Caitlin and Bartley's.' His lips barely move when he talks and his gaze doesn't quite meet mine, although I manage to pick up on his Newcastle accent. I stare at him, taking in the scar above his eyebrow and the deep, barely healed gash across one of his bristly cheeks. I usually love the warmth of a Geordie accent but the aggression in Ryan's stance, as if he's daring me to disagree with him, makes my heart thump in my chest. I remind myself that his thuggish appearance doesn't necessarily reflect his character. 'Two nights a week, you said. I heard you. I've put their uniforms in there. Drop them to Millfield on Monday. We'll grab them from there.'

My mind runs through my brief conversation about

Mockingbird with Robert, wondering whether I'd misinterpreted it. I'm about to say something when Julie appears in the hall, closely followed by the social worker. 'What's going on?' she asks, glancing between us.

'I hadn't planned on taking anyone today –' I start, although I'm already picturing Megan's expression if both Bartley and Caitlin come with me to collect her from school. Having them overnight, especially since my mum is coming round for dinner this evening, will give everyone a chance to feel included.

It's clear that Ryan hasn't discussed his decision with Julie, or the children. When Caitlin appears beside her grandmother, a look passes between the couple. 'I've only got the one spare room,' I continue, running through a mental checklist to make sure I have everything I need if they're to stay. 'They can't share, can they? Not at their age.' I look to Robert for confirmation, but his gaze is focused on Julie. It seems that he's reluctant to take his eyes off the glamorous grandmother.

'Surely it'd be better for Louis to go with Bartley,' Julie suggests, as the two-year-old grabs one of her legs. 'Since he's the most labour-intensive.' She sweeps the toddler up and blows a raspberry on his middle. 'No offence, pickle,' she says playfully, to a gurgle of riotous giggles.

'They're sharing here,' Ryan snaps. 'They shared at Bonnie's. What's the difference?'

Caitlin bursts into tears again. Julie sucks her breath in through her teeth and pulls the nine-year-old into another hug. She gives me a meaningful look over the top of her granddaughter's head, her exasperated expression saying it all. When it comes to decision-making in the marriage, she doesn't get much of a say. 'It's only for the weekend, babe,' she says, planting kisses in Caitlin's hair.

'You sure you're all right with this, Julie?' Robert asks her.

'I suppose it'll give me chance to catch my breath,' she says with a forced bright tone. She leans down to Caitlin and cups her chin. 'Remember what I said yesterday, sweetie, and everything'll be absolutely fine, okay.'

Caitlin manages to stop herself crying. With a few gulping sniffs, she gives her grandmother a brave nod.

Bartley must have been listening because he appears and slips his shoes on, a noisy video playing out on his iPhone. Unfazed, he grabs his case and waits by the door with the air of someone who's not bothered where he goes, as long as he has a gadget along for the ride.

'What about the room situation, Robert?' I have bunkbeds in my fostering room, and an extra pull-out trundle bed for emergencies, but children of the opposite sex and over a certain age aren't supposed to share. Some flexibility has recently been worked into the rules to reduce the frequency of siblings being separated, but it varies between care providers.

'They're used to sharing and they're under eleven. I'm comfortable with it if their grandparents are.'

Ryan grabs his keys, plants a rough kiss on his wife's cheek and lets himself out.

'Come on then, guys,' I say gently, smiling at Caitlin in a way that I hope is reassuring. 'Ah, just a minute,' I pause at the open door. 'Do they have any allergies I need to be aware of?'

It would have been helpful to have a meeting with Robert before taking the children back to mine. Sometimes all a foster carer knows about a child is their name when they arrive on the doorstep, so I'm used to winging it in the first few days of a new placement. It's nicer to know a bit about them before they come to stay, however, if only to give me a chance to shop for some of their favourite foods.

I do try to view scant information at the beginning of a placement as a positive, an opportunity for the child to start over with a clean slate. After all, where would any of us be if all our mistakes over the years were documented, colour-coded and passed around to interested parties?

'Dietary requirements, you mean.'

I frown at Julie. 'Sorry?'

'You're supposed to say dietary requirements these days, not allergies,' Julie smiles. Robert nods in agreement. 'But no, you're all right, they don't have any.'

'Great.' I pause before asking my next question. Foster carers are expected to protect themselves from false allegations by recording any previous injuries on a body plan map provided by the local authority before taking children into their care. It's one of those procedures that a supervising social worker would usually take care of, but since I don't have one at the moment, the onus is on me. It's tempting to leave it to chance and trust, especially since Caitlin is already upset. I certainly don't want her or anyone else to feel awkward, but I've seen the devastating impact that allegations and subsequent investigations can have on fostering families, so I need to do what I can to protect all of us from the outset. 'And do they have any cuts or bruises I need to be aware of?'

'Ah, good point,' Robert says, turning enquiringly to Julie.

'Not that I can think of – do you guys?' Julie asks. Caitlin shakes her head.

'Nope,' Bartley says, but his gaze flicks oddly towards his sister. I suspect she may have come off worse in a scuffle between the siblings, so I'm not unduly worried. Besides, short of asking them to strip off and prove that they're injury-free, I don't have much choice but to take them at their word.

'Come on then,' I say cheerily. 'Let's go to Rosie's house.'

'What's up, bros,' Jamie says when we arrive home. On his way to the living room with a plate piled high, he gives us a casual nod as if the children are already regular fixtures in our home.

I began fostering when Jamie was a young boy. Now in his early 20s, he barely raises any eyebrow when new faces appear. Both he and Emily, my eldest daughter, take morning meltdowns and tears at bedtime in their stride.

Making up for Jamie's laid-back greeting, our dog Mungo bolts towards us, his tail wagging so manically that his whole backside moves along with it. A spaniel–terrier cross, he's been with us a few years now and has helped put many new arrivals quickly at ease.

'Have you left *anything* in the fridge, Jamie?' I say as we pull off our coats.

'It's bulking season, ma,' he throws over his shoulder before settling himself on the sofa and switching on the TV. As the member of a soft-rock band, Jamie often doesn't set off for work until mid-afternoon and then stays out until the early hours. With Emily on midwifery training at our local hospital and often working early, late or night shifts, we're all on different schedules these days. It's rare for all of us to be in the house at the same time.

Most of downstairs is open plan in our house, wide pillars the only obstruction between the hall, living room and kitchen. Bartley watches Jamie with an intrigued expression as I hang up our coats. Caitlin kneels down to fuss Mungo. He rolls around on his back, twisting from side to side and baring his teeth in a soppy grin. A tiny smile appears on Caitlin's lips. Seconds later, Bartley barges her roughly out of the way so that she ends up on her backside.

'Hey, careful, Bartley.' When I first began fostering, nerves at the beginning of a placement meant that I was on high alert for any potential dangers I might be exposing the family to. I'm much more relaxed these days but I try to guard against being sucked into a false sense of security. Knowing that Bartley has a tendency to lash out, I remind myself to conduct a hasty risk assessment once I've shown them round.

'It was her,' he snaps back, as I help Caitlin to her feet. It's not unusual for children who've experienced neglect or abuse to surround themselves with self-constructed emotional barriers, to keep themselves safe. Exposing their true selves is terrifying, and with no idea what they're walking into when they come into care they put so much effort into defending those walls that they often come across as sullen and withdrawn, or surly and hostile. Being met with repeated and unrelenting acceptance and kindness helps build their trust in time.

'Right, let's get you orientated, shall we?' I say, giving Caitlin another reassuring smile. 'What you see is what you get downstairs, although there's a little cubby-hole in here,' I say, opening the door to the 'yellow room', a small office that, when a particularly persuasive social worker goes to town on me, doubles as a bedroom for myself, so that my own can be used for fostering. 'And this here,' I say, pointing to a blank space on the wall near the front door, 'is a worry hook.'

'There's nothing there,' Bartley sniggers, as I'd guessed he would. But Caitlin looks interested.

'It's a special place where you can leave all the bad stuff when you come in through the door,' I explain as we head for the stairs. I've had varying reactions to the worry hook; some children giggle, others give me sidelong glances. A couple of the jeerers eventually came round, hanging up their troubles after a stressful contact session with their birth families, or a bad day at school. One lad of about 13 actually asked if he could take the worry hook with him when he moved onto long-term care. 'Of course,' I told him with a smile. 'It's portable!'

Even for those who don't actually 'use' it, I hope that the worry hook conveys the message that our house is a place of safety, a haven in which they can decompress.

'Bit disturbing but o-kay,' Bartley says, giving me a look that suggests I've lost my mind. He charges up the stairs ahead of us but comes to a sudden stop on the landing. Caitlin and I almost walk into him. 'Oh shit, I just felt a cold shiver up my spine,' he says with a gleeful glance in his sister's direction. 'I think you must have ghosts in the house, or poltergeists.'

'This is where you'll be sleeping,' I say, ignoring him and showing them into a room big enough for bunk-beds, a double wardrobe, a chest of drawers and a small desk with a stool.

Orienting children to their new environment tends to be one of my main aims when they arrive in placement. They've often come from a background of chaos, so I try to make their world as predictable as I can in the first few weeks.

Foster carers are encouraged to draw up a list of house rules so that children know exactly what's what when they arrive. I used to present new house guests with our rules on their first day – NO SWEARING, NO HURTING OTHERS, NO BULLYING – but these days I cut them some slack. Our house rules are pinned to the front of the fridge for all to see, but getting settled is more important than anything else on their first day with us. A list of rules isn't the most welcoming of gifts.

I've learned to reshape the language I use around children over the years as well. I've found it's much more effective to tell children what they can and should do, rather than negatively pointing out all of the 'can'ts' and 'shouldn'ts'. Consequently, our list now reads:

USE KIND WORDS
USE KIND HANDS
USE CALM BOX WHEN FEELING ANXIOUS
   OR OVERWHELMED

Our calm box contains weighted blankets, fidget spinners, chewellery, putty, massagers and all sorts of other gadgets that can help an overwhelmed child regulate their mood.

Des boarded out the cupboard under the stairs for me a couple of years ago and I've transformed it into a sensory area using fairy lights, cushions and textured rugs and blankets. Partly thanks to *Harry Potter*, most children including Megan absolutely adore the space and end up playing in there as well as retreating to unwind.

'No one will come into your bedroom except me,' I tell them. 'And only if I'm invited.'

Bartley goes straight to the window and peers out over the back garden. 'That a rabbit hutch?'

'Yes, that's Boomer and Bomber's home,' I say, giving Caitlin a mock regretful look. 'Blame Megan for those names. You'll meet her in a couple of hours when we collect her from school.'

Caitlin half-smiles from the doorway, her eyes downcast.

'Cool,' Bartley says, climbing up to the top bunk and flinging himself down.

'I'm not sure what Grandad packed for you,' I say, squeezing past Caitlin and reaching into the airing cupboard in the hall. Returning with two 'welcome packs', soft linen bags containing a bath sheet, hand towel, flannel and a few toiletries, I pop one on the top bunk and hand the other to Caitlin. 'If Grandad has packed towels for you and you prefer to use your own ones, it's fine.'

With his phone a few inches from his face, Bartley acknowledges the pack with a soft grunt. Caitlin peeks into hers and bobs her head to say thank you. Knowing that she must be spinning with all the changes of the last week, I turn towards the stairs.

'One second,' I say, confident I have something that will

please her more than toiletries. I return with two large sketchpads and slip one on the top bunk for Bartley. I know he'll show little interest in it, but I don't want to leave him out.

Caitlin's eyes grow wide with astonishment when I hand her the other one, along with some charcoal and artist pencils. She stares at me for a moment, hugging the pad to her chest, then her entire face lights up with a beaming smile of gratitude.

'Right, any special requests for dinner this evening?' Studies have revealed that food often tops the list of anxieties for children coming into care. Making it clear early on that there will always be enough for everyone helps those who've come from a background of neglect. I've found that offering choices is a good way of soothing picky eaters.

Bartley doesn't answer, probably because he's captivated by his game. It's Caitlin that worries me. She looks hesitant, as if she'd like to suggest something, but then bites her lip and stares at the floor.

'Right,' I say with forced brightness. 'I'll make a chicken casserole, I think.'

Caitlin's anxious frown vanishes, but she still doesn't utter a single word.

Chapter Five

After lunch, Jamie invites Bartley to 'shoot some hoops' in the garden. His face a picture, Bartley immediately ditches his phone and runs to get his shoes on. My heart swells as he follows Jamie outside. It's lovely to see the back of his 'grumpy old man' demeanour, and a relief that he's taking a breather from screens.

Technology raises a raft of thorny issues for foster carers. When children come into care they've often been used to unlimited screen time, and naturally expect that routine to continue. With so many other adjustments for them to make, I think it's too harsh to expect them to change their habits overnight, particularly as it's well known that an addiction to screens can be as hard-wired into the brain as a dependence on alcohol or drugs.

To avoid the nightmare of a tech battle, I prefer to introduce children to the wonders of real life by degrees, making it so appealing that they voluntarily sacrifice their own screen time. Since the Powell children won't be staying with me full-time, there seems little point in forcing new habits on them that will only be reversed in a couple of days, when they return home.

Nonetheless, I do find it difficult to swallow Bartley's refusal to leave his phone at home when we're getting ready to pick Megan up from school. He plays a loud shooting game on it throughout the journey, grunting the odd response when I point out the river and the woods, where I plan to take them at the weekend.

Sketching furiously in her notepad, Caitlin pauses every now and then to stare out at the sights. I marvel that Bartley doesn't bump into lampposts as he follows me along the road, he's so involved in his game. 'Megs comes out of that doorway,' I tell Caitlin, pointing towards the school building. She nods and watches with interest, but Bartley doesn't respond.

Megan's face lights up when she catches sight of us. Bolting out of line, she dashes over to her teacher and points us out, then presses her hands together and pleads for an exception to the rule of waiting until reaching the front of the line before being dismissed.

Miss Casey rolls her eyes then nods, and Megan skips across the playground towards us. 'You're Caitlin!' she says breathlessly, immediately taking the nine-year-old's hand. At first, Caitlin looks taken aback by the sudden friendliness, but then she gives Megan a shy smile.

Bartley's gaze flickers briefly in her direction. He gives her a quick appraisal, mumbles something then returns his attention to his screen.

'And *you're* Bartley. Mum told me you're addicted to screens.'

'I didn't quite put it like that, Megs,' I say, with an awkward laugh. I can always rely on my youngest daughter to blurt out observations I'd prefer to remain unsaid. A habit she learned at her older brother's feet. Bartley doesn't seem to have registered the comment but Caitlin meets my gaze and giggles.

Megan insists that Caitlin plays with her when we get home. 'How about I get some craft out?' I say, directing the comment towards Caitlin so she knows she has a say in the matter. She nods shyly, sitting herself at the table as I cover it with an assortment of pens, crayons and multi-coloured papers.

Refusing to reduce himself to colouring, Bartley deposits himself on the sofa with his phone. He lets out a loud groan as he stretches himself out, as if the strain of being vertical for an hour has really taken its toll.

'Des got me some new Hello Kitty stickers,' Megan says as she sits opposite Caitlin. 'You can share them if you like.' The nine-year-old looks pleased and nods.

'She's so dumb even Hello Kitty says goodbye,' Bartley throws out from across the room. It's a jibe typical of siblings, but there's a thread of spite that makes it seem very far from ordinary banter.

Megan looks outraged but Caitlin doesn't react. Not even the flicker of an eyelash. 'Told you,' her brother continues with an unpleasant cackle. 'She's dumb, I mean, literally dumb.'

'No name-calling please, Bartley.'

A keen advocate of justice, Megan's expression relaxes at my intervention, but then she gives Caitlin a penetrating look. 'Do you *ever* talk?'

Caitlin flushes a deep red and makes herself smaller, shrinking like a tortoise retreating into its shell. 'Meggie, really,' I say with a note of admonishment, as I lock all the sharp knives and skewers away in the medicine cabinet in the kitchen.

'What? I haven't heard her say anything yet. Can she actually talk?'

'Of course she can talk,' I say, although I have to admit, I'm beginning to wonder whether the upset of the last few days has rendered her speechless, or whether there's a deeper, long-term issue. 'Maybe she's not feeling comfortable with us just yet.'

'I thought I might need new batteries for a sec,' Megan jokes, grinning as she taps one of her hearing aids. The correction to the cleft palate she was born with went some way in improving her hearing but she relies on hearing aids, as well as her burgeoning lip-reading skills (a practice she refers to as 'pobbing') to communicate. 'I wear n'aids because Christina drank alcohol,' she explains to Caitlin in a matter-of-fact tone, before asking to borrow the charcoal pencil the nine-year-old is holding.

I stroke her long brown hair. 'Megs, that's not why you have difficulty hearing, sweetie,' I say, although I have no idea whether her birth mother's substance and alcohol misuse contributed towards her cleft palate.

After much agonising, I'd decided to gently touch upon Christina's struggles when Megan questioned me about her past. Tempting though it was to sugar coat her life story, she was growing increasingly aware of the attainment gap between herself and her classmates. I felt it was important for her to understand that she's entirely blameless for the obstacles that make learning difficult for her. Ones that most other children don't have to struggle with.

Providing Megan with a peg to hang her difficulties on seemed to come as somewhat of a relief. 'So I'm not actually stupid like Connor says?' she'd responded, smiling despite the tears in her eyes.

'Ah, sweetie, you're one of the brightest buttons I know,' I told her, my stomach clenching with the urge to take young Connor to task.

Megan squeezes some glue into a pot, too absorbed by the activity to pay my correction any attention. Caitlin has paused in her sketching, however, and is watching Megan with a mixture of intrigue and tenderness in her eyes.

The nine-year-old remains at the table when Megan trots off to watch TV, her focus so intense that she jumps when I invite her to join me in peeling some vegetables. She nods and jumps up, seemingly happy to help.

'Do you do any cooking at home, Caitlin?' I say lightly, keen to let her know I'm interested without pressuring her to talk. I hand her a potato and a peeler, remembering a course on childhood anxiety I attended a while back, with selective mutism mentioned as one of the associated issues. As far as I can remember, the condition is more common in girls and often has its roots in childhood trauma. Since many sufferers are able to communicate freely with those close to them, it's a problem that frequently only comes to light when the child starts school and is expected to mix with lots of unfamiliar people.

Caitlin tilts her head from side to side, which I take to mean that she sometimes helps in the kitchen at home. To help her feel comfortable, I chat away about other children who've stayed with us without using any names. It's surprising how keen our senses become attuned when the usual tools of communication are absent. Family conversations are far more animated when Megan is around, and as I tell Caitlin about a nine-year-old who only ate porridge when she first came to us, there's a sharpness to her silence that tells me she's interested. It's almost as if she's bursting to ask more questions about it.

'Bartley,' I call out when all the potatoes are peeled. 'Would you like to set the table?' I can just about see him stretched out on the sofa from where I'm standing. He heard me. I can tell from the way he shifts position. 'Bartley, would you give us a hand, please?'

'I don't have the facilities for that, big man,' he yawns, turning over onto his side.

'Sorry?'

'Nah, you're all right.'

'You've been on that screen a long time now, honey,' I say, as Caitlin busies herself clearing the craft bits and pieces from the table.

'What? This is nothing. I've had screen-time notifications of 12 hours before now,' he tells me, sounding quite proud.

Children don't take too kindly to being separated from their tech, as my poor bruised shins of the past remind me, so I keep an even tone as I call out, 'That's quite a record. I'd rather you didn't try to top that while you're here, though. Ten more minutes, then it's going off.'

Chapter Six

My mother has a key to our house and after letting herself in she waits at the open door for Des, who's taken to picking her up and giving her lifts lately. The social worker's permanent cheeriness sometimes grates on her and his left-wing tendencies drive her up the wall, but she gravitates towards him when he's round, mischievously raising whichever political story is most likely to wind him up. I've long suspected that she thoroughly enjoys their spats.

They rib each other as they hang up their coats in the hall, their banter the perfect background distraction. 'Right, Bartley, pop your screen in the box over here and go and wash your hands. Dinner won't be long. Megsy, Caitlin, wash your hands too.'

Caitlin tiptoes up the hall. Des and my mum pause in their conversation to greet her but she keeps her head bowed and dashes up the stairs.

'Bartley,' I prompt. 'Come on, honey.'

'Yeah, all right, keep your knickers on,' he says as he heaves himself off the sofa and sits at the table.

'It's over here, lovey,' I say, keeping my tone even as I

slip a wooden box on the mantelpiece. I hum quietly as I start mashing the potatoes, watching him out of the corner of my eye.

'Stupid bitch,' he mutters under his breath, his fingers still scrolling over the screen. Mungo, alert to the growing tension, trots over to my side and begins to growl.

'I've asked you to do something, Bartley, love,' I say, abandoning the potatoes and taking the box over to him, so he doesn't even have to get up. My tone is mild but it's the demand that triggers his rage.

Throwing the chair back so that it falls over with a thwack on the floor, he pulls himself up to his full height, which is only an inch or two shorter than me, and squares up. 'You can't tell me what to do, you stupid bitch!'

My heart thuds in my chest. In my heightened state of awareness, I register several things at once. My mother's jaw dropping as she stares at us from the hall. Des's altered position as he moves in front of her, shielding her protectively from the scene. And Mungo, mirroring Des by squeezing himself heroically into the space between myself and Bartley, ears pulled back in distress. It's at times like this I'm relieved that Megan is hard of hearing. Stretched out on a beanbag in front of the television, she's oblivious to everything that's going on around her.

Keeping my gaze low to avoid eye contact, a technique I learned in non-violent resistance training, I set the box gently down on the table. Aware that the slightest display of aggression on my part, a raised voice or threatening body language, is liable to inflame Bartley's temper, I work hard to keep my breathing even while standing firm against him.

After a few seconds he flings his phone into the box and snatches up the chair, slamming it back onto its feet with a loud snarl of fury.

'Thank you,' I say softly. I add that there's a space under the stairs he can go to if he needs some time alone.

Muttered curses tell me that the suggestion hasn't gone down too well but I'm too busy with dinner to show him that I'm not suggesting he lower himself into a dank dark cellar full of rats.

Returning to the kitchen and the steaming potatoes, I shakily find myself wondering where he's picked up such aggression. I suddenly picture Julie practically tripping over herself to get him some chocolate spread when he demanded it. Clearly, his grandmother is used to dancing to his tune so as not to provoke him. And maybe I'm being unfair, but it's all too easy to imagine his grandfather leaning over her and shouting menacingly in her face.

Sprawled across the table with his head buried in his arms, I can't see Bartley's face but his shoulders are trembling as if he's crying. My heart constricts, but when I slip a few tiny bowls and a bottle of ketchup in front of him and ask him to fill them, he sets about the task without complaint. Seemingly, he's as relieved as I am to put the scene behind us.

'I'd like to give him a piece of my mind,' Mum grumbles as I gather utensils from the kitchen drawer. 'He deserves a proper ticking off. I don't know how you keep your patience, I really don't.' I can't help smiling at the note of disapproval in her tone. Old school when it comes to discipline, my mother is always confounded by what she views as the namby-pamby modern ways of dealing with difficult behaviour.

'I could cobble some stocks together in the back garden if you think it'd be helpful,' Des says, joining us in the kitchen.

'I'll give *you* stocks, you cheeky devil,' Mum retorts, batting him on the shoulder with a slatted spoon. She moves to the table and sits opposite Bartley. 'Shouldn't even have a contraption like that at your age,' she mutters, unable to resist a belated rise to my defence. Still red in the face, the ten-year-old studiously avoids her stern gaze.

Des and I exchange amused glances, then he pecks me on the cheek. 'Marry me, Mrs Lewis?'

Des has been asking me to marry him on a regular basis since his return from the US five years ago. My refusals have turned into a standing joke between us. I'm not sure why I don't feel able to fully commit to our relationship – all the children enjoy his company, particularly Megan, and barely a day ever passes without him making at least one of us laugh out loud. I suspect my reluctance has something to do with having witnessed the complex issues that can sometimes arise in blended families, and the fall-out when children feel pushed out by the arrival of an unwanted step-parent.

'I barely know you,' I answer jokingly, before spooning the mashed potatoes and some chicken casserole onto each plate. Des snorts a rueful chuckle as he leaves the kitchen. It's then that Megan finally notices him. Charging over, she throws herself into his arms. He sweeps her up then dangles her upside down, swinging her from side to side.

'Stop it, you maniac,' my mum gasps. 'She's about to eat.'

'Nanny!' Megan shouts when Des sets her on her feet again. She dashes over to my mum and flings her arms around her.

'Ooh, careful now,' Mum winces, on the receiving end of a particularly enthusiastic hug.

Jamie, skilled at smelling a home-cooked meal from any location, arrives home just as the plates touch the table. Bartley watches him with apparent fascination as he and Des discuss his forthcoming gig and the new tracks he and his bandmates have been composing. Having spent many happy years as lead singer of a touring band, Des gets even more animated than usual whenever he and Jamie get together.

Despite hailing from a large family, Caitlin seems entirely overwhelmed by the noisy conversation. Watching Des and Jamie from lowered lashes, she starts so violently when they break into laughter that she drops her fork and knocks over a cup of water as well. Mungo shoots around to her side of the table to gulp down the spillages and looks up at her expectantly, waiting for more.

'You pleb-ite,' Bartley sneers, glancing at Jamie as if expecting approval.

Grabbing a couple of napkins from the centre of the table, Jamie mops up the spillage and, after giving Caitlin a kindly smile, carries on talking to Des.

Caitlin's brow furrows, her gaze lingering on Jamie as if she's puzzled by his consideration. Eventually she picks up her fork again, but prods at her meal warily. 'It's not going to choke you, lovey,' Mum says softly.

'It might,' Bartley pipes up. 'People drop dead from choking every day.' He watches his sister eagerly. When he doesn't get a reaction he adds, 'Mum ate chicken casserole last week and now she's in the nuthouse.'

Megan blinks fiercely between the siblings and then looks at me, expecting me to intervene. 'Dude,' Jamie says, breaking off his conversation with Des and levelling his gaze on Bartley. 'You need to chill.'

Bartley flushes and lowers his gaze.

'I know the *hospital* your mum's in,' I tell Caitlin pointedly. She's so thin, I'm keen for her to eat a good meal. 'It's a lovely place, she'll be well looked after there.'

Caitlin nods and takes a tiny mouthful. When everyone's finished, Jamie dashes back to work. While Des and I clear the table, Mum gets up with a groan and sits next to Caitlin. 'I hear you like drawing. Will you show me some of your sketches?'

Caitlin springs to her feet and flees the room. Mum exchanges a puzzled glance with Des when he returns to the table, but a minute later the nine-year-old returns with her notepad tucked under her arm.

Bartley gives her a slow eyeroll of contempt. 'Oh, Christ, here we go.'

'Let's see it then,' Mum says, doing well to ignore him. She pats the chair beside her and Caitlin sits down. Megan squashes up against Mum's other side and begins leafing through the pages.

'Oh, my, you're quite an artist,' Mum says, sounding genuinely impressed. 'Are they stars?'

Although worlds apart, I think perhaps Mum reminds Caitlin of her own grandmother because she writes something down with a shy, expectant smile. 'Right, let's see,' Mum says, adjusting her glasses. 'So, these are our planets, you say, and over here is the rest of the Milky Way. And what's this swirly area here?' She squints through her bifocals, giving Caitlin a chance to speak. Clearly enjoying herself, the nine-year-old scribbles another note on the page. 'Ah,' Mum says, 'Andromeda?'

Caitlin makes a noise in her throat, the first sound I've heard from her since our introduction yesterday.

'Put a sock in it, smartarse,' Bartley pounces immediately.

Outraged, Megan stares between Des and my mum open-mouthed.

'I've got the measure of you, young man,' Mum warns him. 'You won't half cop it in a minute.'

Bartley sniggers. 'Yeah all right, less of the smoke, old lady.'

Mum glares at him. 'I mean it. Any more rudeness and foul language and I'll have your tongue out.'

Bartley's cheeks flush and his eyes widen as if genuinely shocked. Des starts whistling and staring up at the ceiling. 'Don't *you* start with all your wokery, matey, or I'll cut yours out as well,' Mum adds, but there's a twinkle in her eyes as she looks at him. 'Eye for an eye, that's what society is missing these days. A bit of discipline.'

'An eye for an eye'll just make the whole world blind,' Des returns quickly.

'For heaven's sake, stop it, you two,' I chastise, returning to the table. 'You're worse than all the children put together.' Caitlin grins up at my mum, who hunches up her shoulders with an impish wink. My mother's ability to build relationships with the children I care for has always amazed me. Despite her stern nature and occasional threats of torture, children seem to sense her empathy and her soft heart, and usually end up adoring her.

'You calling me childish?!' Des cries, staring at me in mock outrage. 'Anyway, she started it,' he says, pointing at my mother with such a comical pout that all of us, including Caitlin and Bartley, burst out laughing.

Chapter Seven

Caitlin's tension increases palpably when Des and my mum say their goodbyes. When I come downstairs after reading to Megan, I find her hovering in the hallway, close to tears. 'What is it, sweetie?' I go to her side but resist the urge to put my arm around her, since I don't know how she feels about accepting comfort. Without knowing her history, I have to bear in mind the possibility that physical touch might be linked to trauma in her mind.

Her hands form tight fists at her side. I watch them, wondering if she's trying to summon the courage to talk to me, but then I look at her face. From the way she's clenching her mouth so tightly together, it's almost as if she's literally biting her lips to hold the words in, rather than letting them out.

'I wonder if you're worried about going to bed in an unfamiliar room,' I say gently.

Mungo bounds into the hall. Sensing Caitlin's sombre mood, he rubs an ear against one of her legs and gives a mournful groan. With sagging shoulders, she kneels down and strokes his head. 'I used to feel anxious whenever I stayed away from home.'

She looks up at me with a sharpening gaze.

'Yes, honestly. I could barely sleep the first day or two of a holiday. That was before I took my secret weapon away with me.'

She frowns, watching me intently. 'Come with me, I'll show you.' She follows me into the yellow room and watches as I haul an old-fashioned suitcase out from under the desk. 'My mum and auntie made them,' I say, lifting the lid to reveal dozens of hand-sewn teddies and soft toys. The creations have provided comfort to lots of children over the years, even the older ones you might have thought had long since outgrown them.

Caitlin gasps at the sight and then gives me a beaming smile. 'Would you like to choose one?'

Fear of missing out draws Bartley away from his screen. He peers around the door, but then his face falls. 'Oh, boring. You're such a fucking baby, Caitlin.'

Her smile swiftly evaporates. 'Please use kind words, Bartley. It's not babyish to like soft bears,' I tell him with a disapproving frown. 'You can choose one too, if you'd like.'

'Not babyish? It's fucking embryonic,' he sniggers. Mungo mutters softly as Bartley stamps back down the hall.

'Can you imagine what my mum would say to that?' I say with a grin. 'She'd have his guts for garters.'

Caitlin looks at me and giggles. After a nod of encouragement, she drops to her knees and rummages through the case, finally settling on a small brown bear in a pin-striped suit, which she takes up to bed.

* * *

53

Bartley's gaze doesn't even flicker in my direction when I walk up to the sofa. He's been alternating between the telly and his phone for so long, I feel a bit guilty about allowing him so much screen time. It makes me sad to think of all the experiences children miss these days by spending so much of their childhood online. I'm itching to give him a break, but also to get to know him a little.

He's so engrossed that he barely registers me, even when I say his name. To get his attention, I'm going to have to bring out the big guns. For a boy of his age, that means offering an activity that's both competitive and mildly risky. 'Fancy a game of darts, Bartley?' I say invitingly.

'Darts?' he says, immediately interested. 'You haven't got a board.'

'We have,' I say, opening a slim cabinet fixed to the wall adjacent to the TV.

He sits up sharply. 'Am I allowed?!'

'I don't see why not. You're almost as tall as me.'

He flings the remote control across the sofa and dashes over to inspect the darts I've pulled out of our cabinet drawer. 'Wow, they're really sharp. I could half do some damage to a certain someone using one of these.'

'But that's not the idea, is it, young man?' As soon as I step out of the way, he starts practising. The first few darts sail right over the top of the board and stick in the wall. But he soon gets the hang of it. 'You're good. Have you ever played before?'

He shakes his head. 'Grandad has a board but he never lets me have a go, the …' He proceeds to use a word I find particularly unpleasant so I seize the opportunity, while there's no one else around, to pull him up on it.

'Bartley. You can tell me anything, but we don't use words like that in this house, okay.'

He snorts in annoyance. I move on quickly, so as not to make a big deal of it. 'Right, nearest the bullseye to see who starts.'

We both take a turn. He scowls when I win and I find myself holding my breath, readying myself for another round of expletives. It doesn't happen though; he's excited to get going.

'Drat, you're beating me already,' I say, chalking up our scores after the first round.

He grins and flexes his biceps. 'Made of different stuff, aren't I?' When I laugh and shake my head he adds, 'I heard Jamie say that earlier.'

'Ha, I might have guessed!'

'Ethan would love this,' he beams after winning the next round. Then his face contorts, his eyes rolling towards the ceiling. 'I wish he could have come and not that bloody loser up there.'

I've found that siblings usually pull together when they're uncertain of their environment, but that's certainly not the case with these two. I had thought that Bartley perhaps had a tendency to lash out at anyone in his line of fire, but it does seem as if Caitlin is singled out for his most vicious attacks. There's a thread of heavy spite in his tone, as if he genuinely despises his sister. There doesn't seem to be any love lost when it comes to his grandfather either. It's something I'll need to flag up in my notes to make sure Robert is aware.

'Why do you say that?' I ask mildly, biting my tongue to stop myself complaining about his swearing again.

Throughout the afternoon he'd alternated between calling Caitlin a 'fucking moron', 'gobshite', or 'useless streak of piss', so 'bloody loser' could be considered as a move in the right direction. Besides, it's important to make wise strategic choices early on in a placement. Sometimes, you have to pick your battles. Prolonged disapproval will only serve to make Bartley clam up and my main aim is to establish a relationship and get him talking.

'Because she's a waste of space. Everyone knows it.' He takes aim and fist-punches the air when his dart lands on treble 18. 'I love this! I'm gonna ask if Ethan can come next time we stay here. Can we come next weekend?'

'Ethan won't be able to play darts. I think he's a bit *too* young.'

Bartley shrugs. 'Okay, it'll still be more fun than having that bitch up there.' He throws his next dart. When it hits the wall, he mutters a choice expletive then clamps his hand over his mouth. 'Oops, my bad.' He grins and looks at me. 'Hey, you know what, *he* probably won't let her stay with Nan on her own. Have you got room for all of us?'

A chill runs over the back of my neck. 'I'm not sure,' I say, strongly suspecting that their case is not as cut and dried as it may first have seemed. I take my turn because I don't want Bartley to sense my sharpened interest. 'Who's "he"?'

'Grandad,' he says distractedly, his eyes shooting from the board to my hand as I prepare to throw my second dart.

'Why won't he let Caitlin stay with Nan without you there?'

'He doesn't want Nan questioning her,' he says, watching me eagerly. 'Anything less than a 20 and I win.'

Keeping my gaze fixed on the board, I say, as casually as I can manage, 'What doesn't he want her questioned about?' Having seen them together very briefly, I'm not in a position to make a judgement about Bartley's relationship with his grandfather, but if the scathing tone he uses when he talks about him is anything to go by, there's more than a simple lack of affection there.

He shrugs again. 'I dunno, do I?'

'Then how do you know that's the reason?'

'I heard them arguing about it,' he mumbles, losing patience. 'Come on, Rosie. You gonna take your shot or what?'

Chapter Eight

I'm woken in the early hours of Saturday 2 March by a shrill tone. Accustomed to Megan calling out to make sure I'm nearby, nightly disturbances don't faze me. I am surprised that I'd slept so deeply though. I'm usually so busy thinking about how newly arrived children must be feeling in a strange bed that I rarely manage more than a few hours on the first night of their stay. It takes a second for me to cotton on that the noise is my mobile ringing, rather than Megan or the other children in distress. Worried that my mother has fallen ill, my pulse quickens as I swipe to answer.

'Rosie, so sorry to disturb you,' says a familiar female voice. It's Sonia from the local authority placement's team. She must be covering the out-of-hours shift.

'Hi, Sonia,' I say cheerily, relieved it's not bad news.

'There's a situation at the hospital,' she tells me as I leap out of bed and pull on some clothes. 'Sorry to ask, but would you be able to get yourself over there?'

I'd been warned to expect the unexpected when I joined Mockingbird. Leaving the house at short notice is not something I could have considered when Emily and Jamie were younger, but with one or the other of them usually at home and both officially registered as my back-up carers, I'm mostly free to respond to whatever crisis comes up.

'I'll ping you Millie's profile in a minute,' Sonia says as I grab my car keys and ease an excited Mungo back with my foot so that I can quietly close the door. Inside the car, I flick the call to loudspeaker. Sonia's voice floats out from the dashboard as I drive towards our local hospital. Fifteen-year-old Millie, it seems, has been giving her foster carer, Joan, the run-around since coming to her two months ago.

I've met Joan several times over the years – she cared for Archie and Bobbi, siblings who came to me after a short period of time in her care – so I know she's an experienced, safe pair of hands. 'She's pleasant enough to Joan when she's around,' Sonia goes on, 'but she's up at all hours, prone to running off, and for some reason she's developed an obsession with her orthodontist. She's stalking him, I mean, literally. He's had to arrange security at the practice, so now Mille's taken to following him home. She must have waited until Joan went to bed then did a runner again.'

'And turned up at the orthodontist's house?' I say, pulling into the hospital car park.

'You've got it,' Sonia says with a sigh. 'Banging on the door. When she got no joy there, she climbed over their side gate.'

'Oh dear, and fell?'

'No.'

'So how come she's in hospital?'

'The dentist's wife called the police. She's had enough of it. So anyway, the police woke Joan up to let her know, she hadn't a clue it was all going on, then when the bobbies turned up and tried to remove Millie from their property she kicked off.'

'Oh no, and she got injured?'

'No, no, nothing like that. They *were* going to take her back to Joan's but she started clawing at her own face and drawing blood so they took her to A&E instead.'

'Ah,' I say with a pang. No matter how many times I hear about children self-harming, I never quite get over the shock of it. It's awful to think of a girl Millie's age in such turmoil, and so desperate to get some release. 'Well, I'm here now.' I cut the engine and zip up my coat, promising to update her in the morning.

The icy air hits me as soon as I step out of the car, so the wave of warm air that greets me as I enter the emergency department is a welcome relief.

I'm about to let the receptionist know I've arrived, when my attention is drawn to a commotion at the far end of the waiting area. With their backs towards me, two uniformed officers are blocking the path of a young teen. From what I can see of her – a painfully thin girl in leggings and a long-sleeved top with unicorns all over it – she looks no more than 11 or 12. I'm pretty sure it's Millie, especially when I notice the long scratches down her cheeks.

'Um, hello,' I say as I approach the group. The police officers turn to me with weary expressions, but they soften when I introduce myself.

Millie greets me like an old friend. 'Hiya, Rosie,' she smiles, revealing twin tracks of braces across her teeth.

There's a slight lisp to her high voice which makes her sound even younger than she looks. 'Want a Coke or something?' she offers, as if she's hostess at her own dinner party. She nods towards one of the officers, a young man with a kindly face and spiky gelled hair. 'He'll get you one, won't you, Sean.'

'Mil-lie,' the officer warns, his tone exasperated. 'This isn't a social. Stop mucking us about and get yourself back in there.' His tone is stern but he's looking at her in the manner of a kindly older brother as he raises a hand and gestures towards a set of double doors marked 'MINORS'.

'Millie's had a check-over,' the other officer tells me, a young woman with a blonde bun. 'Everything's fine but they've done some blood tests, just to dot the I's and cross the T's, and the results aren't back yet. We'll leave her in your capable hands now you're here. Her guardian will need to bring her to the station on Monday morning for processing and we'll, oof – what you doing, Millie?' she gasps, as the teen barges past her.

Sean catches her by the arm. 'Oh no you don't, missus.'

'I need some air!' Millie says, thrashing around so wildly that she catches him in the face with her elbow. 'I told you I can't stay in here, it's too hot!'

'Shall I take her out?' I offer. A moment alone with Millie might give us a chance to make a connection, so she won't be fearful of staying with me while we wait for her results.

'Cheers, Rosie,' Millie says, smiling at me gratefully. 'You're really kind.'

'I'll go with them,' the female officer tells Sean. He gives her a wary nod. 'I'm Poppy, by the way,' she says as she follows us into the car park. She waits beside a huge planter that has dozens of cigarette stubs sticking out of the soil. 'I'll be here if you need me.'

I nod and follow Millie to a bench. We both sit down. Shivering, she hunches over and takes great gasps of air. 'You must be shattered, honey,' I say sympathetically. 'And very cold. Do you want my coat while we're out here?'

'You're so nice,' she says, meeting my eye and smiling. 'I'm really sorry about this,' she adds before leaping to her feet and dashing across the road that runs parallel to the car park.

'I knew it!' Poppy shrieks, tearing past me. There's the hammering of feet on tarmac, a flash of colour as the streetlights flicker over Poppy's high-vis tunic, then both of them disappear from view. Sean appears at the doors just as I reach them.

'Bolted again?' he puffs, his rapid breaths misting the air.

'I'm sorry, there was just no warning.' Feeling responsible, I cover my face with my hands.

'Not your fault, love,' Sean says, twisting the dial on his buzzing pocket radio. 'Like lightning, that one. Don't s'pose Poppy'll catch her. Don't worry, though. At least we know where she'll turn up.'

Shivering, I tiptoe back into the house half an hour later. The thought of my warm bed is tempting, but I'm so wide awake that there's little point in going up now. It's almost 5 a.m. By the time I drop off to sleep, Megan will no doubt be up and pottering down the hall with a cheery hello.

'Stop it, rascal,' I whisper as Mungo plays tug-of-war with the draught excluder I'm trying to lay at the front door. Releasing it, he sits back on his haunches and gazes up at me with his head bowed, tiny slits of white showing beneath his dark brown eyes. I grab a treat from the jar in the hall. 'You know exactly how to get round me, you monster.'

Chew dangling from his mouth, he pads into the kitchen after me. His head tilts from side to side as I boil the kettle to brew some coffee, no doubt puzzled by the change in routine. I pour myself a drink, savouring the warmth of the cup on my cold fingers, and go through to the living area. My thoughts return to Millie as I pile a couple of logs onto some kindling and light a fire. It's awful to think of her wandering the streets on her own, at the mercy of so-called 'kingpins' who are always on the lookout to recruit disenfranchised youths into county lines. Apart from her vulnerability and the dangers she might be exposing herself to, there's barely anything of her and it's a freezing cold night.

Snuggling down on the sofa under one of my mum's goose-down quilts is bliss. Mungo settles himself at my feet and rests his nose on his paws. It doesn't take long for his warmth to seep into my toes. I keep my mobile at my side, willing it to ring with news that Millie is safe and sound.

Sipping my warm drink, my eyes settle on the dartboard across the room. Suddenly, Bartley's words come back to me. I'll need to log our conversation in my daily diary while it's fresh in my mind and send it over to Robert by the end of the day.

Foster carers are strongly encouraged to carefully record anything of note that happens during the day, even if doing so might paint themselves in a less than positive light. For instance, while it may be tempting for a carer to brush a flaming row with the teenager living with them under the carpet, it's important to report the incident accurately. Nothing raises suspicions in a social worker more than a foster carer who has failed to report significant events in their log. Emailing our diaries to the case worker every day makes it impossible to add or delete details after the event, and evidences that the record hasn't been tampered with.

I close my eyes, trying to remember exactly what Bartley said. Something about Ryan sending Caitlin away because he didn't want Julie to question her.

The skin at the back of my neck tingles again, as it had during our game. Does Julie suspect that Caitlin is keeping secrets, I wonder. Ones that Ryan is keen to keep quiet.

My thoughts drift to Phoebe, a girl who was the same age as Caitlin when we fostered her a decade earlier. I wrote about our experiences of caring for Phoebe in *Trapped*. Her parents had subjected her to years of sexual abuse, but her loyalty to them had been so absolute that despite all the suffering and the damage to her psyche, she still did her best to protect them.

An image of the ferrety-looking man who barged past me on my first visit to the Powells' house flashes into my mind. And then my thoughts turn to Bonnie, Caitlin's mother, and her flight from home on an equally freezing cold night. 'What were you running from?' I murmur, shivering despite the warmth from Mungo's snoozing form and the blazing fire a few feet away.

I'm so deep in thought that I don't register the sound of footsteps straight away. 'Hello, sweetheart,' I say, as Caitlin slides into the room. 'Did you sleep okay?'

Silenced

She nods but doesn't meet my gaze. Mungo stretches himself, arching his back, then slowly pads over to say hello. Caitlin puts her notepad and pencils on the floor so that she's free to pet him. 'Would you like a drink? Hot chocolate?'

Her eyes light up. She nods with a half-smile. 'Here you go then,' I say, lifting the quilt and gesturing for her to take my place. 'Snuggle yourself under there and I'll get us both a nice warm drink.' She doesn't say anything as I tuck her in but another faint smile tells me she's comfortable with the attention. When I return a few minutes later, her eyes widen in surprise. I've gone to town with the hot chocolate, lavishing it with some whirly cream and marshmallows.

The rain pattering against the windows and the wind howling down the chimney make it feel even cosier as I work on a patchwork quilt for my mum and Caitlin quietly sketches in her pad. She works with focused intensity, creating page after page of intricate fractals. When I ask her what she's drawing she lifts the pad to give me a better view but doesn't say anything.

'Our galaxy, or Andromeda?'

She grins at that, seemingly delighted that I've remembered her 'conversation' with my mum, but she still doesn't utter a word.

At the back of my mind lurks a strange sense that there's a lot she's trying *not* to say.

Chapter Nine

I finally hear news of Millie just before 9 o'clock. 'You've had a night of it, I gather?' Joan says over the phone.

'Oh, Joan, I've been on tenterhooks since I got home.' I cradle my mobile phone between shoulder and ear so I can carry on whisking some pancake mix. 'Is she okay?'

The foster carer lets out a deep sigh. 'Almost blue with cold and thoroughly worn out. That's my fault really. I hid her coat away hoping it would put her off going out. But yes, she's all right. The police found her at the dentist's house again. She's tucked up in bed at the moment. No doubt she'll sleep most of the day so she's ready for another escapade this evening.'

My heart sinks. 'Oh, don't say that.'

'Sorry you got dragged into it, Rosie, but with two smallies in placement I can't be running about here, there and everywhere after her. I've just taken a newborn with NAS as well and you know what that's like.' I do indeed, having cared for several babies with Neonatal Abstinence Syndrome. When babies are born addicted to drugs, they need weeks, sometimes months, of intensive love and

66

attention to nurse them through the jitters, shakes and stomach cramps that characterise withdrawal.

'Of course you can't,' I say, handing the whisk to Caitlin, who's been loitering at my side. 'What's going to happen to her? The police said she's to be processed first thing on Monday.'

'Someone's coming round in an hour to do a Return to Home interview, then I'm supposed to get her to the police station for processing this afternoon. If I can get her out of bed, that is. Honestly, it's too much sometimes.'

When children missing from care return home, an independent worker is appointed to conduct a Return to Home interview, to find out why they went missing and to avoid it happening again.

I listen as Joan lets off steam, knowing full well that she loves fostering as much as I do. I get the impression she doesn't have much of a support network so I'm happy to be her sounding board. I count myself lucky in that regard, what with my wonderful mum as my keystone. My children are both great listeners as well. Then there's Des of course, whose experience as a social worker gives me a different perspective on any fostering issues that come up. 'I'm her fourth carer in as many months. You know what she's up to, don't you.'

'Hmm, she thinks she'll get back home?'

'Yep, not that she stands much chance of going back there,' Joan says, sounding thoroughly fed up. She lowers her voice and tells me that Millie's first 12 years of life were relatively stable. It was only once Luke, her mother's new partner, appeared on the scene that life at home began to deteriorate. The roofer seemed to feel that having a child around cramped his clubbing lifestyle. 'I'll not give her the satisfaction of getting rid of me, though. I've told her straight. She's got a place here for the foreseeable, however much she plays up.'

'You're lovely, Joan,' I say, knowing that she's done the best thing for Millie. Children find it hard to accept that their own parents have rejected them. It's easier to blame social workers, the authorities, even the government, rather than face the fact that they can't return home because their parent doesn't want them. Delusional thinking can lead them to deliberately sabotage their foster placements under the false assumption that if they work their way through lots of carers in a short space of time, the authorities will have no choice but to send them back home.

'Right, breakfast's ready, guys!' I call, after telling Joan I'll be in touch soon.

Glued to his phone, Bartley doesn't respond. As he's not been up long, I decide not to make an issue of it and let him eat his pancakes on the sofa. Fork in one hand, he scoffs his pancakes while scrolling through the iPhone that's balanced on a tray on his lap.

Caitlin eats silently and leaves the table without a word, though she seems content enough sketching in her notebook for the rest of the morning.

The weather is dry and bright, and in the afternoon Caitlin, Megan and I brave the cold and venture into the garden while Bartley hangs out under the stairs. I'd shown him the space when I sensed his anger boiling over and it had immediately taken the wind out of his sails. 'Oh my life, this is so cool!' he'd exclaimed, throwing himself in as if diving into a pool.

Tucking the rabbits inside her coat to keep them warm, Caitlin retreats to the swing at the bottom of the garden. In her element with hosepipe and wellies, Megan scrubs out the hutch and sweeps the patio.

'Meggie, no! I'm too cold for that!' I shriek as she tilts the hosepipe skywards and creates an arch of water over my head.

'Oops, sorry, Mummy,' she says, giggling. Caitlin lets out a chuckle from the swing. Deciding that it'll be safer to watch Megan's antics from a safe distance, I head down the garden towards her. Halfway down, I catch a soft murmur. Feigning a sudden interest in the borders, I sneak a side glance and see that Caitlin is whispering softly to the rabbits as they sniff inquisitively around her neck. I can't make out what she's saying but it's heartening to know that she's feeling relaxed.

Given some more time and space, I'm hopeful that she'll be able to find her voice.

Sunday morning passes peacefully enough, Bartley lounging on the sofa, his sister moving around the house like a little ghost, keeping to the shadows of every room, always with her sketchpad in her hand. After lunch we take Mungo for a walk along the river. On a rest day, Emily joins us.

At the tea hut we share some cheesy chips, then let Mungo off the lead. He charges along the riverside path and over a black wrought-iron bridge, stopping halfway along to sniff at some flowers that have been tied to the railings.

'Don't you dare, Mungo!' Emily calls out, running to shoo him away before he cocks his leg over the tributes. The site is well known to locals, a victim of bullying at one of our local high schools having tragically thrown himself into the river one dark day the winter before last.

'Is it someone's birthday?' says Megan when we catch up.

'Not a birthday, no,' I say carefully, slipping Mungo back on the lead. 'But an anniversary, of sorts.'

We set off again at a slow pace. After a few steps I become aware that Bartley isn't keeping up. Next thing I know, Emily is charging back past me. 'What the heck are you doing, Bartley?' she cries, and then the reason for her outrage becomes clear. Having pulled several flowers from one of the bunches, Bartley is now clumping them together on a nearby bench.

Emily makes a grab for them but Bartley rounds on her. 'Mind your own beeswax, you stupid bitch!'

'Those flowers have been put there for a reason!' Emily rages. 'You can't go vandalising them! Who does that?!'

With his face contorted and puce, Bartley screams in her face. 'All right, bitch, no need to shout!'

'I didn't shout,' Emily returns in a mild but firm tone. She raises her eyebrows at me, takes Megan's hand and then walks off shaking her head. Megan can't help twisting around as she goes, giving Bartley daggers for upsetting her adored older sister.

Caitlin follows quietly behind.

'They were for you, okay?!' Bartley yells at me in wounded fury. 'Sorry for trying to be nice for once!'

'Well, it's lovely of you to think of me, Bartley,' I say quietly, genuinely quite touched. 'But these flowers have been left as a tribute to someone who died, honey. That's why Emily was sad.'

'I know that, but I was only going to take a few of the nicest ones. Fat lot of good they are to someone if they're dead.'

'Aw, well, I appreciate the sentiment, Bartley, but they're not ours to take.'

'We usually stamp on them,' Bartley grumbles defensively. 'I wasn't going to do that. I was going to give them to you,' he reiterates. 'I was being bloody nice!'

I'm tempted to ask who allows him to stamp on shrines, but his voice, high-pitched and full of resentment, tells me that it might be wiser to take a leaf out of Caitlin's book, and not say another word.

The telephone rings as soon as we step indoors.

'I won't come out today if you don't mind, lovey,' my mum says as soon as I pick up. 'It's so chilly out there. I'm going to batten down the hatches and catch up with a few episodes of *The Repair Shop*.'

'Okay. Shall we drop you something round?'

'I'm not at the Meals on Wheels stage quite yet, thank you very much,' she laughs. 'No, really. I've got some stew left over from yesterday. I'll warm that up with a nice bit of granary.'

'Okay, let me know if you need anything.' My mobile phone buzzes in my coat pocket as soon as I replace the receiver. It's a text from Des, telling me he can't make it over for dinner either. I stare at the message, frowning.

'Literally no one uses a landline these days,' Bartley calls out from the sofa. Stretched out on his side, he's already got his phone in his hand.

'I like my landline,' I say in a mock defensive voice, popping my mobile on the stairs and taking off my coat. We didn't celebrate my birthday last year because of the arrival of a last-minute placement. I'm wondering whether my mother and Des are up to something, or whether it's simply a coincidence that they've both cried off at the same time. 'Right, dinner won't be long. Twenty minutes, then that phone has to go in its box, okay, Bartley.'

Since my guest list is lighter than planned, I freeze half of the minced beef I'd fried earlier and add some spice to the rest. Caitlin and Megan set the table as I prepare a soya alternative for Emily, who's on a mission to lower her carbon footprint. 'Bartley,' I call out lightly, as I set out bowls of grated cheese, salsa and wraps. 'Time for you to put your phone in the box, honey.'

No answer. I leave it a minute or so then try again, deciding to simplify the request in case he has processing difficulties. I've learned a lot in the last few years about the effect of early trauma on the brain. Language deficits are common in children from challenging backgrounds, and I know that an overwhelmed brain can pull the shutters down when lots of instructions are given all at once. 'Bartley,' I say, repeating his name until he deigns to look at me. 'Phone in the box, then wash your hands.'

Satisfied that I've delivered a clear instruction in a firm tone, I busy myself with the cutlery so that he's free to back down without humiliation.

Nothing happens. I turn so that I'm facing the sofa. 'Bartley, now please.'

'God, you're always on at me!' he roars. Leaping from the sofa, he charges over and presses himself right up against me so that I'm pinned against the kitchen worktop.

Mungo springs from nowhere, lip curled back so that one fang is on display. He's usually such a gentle character that the sight is enough to make my pulse soar, even without the sound of his heart-wrenching whines and Megan and Caitlin's expressions of horror.

Taking a slow, calming breath, I remind myself of the non-violent resistance techniques.

Do not react

Do not talk much

Do not lecture

Do not use sarcasm

Be aware of body language

'Bartley, be gentle with me please,' I manage calmly. He presses his hips against mine by way of reply, and then cocks two fingers and a thumb to imitate a gun, making a clicking noise as he 'fires' against my forehead. Tension makes my neck and shoulders stiffen. 'Come on, Bartley, you're better than this.'

It isn't easy to fake optimism at times like this, but it's effective. As his failure to rile me sinks in, I get the sense that he's already losing steam. He drops his hand. There's an easing of the pressure against my hips, so that the edges of the worktop aren't pressing quite as painfully into my back.

My pulse begins to drop. But then, with a sinking heart, I register the sound of rapid footsteps on the stairs. And then Jamie appears in the hall. I hadn't even realised he was home.

Knowing how protective he is of me, my stomach flips. I needn't have worried.

'Not cool, bro,' is all he says as he walks steadily past us. Suddenly frozen, Bartley watches as Jamie fills a glass with water, takes a few large gulps then lays it gently in the sink. 'Seriously not cool,' he says as he passes us again, pausing for half a second to look Bartley in the eye.

It's a gentle rebuke but a powerful one. Shame-faced, Bartley overtakes Jamie in the hall, dives into the cupboard under the stairs and slams the door after him.

Halfway through our meal, Bartley returns sulkily to the table. Cheeks still glowing red, he glances at Jamie a couple of times but doesn't make any attempt to eat. Keen to make him feel comfortable and lower his feeling of shame, I try to jolly things along and draw him into our conversation.

Nothing works, but then Jamie looks at me. 'Did you know there's a company that makes rucksacks to capture cow farts?'

'Wait, what?' Bartley pipes up, intrigue dissolving his shame in an instant.

'Cow farts,' Jamie answers casually as he pours himself a glass of water. 'Full of methane that can be turned into electricity.'

'Very eco-friendly,' Emily nods. 'I approve.'

Bartley snorts with laughter and grabs himself a plate. 'That's so gross,' he grins as he fills a fajita with chicken.

I flash Jamie a grateful look, marvelling at the transformative power of positive role models.

Silenced

Sometimes, all it takes to turn a child's life around is one interested adult. That's why advocacy schemes are so important for children in care, particularly for adolescents. The Children's Society often recruits volunteers to work directly with children in the care system. Advocates may only spend one or two hours a week listening and supporting the child, but I've seen the positive effect their involvement can have.

Bartley beams as the banter around the table picks up pace. I watch his face, wondering about the other adults in his life, and exactly which of them he's been modelling himself on.

Chapter Ten

Never happier than when the house is full of hubbub, I'm almost sorry when Monday morning arrives. On early turn, Emily left the house before any of us woke. With Jamie in bed after his late gig, the only sound as we eat breakfast is Megan's constant cheery chatter and Mungo's snorty breathing as he hoovers up the toast crusts that she accidentally on purpose drops on the floor.

Bartley and Caitlin show no interest in his antics. Picking at their cereal with glum expressions, they answer my cheery questions about their school day with muted nods and shrugs. I wonder if it's school they're not keen on, or the idea of returning back home.

Sipping my coffee, I'm about to text my mum to see if she's free for a cuppa after the school run, when a message from Joan appears on the screen:

Millie's been bailed to appear at youth court at 11 a.m. C has a health review that I can't miss this morning. Any chance you can attend as appropriate adult instead?

Silenced

The Appropriate Adult scheme exists to make sure that vulnerable adults and young people have their rights, mental health and emotional wellbeing safeguarded when being processed through the criminal justice system. To comply with the Police and Criminal Evidence Act 1984 (PACE) codes of practice, an appropriate adult is appointed if the young person's parent or guardian isn't able to accompany them. While a solicitor is always made available for legal representation, it's not necessarily someone a young person would feel comfortable opening up to if, for example, they're feeling sick, or they're simply overwhelmed.

With a sense of anticipation, I send Joan a thumbs-up emoji and ask for more details. Acting as an appropriate adult isn't new to me. I've accompanied a number of children I've cared for during police interviews, but I've only ever been to court once before and that was for Megan's adoption. Magistrates' court is going to be a new experience for me.

After dropping Megan off at school, we set off towards Millfield Primary. As soon as I enter the colourful playground, I'm reminded of the first day I brought Archie and Bobbi here, the siblings who had initially been placed with Joan. Then five years old, Bobbi couldn't have been more different from Caitlin in terms of behaviour. Barely pausing long enough between sentences to draw breath, the young girl would throw herself around and constantly make a noise to remind me of her existence. It took a while for me to realise that Bobbi's verboseness was a manifestation of high anxiety, and while Caitlin's silence seemingly

77

places her at the opposite end of the behavioural spectrum, I suspect the same root cause for both.

Having fostered several other Millfield pupils in the past, I know that staff at the school are particularly good at keeping parents and carers informed. Their senior leadership team are less progressive than some when it comes to behaviour management, however, evidenced by the painful number of past exclusions under their belt.

Bartley charges across the playground when the bell goes, shouldering his way through a group of younger children.

'I've so enjoyed our weekend,' I tell Caitlin, as the playground empties around us.

Biting her lip, she hovers at my side, seemingly reluctant to go in. 'Nan or Grandad will pick you up, okay, sweetie? And I'll see you again tomorrow.'

She meets my gaze and nods, then trudges off towards her class. I keep her in my sights as I make my way over to reception and notice two girls about her age nudging each other as she walks past. Their eyes slide over her and then they giggle and walk away.

She looks so unhappy as she passes other groups of girls, their arms looped around each other, that my heart turns in on itself in sympathy. While writers like Jacqueline Wilson, J.K. Rowling and David Walliams have done wonders for the reputation of the underdog, it's still not unusual for children in the care system to be on the receiving end of relational aggression. Being ostracised by their peers is an insidious problem for young people. One that's sometimes so subtle that teachers often miss the signs.

Trouble forming friendships is common for children with a history of trauma. Sometimes it's because the neglect the child experienced in their early years prevents them from developing their social skills. Often the cause is difficult to identify. It's almost as if others can sense that the child hasn't been properly cared for and instinctively avoid them through fear of being tarnished by association.

'That's thoughtful of you,' the white-haired, rather stern-looking receptionist says, when I introduce myself. I don't recognise her from my previous visits, but she has the manner of someone who's been in post for decades and likes to keep everything ship-shape. 'If only all of our parents were as considerate. But we knew you were coming. The MASH team already informed us.'

'Ah, great.' The MASH team, or Multi-Agency Safeguarding Hub, is an amalgamation of all the critical agencies involved in keeping children safe – health, education, social services, mental health and youth offending teams, as well as police and probation. With representatives from each profession co-located in one place, it's harder for children to slip through the net nowadays, as they may have done in the past. Improved communication between the disparate agencies means that schools quickly become aware of any trauma their pupils may have experienced overnight. Armed with fast-time information, teachers are then able to contextualise a child's distressed or difficult behaviour, and react compassionately instead of imposing detentions or sending them off to isolation.

Steps are being taken across the social care system to ensure that children are not blamed for circumstances beyond their control. The NHS, for example, has adapted its policy on 'no shows'. Now, when a child misses a planned appointment, their notes are marked with the words 'WAS NOT BROUGHT' instead of 'FAILED TO ATTEND'. It may seem like a trivial distinction but it's an important one, shifting the burden of responsibility where it rightly belongs. After all, what chance does a young child have of visiting a doctor, if their parent or guardian has no intention of taking them?

I bid the receptionist a cheery farewell, but when I'm halfway across the playground I hear someone calling my name. I turn to see a tall dark-haired woman hurrying over. 'I thought I recognised you,' she says. 'Rosie, isn't it?'

'Clare,' I smile, pleased to see the Special Educational Needs Co-ordinator again. Clare Barnard had been in post when Archie and Bobbi attended Millfield. The SENCo was very supportive in establishing some strategies to lower Bobbi's anxiety at school – she helped me erect a small tent in the classroom, for example, a place for the little girl to retreat to when feeling overwhelmed. The headteacher had initially been reluctant to try what she viewed as new age nonsense. Even she came round when she saw how the sanctuary transformed Bobbi's view of school as a scary, unforgiving place. 'Still here then?'

'For my sins,' she says with a grin. 'I spotted you bringing Caitlin and Bartley in. I'm so pleased you're involved. Do you have a minute?'

Clare seems disappointed when I tell her there are no plans for Caitlin and Bartley to stay with me permanently. Opening the door to her office, she gestures for me to go in first. 'It'd be good for everyone if they could stay with you for a while,' she says, gesturing for me to take a seat on a small sofa beside a desk. 'Poor Julie could do with the break, I imagine,' she says sympathetically as she sits beside me. 'I think she finds Bartley particularly hard.' She gives me a rueful smile. 'Well, we all do, if I'm honest.'

According to Clare, Bartley has been suspended twice in the last few months for spiteful behaviour towards some of the other children. 'There's a lovely kid lurking in there somewhere. But we're having to dig deep to try and reach him. How have you found him?'

'Changeable,' I say with a half-smile. She snickers at that. 'So, do any of the children have an EHCP, Clare?'

Once known as a Statement of Special Educational Needs, Education, Health and Care Plans are awarded to children whose learning needs or disabilities are significant enough to prevent them from accessing the curriculum. If a child has an EHCP they are legally entitled to additional support until the age of 25. Almost half of children in need (CIN) have special educational needs, compared with only 15 per cent of the general pupil population. While they may be very bright, it is well known that trauma during childhood has a dramatic impact on educational attainment and the ability to learn.

The funding secured when an EHCP is awarded allows schools to put extra support in place such as a 1:1 teaching assistant dedicated to the child, as well as occupational and SALT, speech and language therapy.

The heavy cost burden of EHCPs on local authorities means that they try to avoid issuing them if they possibly can. It's a false economy; children who fail in education reach adulthood feeling as if they have no stake in their own community. And that spells trouble for everyone.

It remains a sad fact that the care system in the UK performs consistently well at acting as a feeder institution for prisons. Nearly half of all children in care will spend a proportion of their adult lives incarcerated and at any one time almost a quarter of the prison population in the UK spent their childhood in care. Almost all of those remaining experienced severe adversity as children. Ironically, it's often the case that prisoners are victims of crimes far more serious than those they've been convicted of.

In a bid to interrupt what has become known as the care-to-prison pipeline, CIN are now automatically registered for basic SEN, or Special Educational Needs, support at school.

Clare sighs. 'You know how it is. EHCPs are like gold dust at the moment, but I really feel that Bartley has a good chance of getting one for his social and emotional needs. Apart from his volatility, he really struggles to focus in class. We've put the scaffold in place to support him but he's nearly 18 months behind in maths.'

I frown. 'Then why –'

Clare exhales loudly. 'Mum simply won't hear of it.'

'Ah.'

'I know how much of a shock it is to hear your child has learning needs,' Clare says with a regretful look. 'It's hard breaking the news to a parent who isn't expecting it. They're often stunned. Some even feel ashamed. There's usually some denial at first, or anger. They blame the school, as if it's our fault, or trawl through Google to find a quick cure. It takes a while to accept that the child they thought they had doesn't exist. And I understand that, of course I do. It's hard. They have to grieve for what they feel they've lost.

But most come round to the idea of putting support in place, when they recognise that their child is struggling.'

Clare presses her lips together. 'Ms Powell is one of the most –' She pauses. 'I hesitate to use the word stubborn. Put it this way, she's still adjusting to the fact that Bartley is not a perfect child.'

I blow out some air. I haven't met Bonnie, but it sounds like she's one of those parents who finds it difficult to put her child's needs ahead of her own. I'd met many of those over the years. 'How about Caitlin?'

'She's extremely bright. She does very well,' Clare pauses. 'Some of the time.'

I shake my head, not following. The SENCo sighs again. 'When she focuses she's up there with the most able in her year, but some days she can barely remember how to write her own name. It's like teaching an entirely different child from one day to the next.'

'How is that possible?'

'I have no idea. It's like the silence. We all know she *can* speak. She just won't.'

Won't strikes me as a bit of a judgemental word when we don't have any idea what's driving Caitlin's behaviour. I raise my eyebrows.

Clare opens her hands. 'Don't get me wrong, I don't think for a second that she's attention-seeking or anything like that. It's the changeability that puzzles us, with all the children actually.'

'Ethan too?'

'Ethan's a sweetheart but he can't sit still, can't focus. We're following the protocol for ADHD kids, even though he doesn't have a diagnosis, *yet*. He's always at the front of every line. He's book monitor, register monitor. And,' Clare adds, 'we have him delivering an extraordinary number of messages around the school every day.'

I laugh. 'We have to be inventive, in our lines of work.'

She grins. 'Every note buys his teacher, and the other kids, about five minutes' peace.'

As a foster carer I'm supposed to interpret a child's behaviour as communication, and as I drive towards the magistrates' court I go over my conversation with Claire. According to the SENCo, Caitlin has grown increasingly mute since starting school. It's clear from their behaviour in the classroom that her siblings are running on high levels of anxiety as well.

I had hoped that some time in their grandparents' care, away from the chaos that a parent with substance issues brings, would allow their nervous system to reset. That doesn't seem to have happened yet.

A nagging sensation in my gut tells me that I'm missing something.

I run over all I know so far in my mind, trying to make sense of it. Materially, there doesn't seem to be an issue. Their grandparents' home is warm and comfortable, salubrious, even. When I first met the children, their clothes were worn and over-small, but their shopping trip with Julie took care of that. The strained relationship between Bartley and his grandfather could simply be down to the fact that Bonnie failed to put boundaries in place, and the ten-year-old resents Ryan trying to put his foot down.

Bartley's hatred of Caitlin is difficult to explain away. An image of one of Caitlin's fractals pops into my mind. It's almost as if her passion for drawing the intricate, uniform patterns is an attempt at imposing some order on the chaos of her inner world.

Pulling up outside the court, I wonder what trauma the nine-year-old might have experienced in her young life, and whether she'll ever find the courage to tell me about it.

Chapter Eleven

There's a forlorn expression on Millie's face as she sits in the lobby outside Youth Court 7. With the scratches on her face barely healed, she looks more like a victim waiting to give evidence, rather than a defendant. But when she looks up and catches sight of me, she leaps to her feet with a beaming smile. 'Rosie, what's good?'

A young man in a pin-striped suit, whom I take to be Millie's solicitor, looks up and gives me a friendly nod. 'S'my brief,' Millie confirms with a smirk. I can't help but get the feeling that all this attention is quite enjoyable for her.

I perch on one of the nearby screwed-down seats and introduce myself, but just as the solicitor opens his mouth to speak, Millie slips her track-suited arm through mine and half-pulls me to my feet. 'Can we walk?'

'Don't go far,' the solicitor warns with a wary look, although I doubt Millie stands much chance of absconding from here.

We pace slowly away. Two ushers clutching box files hurry past us. Ohers rush in and out of closed doors. 'Feeling a bit nervous, lovey?'

'Nah, been here loads of times, haven't I,' she says with a shrug, then her eyes light up. 'Hey,' she shouts over an announcement on the Tannoy, 'shall we take off somewhere after this?'

I'm not certain of the wisdom of rewarding a trip to court with a pleasant outing, but I'm rescued from coming up with an instant answer when a nearby door opens. We turn as a smartly dressed, homely-looking woman in her mid-50s leans through the gap. 'Millie, we're ready for you now, sweetheart.'

My heart rate picks up as we file into the room. The walls are painted a bright magnolia instead of the dark wood panelling I associate with courtrooms in my mind, and there's a long oval table in the middle of the room instead of the traditional dock, but there's something intrinsically intimidating about the space nevertheless. For me, at least.

Millie doesn't seem to think so. She smiles as other smartly dressed professionals fill up the chairs next to ours, then asks me again if we can go for a drive afterwards.

'All rise,' the court usher requests, before I have time to answer. A hush falls over us as the district judge, His Honour Judge Symonds QC, is introduced. The tall bespectacled man sits himself down behind a raised bench in front of us. I swallow nervously. Without the robes and sash of a judge in the High Court, he looks like any ordinary middle-aged, if well-groomed gentleman, but there's still something imposing about his demeanour.

'Hello, Millie,' he says eventually, after studying the papers in front of him. He waits expectantly. The teenager shows a sudden interest in the ceiling and doesn't reply. He clears his throat. 'Could everyone introduce themselves please?'

Social workers from the Youth Justice Team speak up first, then the solicitor and a Crown Prosecution Service (CPS) caseworker. The judge smiles at me when I tell him who I am, peering at me over the top of his spectacles. 'Thank you for your time,' he says warmly. 'See, Millie. You have lots of people who want the best for you. Giving up their precious time. Going out of their way to support you, eh?'

I know he's trying to be kind, but I find myself cringing at his words. Few children choose to come into care and I'm sensitive to the likelihood that Millie has been rejected by those who are supposed to protect her. Intimating that she's a nuisance who's putting people out isn't going to do much to boost her depleted self-esteem.

Millie snorts derisively. Tilting her chair back, she lifts her legs up, supporting herself by bracing her trainers against the edge of the table.

'This is your fourth appearance in as many weeks, young lady. I was hoping not to see you here again. You promised me last time, did you not? Promised me that you'd leave this' – he pauses, looking down to examine his notes – 'poor Mr Baldwin alone, didn't you, hmm? But once again you've broken the conditions of your bail, as well as breaching your restraining order. I'm going to have to consider relocating you to a different area altogether if this persistent offending carries on. It might well be the only option left available to us.'

'What the fuck you on about now?' Millie barks, her sweet voice suddenly husky, like that of a long-term, heavy smoker. She glares around the assembled group of professionals then settles her hostile gaze back on the judge. 'I was falsely arrested, man.'

On top of the physical transformation and the gravelly voice, total amnesia seems to have set in, as far as Millie's night-time jaunts to the orthodontist's house go. 'You're saying you have no recollection of returning to Park Road in the last 48 hours?' the judge says patiently.

'Never heard of the place.'

'Mrs Baldwin is reaching the end of her tether, Millie.'

'She needs to stop dissing me and chill. Why's everyone so vexed, man?'

'I'm concerned that you don't seem to be taking any of this seriously, Millie.'

Millie's lip curls into a smirk. 'Can I help it if her husband wants to shop around?'

'As I made clear at your last appearance, when was it,' the judge flicks through his file again. 'Ah yes, three days ago. As I explained then, stalking is a criminal offence.'

'You calling me one of them dirty Peeping Toms?'

'What would you call it? Waiting outside someone's home, peering through their windows. Following them to work …'

'What can I say, we entwined, innit?'

I stare at her, hardly able to believe the contrast with the sweet girl in the corridor not 20 minutes earlier.

'You're claiming there's a relationship between you?'

'Maybe,' she shrugs at the judge. 'If you call him liking some of my posts on Insta a relationship. Not to mention the private messages.'

The clerk to the court, a young woman with long auburn hair, pauses in her tapping of her keyboard. The judge raises his eyebrows. 'Do you have evidence of correspondence between you?'

'Nope.'

'Why not?'

'Snapchat mainly, innit. God, don't you know *anything*?'

The judge removes his glasses and leans forward, peering at Millie closely. 'You're claiming that Mr Baldwin has been grooming you?'

Millie sticks out her chin obstinately and mumbles something under her breath.

'Is that your claim?' He studies her patiently.

The teenager picks at something on her scalp, examines her fingernails then flicks them nonchalantly in the air.

The rigid shoulders and flared nostrils of the middle-aged court usher standing to the right of the judge tell me that she's had enough of the teen's obstructiveness.

'So that's your story. That Mr Baldwin has been pursuing you?'

'S'right. That's what I'm saying. And can you stop looking down my top, you dirty old man.'

My role as appropriate adult is to make sure Millie doesn't feel intimidated by the court process, but at this moment I'm feeling more protective towards the judge. Red-faced, he pulls at the collar of his shirt then rubs the back of his neck and sucks in an audible breath before replacing his glasses. 'Don't you like it where you are, Millie?' the judge tries again. 'Is your foster carer not considerate towards you?'

For the first time since she sat down, Millie's scowl

dissolves. 'I wanna go back to my mum,' she says tearfully. Suddenly, she seems much younger than her years again.

'That's not an option at the moment, my dear,' the judge says softly. He glances at me over the top of his spectacles. His look says it all. *What a sorry state of affairs.*

'Stop calling me your dear, you perv,' Millie snaps, a scathing expression back on her face.

I stop off at the Co-op to get Millie a meal deal after leaving court, something she seems surprised and overly delighted about – 'I can get a sandwich *and* a drink, *and* crisps?!'

Driving towards home after dropping the teenager back to Joan, I wonder whether I'd be nearly so captivated working nine to five in an office.

Foster carers are exposed to the full gamut of human frailties and the seemingly endless ways people do harm to each other, and to their children, without the benefit of sick or holiday pay that almost everyone else in society enjoys. There are no industry standards as far as foster carers' employment goes. No security, pension or minimum wage. Some days pass in what might only be described as organised chaos, but I can't think of a single job I'm qualified to do that offers such joy and heartbreak in equal measure. One that makes me laugh out loud one minute and has me struggling not to weep the next.

Chapter Twelve

My phone rings as I leave the playground of Megan's school the next morning.

'She's done a runner again,' says Joan, sounding exasperated. 'She was supposed to be in school early this morning for some remedial work. She left here at half seven but her head of year just called. She's not turned up and I can't get hold of her. She's not picking up her mobile, the little so and so. I'm so sorry, Rosie. I'd go but I've got to take these two to contact this morning.'

'It's not a problem, Joan, really.'

'Ordinarily I'd spend some time with her, get to know her a bit better so that maybe she'd open up. I've just been that tied up with the little ones, I've barely had the chance to exchange the time of day with her.' The foster carer's voice cracks. 'I feel that bad about it. And she refuses to talk to anyone else. She wouldn't even engage in the Return to Home interview. She just outright refused.'

Joan clears her throat and adopts a brisk tone. 'The police have her up-to-date grab pack. I've let them and her social worker know. I'm not really sure what else I can do.'

If a child in care is prone to running away, their social worker prepares a Looked After Child Information Sharing Form. Known as a 'grab pack', it contains all relevant information about the child so the police are able to mount a rapid response to locate them without wasting valuable time.

'You've only got one pair of hands, Joan,' I say gently, assuring her that I'll update her as soon as I can.

As I pull away from the kerb, I wonder how many police hours are spent supporting social services in this way.

With a restraining order in place at the orthodontist's home and place of work, I wonder whether Millie might gravitate towards some other place connected to him. If she's been following him for a while, she must know something about his routine. Perhaps he stops off for a coffee every day on his way to work, I reason, or nips into a particular bakery for a sugar-free treat. As I drive towards the vicinity of his home address, I mentally visualise his morning journey and the local shops he might pass en route.

Before retracing his steps, however, I decide to do a quick drive-by of his home address. If Millie's obsession is that strong, a piece of paper isn't going to be enough to keep her away. Sure enough, as soon as I pull into Park Road, I spot her. Sitting on a wall, she's swinging her legs over a Tesco's carrier bag and chewing some gum in a care-free way, as if she's fully prepared to wait all day, if that's what it will take to see the target of her affection.

I wonder if she'll do a runner when she catches sight of me, but when I pull into the kerb she looks up, squints, then gives me a beaming smile.

'Hey, Rosie,' she says cheerfully as I roll the window down. She comes over and leans through the gap, her elbows resting on the ledge.

'Millie, you've got everybody worried sick, honey.'

Her eyes widen. 'Oh no, I'm sorry, no one needs to worry! I can look after myself.'

I quickly text Joan, then offer Millie a lift to school. I suspect I'll have a job persuading her to come with me, but she grabs her bags and slides in compliantly.

'I'm starving,' is all she says, when I tell her that Joan has been endlessly calling her.

'Would you like to stop for something before I drop you at school?' Having spotted a Subway café, I indicate to pull over and slow the car down.

Millie looks out the window as I park outside a branch of the Co-op. 'Meal deals are three quid. I don't get my pocket money 'til next week.'

'That's okay. My treat. I wouldn't mind getting a wrap or something myself.'

Her jaw drops. 'We're going Subway?'

'If you'd like to?'

'Ye-ah!' She gives a little skip as we leave the car, as if we're off for a week's holiday in the sun. 'I can have a drink as *well*?' she exclaims, when I point to a rack of cans and cartons.

'Of course. Nothing fizzy though.' Goodness only knows she has enough energy for running off as it is.

I move towards a free table when our food is served, but Millie asks if we can take it outside. I give her a look. 'I'm not going to run, I swear to God.' She crosses her hands over her chest. 'I prefer to walk while I'm eating.'

'We could sit in the car,' I suggest when we reach the pavement. The air is icy, my feet are already tingling with cold and I don't have complete faith in her promise not to scarper.

'Okay,' she says, but her crumpled expression betrays the turmoil she must feel inside.

'Actually, you know what, I know a place away from the traffic. Follow me.' I lead her to a ginnel, telling her that the narrow walkway between shops was once used to control sheep on their way to the square on market day.

'I love animals,' she says as we cross over another road and into another ginnel that leads to open fields. 'We've got so many.'

'Pets?' When we reach the meadow I pass her the small paper bag containing her lunch, presuming she's talking about her birth family. I don't remember seeing any pets at Joan's.

She smiles. 'Yep. There's Ziggy. She's a Staffie. She had a litter a few days before Luke kicked me out.' There's a pause, then she pulls out her wrap and nibbles at the end.

I ask who Luke is to get the conversation going, though from my chat with Joan I already know that he's her mother's younger partner.

'Mum's boyfriend,' she mutters, slowing her step and dropping the arm holding her wrap, as if she's suddenly lost her appetite.

'I see. So, there's Ziggy,' I prompt, hoping to steer the conversation towards more pleasant territory so that she can finish her lunch. She's so thin, it's a wonder the cold wind doesn't blow her along ahead of me.

'Yep, Ziggy,' she echoes with a sigh, 'then all the pups. I don't know if they've been re-homed yet or not, then there's Emma, our black cat, and we've got guinea pigs and a snake.'

We walk some more. I spend the next few minutes telling her about Mungo and the rabbits. When she's finished eating and she's halfway through her drink, I ask her what happened at home, and why she had to leave.

'Luke did sicko things to me whenever Mum was too pissed to notice,' she discloses in a resigned tone, as if he'd let her down over something mundane, like taking his turn to wash the dishes. 'He denied it, the tosser. Said I was making shit up. She believed him, I dunno why.' Her voice cracks. I try to say something but a wave of sadness makes the words stick in my throat.

'Kept picking on everything I said and did after that,' she goes on. 'First his tea was too cold, so I microwave it, then it's too hot. He just wanted me gone but I didn't want to leave Mum so I did everything he said. Then he starts storing his tools and stuff in my room cos he said there's nowhere else to keep them, then all the materials, planks of wood and stuff. I could hardly get into my bed.' There's another catch in her throat but then she undergoes the same metamorphosis that came over her in court. Her tone takes on a harsh edge, her step turning into a swagger. 'I had enough of it, to be honest. I chucked my clothes out the window then jumped out. I'm not a complete mug.'

What really happened is clearly too painful for her to repeat. According to the profile emailed to me by the out-of-hours team, the teenager got home from school and found that her key no longer worked in the lock. When she hammered on the door, Luke shoved some of her clothes into a bin bag and threw them out of one of the upstairs windows.

I don't remember reading anything about Millie being the victim of abuse. I try to keep a mental note of the teenager's exact words, in case this is her first disclosure.

'Does anyone else know about what Luke did, sweetheart?'

She shakes her head. 'Mum was so upset. She said I needed to stop' – she hooks the air with her fingers – 'spreading lies.'

'Oh, Millie, I'm so sorry you went through all that. Have you spoken to Joan about it?'

'She's always too busy with the babies. Don't matter anyway, I don't like thinking about it.'

A swell of anger rises in my throat at the thought of this Luke character getting away scot-free. 'We need to let someone know about it though, sweetheart, otherwise he might do the same to someone else.'

She looks at me and nods, her lips pressed together in resignation. I'm surprised by the meekness of her reaction – children often beg and plead with you to keep quiet after making a disclosure. Then again, victims often need a significant length of time to pass before they're able to open up about what they've been through. Although it sounded as if Millie felt pushed out by the younger children at Joan's, she'd been given sanctuary by the foster carer, a place of safety to lick her wounds. Joan had laid the groundwork. All Millie needed from me was a listening ear.

'Must be hard, not seeing your mum,' I say gently. According to Joan, Millie's mother claimed she couldn't afford to make the short trip to see her daughter, despite her social worker offering to pay for transport so that they could meet.

'It's all his fault. Mum wants me back.' A tear escapes and rolls down Millie's cheek. She swipes at it angrily with the sleeve of her top. 'It's him, he won't let her.'

There's a pause while I mentally rehearse my next question, trying to get the phrasing right so that it doesn't sound accusatory. 'And what is it about Mr Braces that draws you?'

She giggles delightedly at that. 'I like that. I think that'll be my pet name for him from now on. Mr Braces.' She laughs again and takes a sip of her drink. 'Dunno really. I s'pose it's cos he was so nice to me.'

'Nice to you when …'

'When I got my braces fitted. I was scared and he patted my shoulder, told me not to worry.'

I gulp down a rush of sudden emotion. The orthodontist's small gesture of kindness must have been extraordinarily unfamiliar to the young teen to have had such a lasting impact on her.

'He made some lame dad jokes too,' she grins, without a touch of self-pity, 'but I was willing to overlook those.'

I force a smile, my heart constricting in my chest.

Chapter Thirteen

It takes a while to log Millie's disclosure and email it to her social worker. When I update Joan, she sounds so choked to hear what the teenager went through at home that I can't rush to end the call. Consequently, it's after three by the time I make it to the Chambers' house.

'Sorry I'm a bit later than planned,' I say as Julie welcomes me in.

'No school run for little Meg today then?' she says as she waves me ahead of her. 'Bartley was telling us all about her. She sounds quite a character.'

'She most definitely is,' I say with a smile. 'She's at her friend's house for tea so I've an hour or two before I need to pick her up.'

I walk into their large open-plan kitchen and come face to face with Ryan.

In complete contrast to our previous meetings, he meets my gaze and makes friendly conversation. Somehow, we get onto the subject of sport. I tell him about Jamie's passion for cricket and he talks about playing rugby in his army days, and how he still loves the game, joining the veterans whenever he gets the chance.

'He's too old for all that now,' Julie tuts as she switches the kettle on. 'I keep telling him but he won't have it, will you?' She goes over to him and pecks him affectionately on the nose.

He grins and pulls her into a hug, his hand slipping down and resting just above her bottom. 'Cheeky,' she half-whispers before kissing him on the lips.

Feeling uncomfortable, I look briskly away.

It's then I notice Caitlin. Sitting on the sofa on the other side of the large room, there's an indefinable expression on her face as she watches her grandparents canoodling. Perhaps feeling the pressure of my gaze, she meets my eye and then flushes deeply.

'How was school, honey?'

Eyelids heavy and drooping, she gives a polite little nod by way of reply. She looks exhausted.

'Fancy a game?' I say, pulling a pack of UNO out of my handbag. It's a special edition pack with a space theme that I'd spotted in the toy cupboard yesterday evening. Her eyes light up as she shuffles to the end of the sofa to make room for me.

'Oh, someone needed a quick forty winks, I see,' I say with a grin when I catch sight of Louis. Prostrate on a nearby beanbag, he's still clutching his digger in one hand so it looks as if he collapsed with exhaustion in the middle of playing.

There's the sound of footsteps on the stairs, and just as I sit beside Caitlin and begin to shuffle the cards, Linzi sash-ays into the room in a tight pair of shiny black leggings. The black crop top she's wearing looks more like a bra.

'Hi, Rosie,' she says brightly, her lips shiny with pink gloss. 'Count me in.'

'Of course,' I say, smiling as Bartley and Ethan storm in. 'Would you like to play as well, boys?'

'I will!' Ethan says, throwing himself in the gap between Caitlin and me.

'Nah, you're all right,' Bartley yawns, lolloping on the other sofa and pulling out his phone. After dealing out the cards, Linzi takes hers and perches on the arm of the sofa, then we all shift around so that we can't see each other's hands.

Caitlin's eyes run over her cards with delight. She's so absorbed that we have to nudge her every time it comes round to her turn. 'God, you're such a fucking loser, Caitlin,' Bartley sneers from across the room.

'I think she's enjoying looking at the pictures more than the actual game, aren't you, love?' I say with a smile.

Even though Ethan is sitting down, his limbs never stop moving. He wriggles so much that he continually drops his cards, scattering them all over the place. No one complains, but they have plenty to say when Caitlin doesn't move quickly enough to take her turn. I'm about to prod her again when Linzi lets out a shout of jubilation. 'Ha, I've been waiting for that one!' she says, laying one of her own cards and then yelling, 'UNO!'

'Ah, but it's Caitlin's turn,' I remind her. 'Come on, Caitlin, let's see what you've got. Linzi's excited to have her go.'

'Too late!' Linzi argues, slapping her hand down on her card when I try to return it to her. 'If *she* can't be bothered to keep track of whose turn it is, it's her problem.'

Children usually possess a strong sense of justice, in my experience, so I wait, giving Caitlin a chance to stand up for herself, or Ethan the opportunity to step in and defend her. Neither of them stir. After a few seconds, I summon a light tone. 'Got to play fair, Linzi, or there's no point in playing at all.'

Care leavers are sometimes interviewed about their experiences of growing up with the state as corporate parent. When asked about the qualities they believe foster carers should possess, fairness is almost always listed as the most important. One girl reported that her foster carer wouldn't let her keep a night light on in her bedroom, even though she was terrified of the dark. The carer cited rising energy bills as her reason for the refusal, even though her birth daughter, of similar age, was allowed the same 'privilege'.

Aware of the deep flush of fury creeping up Linzi's neck, I hurry Caitlin along. 'Come on, honey, have your go and then we'll see what Linzi can do.' She hesitates, flicking a nervous glance at her auntie.

'Nope, she's missed her turn,' Linzi says firmly. 'I've already laid my card.'

Caitlin doesn't object. Julie and Ryan, who had been giggling behind their marble kitchen island, stare across the room at us. Ryan watches with an air of intense vigilance, but I get the distinct impression that it's not because he wants his daughter to do the right thing. His eyes are on Caitlin, as if he can't wait for her to put a foot out of line.

'But you shouldn't have done,' I tell Linzi, trying to maintain some light-heartedness to my tone. 'It's Caitlin's turn.'

Bartley briefly turns his attention away from his screen to look at us, and from the way Ethan is goggling at me I get the impression that it's unusual for any of the children to be told 'no'. My mother would have a field day in this house. 'Are you going to pick your card up, Linzi, or do you want to quit the game?'

A noise across the room catches my attention; Ryan is moving towards us with a deep scowl on his face, his skin red with irritation. Julie catches his arm. She shakes her head with a pleading expression.

Linzi stares between me and her parents in disbelief. Then her face crumples. She flings her cards at Caitlin's bowed head, then rushes over to Julie with a wail. 'Oh, sweetie,' Julie says, cradling her against her chest.

'That woman is a total nightmare!' Linzi shrieks, tossing her head. She steps away from Julie and puts her hands on her hips. 'I want her out of our house!'

Suddenly, it's as if all the air has been sucked out of the room. The atmosphere prickles with tension as Ryan throws me a look of disgust then stamps towards the front door. 'Caitlin, come,' he barks, grabbing his coat from the banister.

'Oh no, don't, Ryan,' Julie pleads. 'It's swimming tomorrow, you know she loves that.'

Caitlin looks between them, her face an agony of uncertainty. 'Caitlin,' Ryan says through gritted teeth. 'Now.' The contrast with his earlier cheeriness is stark, telling me that the man is a highly unpredictable individual.

After another quick glance in her grandmother's direction, Caitlin scrambles to her feet and rushes to the hall.

Silently, she slips her shoes and coat on, then follows her grandfather obediently out the door.

Julie meets my gaze and blows out her cheeks. Linzi, seemingly unaware of her mother's expression of utter defeat, flounces around the kitchen throwing her arms around. 'I can't believe you're not supporting me, Mum?!' she declares dramatically. 'I want you to get her sacked!'

Ethan drags his hands down his face and looks at me with an exasperated expression. Julie croons and makes all sorts of efforts to calm her daughter down. 'How about choosing yourself a new top, baby?' She reaches out and touches her daughter's shoulder. 'Get yourself on your laptop –'

'Get away from me!' Linzi growls, batting her mother's hand away. 'Can't you see I'm distressed?!' She spins on her heel and stamps down the hall, throwing me a petulant look of disgust over her shoulder before sweeping into the downstairs bathroom and slamming the door.

A few seconds later, Ethan taps my arm. 'Can we play a different game, Rosie?' Clearly, highly emotional outbursts are something he and his brother are accustomed to; Bartley's gaze barely flickered from his screen during the entire exchange.

'Of course we can, sweetheart.' The muscles in my face are tense but I force a smile. 'What would you like to play?'

He dashes upstairs just as Louis begins to stir. I open my arms as the toddler lifts his head and blinks, his eyes cloudy with confusion. When he realises where he is his expression clears and he crawls unsteadily towards me, digger in hand. Aware of Julie trying to cajole Linzi out of the bathroom, I welcome him onto my lap and give him a hug.

'Get off!' Ethan screeches a minute or so later. Charging over, he lets the plastic box he was holding clatter to the floor and whacks his small brother over the head with the lid.

'Hey, kind hands, Ethan,' I say as Louis's yowls fill the air.

'But you said you'd play with *me*! That's not fair!' the six-year-old yells, his face screwed up with fury as he tries to bat his brother over the head again.

'And I will,' I say soothingly, while rocking poor Louis back and forth. 'Ooh, that looks interesting. Is that an elephant I can see in there?'

Meltdown averted, Ethan tips the box over. An assortment of plastic animals spills out over the floor. Louis sucks docilely on the tail of a dinosaur as I help Ethan sort them into groups so they can have a race.

We manage a few circuits – debating about which animals are fastest – before the drama kicks off again, Linzi emerging from the bathroom and marching straight over to me. 'I want the name of your boss,' she demands, standing so close that her trainers ruffle the hem of my skirt. Since she didn't use my name and failed to ask politely, I give her a look and carry on playing with Ethan.

'Can you *please* answer me, Ro-sie?' she says, folding her arms and throwing her hip out. 'I *said*, I want the name of your boss.'

'I will answer you, Linzi, since you've asked politely this time.'

Her cheeks redden under my steady gaze and she shuffles her trainer back slightly. 'You can direct any complaint against me to the fostering team. If you fetch me a pen, I'll write the details down for you.'

Chapter Fourteen

'Can you believe it?' Julie whispers 20 minutes later, as she makes me a cup of tea in the kitchen. She tilts her head towards her daughter who's sitting at a desk on the other side of the space, tapping ferociously at the keyboard of a laptop. 'Typical, isn't it? Can't get her to do her homework but there she is writing a two-page report about UNO.' Her tone is friendly but she clearly doesn't feel the need to apologise for her daughter's outburst, or her blatant attempt to get me sacked.

'Quite the keyboard warrior.' Sitting on a stool at the breakfast bar, I thank Julie as she sets the hot drink down in front of me.

'She's always been strong-minded,' Julie says, sounding quite proud. She pulls an e-cig out of a nearby drawer, sits on the stool on the other side of the bar and sucks on it deeply. Up close, her lips appear swollen. There's also a couple of dark shadows below her eyes that are clogged with concealer. I realise that my gaze must have noticeably lingered because she gives me a rueful grin and says, 'Botox.'

'Ah,' I say, half wondering whether she's being honest. She looks like she's been punched.

'And filler. You should a hundred per cent try it,' she adds, her own gaze sweeping over my face and pausing on my chin. She pats her manicured hands over her cheeks, her eyes scrutinising my face. 'Would do wonders for those jowls.'

A little taken aback by the sizing up, I manage a half-laugh and then steer the conversation back to the children. Far more familiar territory for me. 'She's strong-minded, you say. Linzi, I mean.'

'Totally. Not a bad trait for a woman to have these days,' she adds, breathing out a cloud of cherry-flavoured smoke.

I make a non-committal noise, reminded of the course I'd recently attended at the local authority training suite. In an effort to provide children in care with a record of their childhood – something that happens naturally in birth families in myriad ways, from the saving of precious items like a baby's first weaning spoon, to the reminiscing of treasured moments over the dinner table – foster carers are now expected to write to the children they're caring for twice a year.

The letter is supposed to be an honest account of the preceding six months of the placement including the highs and lows, so that the child has an accurate record of their young life to take with them to adulthood. It's a particularly helpful exercise for children who move placements often, those with fractured childhoods who might otherwise lose memories of achievements like winning the cross-country race, or the handwriting competition at school.

Silenced

The course is designed to help foster carers recognise the importance of language when communicating with children, and to be able to reframe negative experiences in a positive light. We learned that when writing to a child who has tested us to the limit, we could talk instead about their determination and single-mindedness. A child who is hyperactive could be described as lively, stubbornness could be reframed as being committed, impulsivity as creativity, clinginess as affection, and having a dramatic nature as being expressive.

I'm all for reframing negatives and giving everyone the opportunity to shine in a positive light, but describing Linzi's efforts to get me sacked as strong-mindedness strikes me as a touch overgenerous.

Julie taps her vape lightly on the counter and sighs. 'I've got one who won't say boo to a goose and one who wants to run for election.' She smiles and shakes her head. 'Talk about how different kids can be, even in the same family. Mind you, they didn't have the best start, what with Bon and her – choices.'

'I gather she's been struggling for a long time?' I'd read about Bonnie's history of drug and alcohol misuse in the children's profiles, but that was the clinical version and possibly differed from Julie's lived experience at the sharp end.

'Ever since 16 or so,' Julie says with a sigh. She rubs her eyes delicately, presumably to avoid the bruises and the mascara, then cups her cheeks in her hands. 'Always flitting from one boyfriend to the next, she was, shrugging one off without a backward glance as soon as the next one came along. When she fell with Bartley I thought things might change but she got worse, if anything.' Julie looks at me, her eyes shiny with tears. 'You just can't do that when you've got kids, can you?'

I grimace. 'Caitlin seems most noticeably affected by it. How long has she been silent for?'

Julie presses her lips together. 'Hmm, she's not all she seems, that one. Of all of them, she's the crafty one.'

I'm a bit taken aback. 'Oh? She seems very sweet.'

'She can be, but she's quite sly as well. And a bit of a liar, like her mum I'm afraid.'

A prickle of unease runs across my shoulders. I've lost count of the number of children condemned as liars by relatives who prefer to bury their heads in the sand when it comes to secrets lurking in their family. My thoughts spring to Millie. I give my head a little shake and try to focus on what Julie's saying about her efforts to encourage Bonnie to turn her back on her partying lifestyle and settle down. I know I mustn't let Millie's disclosure colour my judgement here.

'I spoke to the SENCo yesterday,' I say after a pause.

Julie sniffs. 'They're *not* special needs.' There's an offended edge to her tone, as if having a child with learning needs might reflect badly on her. 'It's that school. They're useless.'

'I know Millfield quite well. The headmistress is a bit old school but –'

'Principal,' Julie interrupts. 'You can't say headmistress these days, or even head teacher. They're principals.'

I nod, mildly irritated by her pedantry. Then I remind myself that her quickness to correct could well be a sign of someone who's used to living on eggshells, and my empathy kicks in. 'The children are obviously bright,' I say gently. 'Could be they just need a more visual approach to learning. My daughter has an education plan and she's as sharp as anything, she just learns differently and –'

'If they'd come to me earlier, they'd be the top of the class by now,' Julie cuts in bitterly. She takes another long draw on her vape then turns her head to exhale.

'You mustn't blame yourself.'

'I don't,' she says quickly, swatting at the smoky cloud between us. 'Why would I? I did everything for that girl. Everything. I offered to take them all in when Ethan was born, then she went and got herself pregnant again. I couldn't believe it when she started showing. It's like one of those stories you read in *Take a Break* magazine. *I can't cope with the children I've got so what shall I do? I know, I'll go and have another one!* Honestly, I don't know what I've done to deserve all this. I'm at my wits', end with it all. Never would have thought it of my own daughter.'

I sympathise. I've seen it so many times before; women who lack healthy connections in society putting themselves through repeated cycles of pregnancy, sometimes in the certain knowledge that their babies will be removed from their care at birth. It seems such an irresponsible, damaging way to live, but it's easy to judge someone else's behaviour as nonsensical when you aren't walking in their shoes. Enduring multiple pregnancies when they can easily be avoided always strikes me as a desperate cry for help. Sadly, political correctness often means that social workers shy away from the straight talking these women so obviously need. 'I think the temptation to keep pressing the self-destruct button is irresistible when life doesn't offer much hope.'

Julie snorts. 'Well, we could all do that, couldn't we? But some of us have to show a bit of responsibility. God knows I've had more reason that most to run away from it all, but where would we all be then?'

'It's not been easy for you,' I say softly, thinking of all the grandparents I've known who have stepped into the breech and become kinship carers to their grandchildren. Sometimes, the only stability a child has in their lives comes from the extended family.

'No, it hasn't. Especially as they're not even anything to do with Ryan.'

'How does he feel about them being here?'

She gives a little groan and looks at me. 'Are you married, Rosie?' I shake my head. 'You have a partner though? Surely you can't do what you do as a single person?'

'Oh, you'd be surprised,' I say evasively, at a loss as to how to describe my relationship with Des these days. Besides, I'm keen to keep the focus of the conversation away from myself.

'We were just getting back on track after Linzi was born,' Julie explains. 'She wasn't a planned baby. Then Bonnie fell pregnant with Caitlin, even though Bartley was only two months old and she couldn't cope with him as it was. I had to give up my job when Ethan came along because so much of my time was swallowed up with supporting them all. Ryan wasn't best pleased with all the time I spent with them as it was. And now all this.'

I rehearse my next question in my head so that when I

speak I manage to keep a suspicious tone out of my voice. 'Where's he taken her? Caitlin, I mean.'

She scratches the surface of the worktop with a long nail. 'He's a haulage driver. He's doing an overnight run tonight.'

I stare at her in disbelief. 'Caitlin's gone for the whole night? Where will she sleep?'

Julie takes a long draw on her vape. 'In the cab. It's surprisingly roomy in there.'

My stomach flips over. Why would a man who resents the children being around take his step-granddaughter to work with him, I can't help but wonder.

'Don't look so appalled, Rosie. She enjoys going.'

'But it's February. Surely, she'll be freezing. And she'll miss school tomorrow.'

'She'll only miss half a day,' Julie says defensively. 'He'll drop her in at lunchtime when his shift ends. He's only trying to give me a break. He does it now and then. Takes one or two of them to work with him. Divide and conquer, isn't that what they say? And she won't be cold. It's actually quite cosy in the cab. The kids love it.'

I pull a doubtful expression. The memory of Ryan's thunderous expression makes me suspect that he's taken Caitlin out to have a go at her. That's best-case scenario. Another deeply unsettling possibility nags at me, but I push it to the back of my mind.

'Don't tell Robert, will you?'

After a pause, I explain that I can't keep anything that might impact on the children's welfare to myself. Julie bristles. I find myself cringing a little. Explaining to children that I can't keep their disclosures secret is something

I'm used to, but refusing to honour someone's plea for discretion feels awkward when I'm sitting in their home, enjoying their hospitality. 'I'd be struck off if I failed to report something that might impact on them,' I add quickly, passing the buck. 'But I'm more than happy to provide a shoulder to cry on, whenever you need it.'

'Ryan's very good really,' backtracks Julie as she collects my half-full cup and puts it in the sink. Returning to the island, she leans towards me and lowers her voice. 'It's been so hard on us as a couple, all of this. Ry gets pent-up if he doesn't get me to himself on a regular basis, if you get what I'm driving at.' She raises her brows meaningfully. 'We don't get much alone time at the moment and he gets … grumpy.'

'Ah right, I see,' I say, surprised by her openness and ever so slightly uncomfortable. 'If there's anything I can do to help, just let me know.'

'It would take some of the pressure off if Louis isn't here when he gets back.'

Sympathetic to the difficult position she's been catapulted into, I agree to take Louis home with me for a couple of days, and to pick the others up from school tomorrow.

I don't waste any time in helping the toddler into his shoes and coat. I'm always more than happy to put the fostering bedroom to good use, but it's more than that. Something doesn't quite feel right. It's a relief when I lift Louis into my arms and take him out into the cool evening air.

Chapter Fifteen

Readying myself for an excitable onslaught as soon as Megan sets eyes on Louis, I lower the toddler to the ground when we arrive at her friend's house, so neither of us get bowled over by the charge. A rush of warmth and light greets us when Maya's mother, Lynn, opens the door. It takes a second or two for my eyes to adjust, but then I'm surprised to see Megan standing quietly behind Lynn in the hallway. Usually, we have to prise the two girls apart at the end of a playdate, but she's already in her shoes and coat.

'Hello, sweetheart. This is Louis.' I pat the toddler on the head. Lynn smiles warmly.

'Hello, Louis!' she croons, leaning down to his level. Louis grins up at her then stares at Megan. Her sombre expression barely alters. Grabbing her book bag, she thanks Lynn politely then edges past her to join me on the path.

I slip my arm around her. 'Rough day, poppet?'

'It was okay.' Barely looking at Louis, she leans into me for a hug then trudges off towards the gate.

'They haven't had a fall-out or anything,' Lynn explains quietly, joining me on the path in her slippers. 'She's been quiet since I picked her up. She insists there's nothing wrong but I'm wondering,' she says, peering over at Megan's retreating form and then lowering her voice still further. 'I'm wondering whether it has something to do with their science lesson today. Maya told me they were talking about inherited characteristics. Nothing too deep, but apparently they have to take photos of their mum and dad into school tomorrow.'

'Ah.' I glance at Megan, faint in the twilight as she waits at the gate, and my stomach contracts with pity.

Maya appears in the doorway at that moment, looking somewhat deflated herself. A calm, quiet girl by nature, she can usually rely on Megan to bring her out of herself. She looks at Louis, who's beginning to get impatient, kicking out at the potted plants flanking Lynn's front door. Then she peers at Megan.

'See you tomorrow, Megs,' she calls. Her expression doesn't alter when Megan fails to turn around, no doubt understanding that she struggles to hear anything over and above background noise like traffic. 'Bye, Rosie.'

'Bye, honey,' I say fondly, grateful that Megan has such caring, loyal friends.

'Why the need to make it personal?' Lynn seethes, after Maya has retreated into the house and I've lifted Louis back into my arms. She folds her arms. 'They could easily teach the basics of genetics without the need for photos. It does make me cross.'

I nod in grateful agreement. I became friendly with Lynn a couple of years ago, when Maya and Megan's friendship took off. Knowing a little about Megan's past seems to have brought out the protective lioness in her. She's always very quick to jump to Megan's defence.

'Thanks, Lynn. See you tomorrow, no doubt.'

After a snack and a warm drink, Megan brightens up. 'What did you do today, Mummy?' she asks as I plant a box of Duplo between her and Louis in the living area.

I think about my time with Millie earlier. It feels like a week ago. I can hardly believe it was only this morning that I was with the teenager. 'Hmm, let me think. I played hide-and-seek.'

Megan pauses in her rummaging through the box and looks up at me. 'Who with?'

'A girl called Millie.'

'Who won?'

I pause, wondering how to sum it all up. 'No one did, darling, I'm afraid.'

She nods as if it makes sense, then continues rifling through the box. 'Look, Mum!' she exclaims when she comes across a small red pram with a Duplo baby inside. 'I haven't seen this for ages!' She pulls Louis into a hug. 'I love playing with you, Louis,' she cries, squeezing so hard that one cheek rides up and forces his eye closed.

Louis bashes her over the top of the head with one of the colourful bricks and she swiftly releases him. Mungo, watching them from his refuge beneath the dining table, softly growls. 'You're sweet,' Megan says unresentfully, rubbing the cowlicks on top of Louis's head. 'Do you want to stay here forever? You can be my brother if you like.'

'Louis is only here for a couple of nights, Megs,' I remind her. Broken attachments early on in life have long-term effects on a child's perception. Despite several years of stability within our family, Megan still doesn't quite understand the concept of permanence. Securely attached children assume that their place in their family is fixed. Megan and many other children I've cared for seem to think that belonging is a fluid thing that might be changed on a whim.

As they play, I sit at the dining table nearby and pull out my phone to check my emails.

My heart leaps into my throat at the sight of an email from FT, the fostering team, entitled 'COMPLAINT'.

When I open it up, however, my pulse quickly resets itself. Lorraine Harvey, the FT manager, briefly summarised the complaint received from Linzi and dismissed it with one sentence:

> While it's pleasing to know that children of Linzi's age feel empowered to call out injustices, as they see them, I'm satisfied that there has been no failure in Rosie's duty of care and consider the matter of the UNO disagreement not worthy of further investigation.

Amused, I thank her for letting me know and hesitate for only a moment before copying her into a report I address to Robert, about Ryan taking Caitlin to work with him.

Breaking confidences doesn't sit comfortably with me, but I had made it clear to Julie that I couldn't keep the information to myself. Despite the friendly nature of our relationship, I tell myself that the welfare of the children trumps any loyalty I feel towards their grandmother.

My phone buzzes with a notification less than two minutes later. I swipe the screen, anticipating one of the seemingly never-ending notifications from the homework app I had to download from Megan's school. Instead, it's a text from a number I don't recognise:

> Rosie, couldn't help overhearing you earlier saying that kangaroos are one of the fastest animals on the planet. Not sure where you're getting your info from. I always find this site a reliable source … Jules x

The link pasted beneath Julie's message takes me to an article featured on a nature magazine about the world's fastest animals and their maximum speeds. Bemused, I run my eyes over the piece (in which kangaroos don't appear), then return to Julie's message. I find myself re-reading it a couple of times, puzzled that a woman who has more than enough on her plate at the moment took time out of her busy day to check the veracity of one of my off-the-cuff comments, and then went to the trouble of pointing out my mistake.

A few feet away, Louis takes the tower Megan has built and smashes it violently against the side of the armchair, then hits her over the head with the remnant. 'Bad boy!' Megan cries, tearfully cradling her head. As I cross the room to give her a hug I wonder, not for the first time, whether Julie's pedantry might be attributed to living within the crosshairs of an aggressive man for too many years. When someone is constantly criticised, perhaps they end up nervously overthinking everything they or anyone else says or does.

If Ryan is as volatile as Bonnie's neighbour suggested, it could be that Julie has grown used to carefully correcting herself and others around her, in an attempt to keep everyone safe.

'Everyone has a daddy, Megs,' I tell the seven-year-old later, after tucking Louis up in a portable cot in my room.

Opinions differ among adopters as to how frequently their child's birth family should be discussed. Some leave the life-story book given to them by social services – an album about the child's birth family, sometimes containing photos and a simplified version of the events that led them to becoming a ward of the state – within easy reach so that it can be flicked through on impulse. Others prefer to stow the book away on top of the wardrobe so that it's easier to pretend it doesn't exist.

I find myself hovering somewhere in the middle. While I wouldn't like to return to the old days, when adoption was a secret to be hushed up, I don't believe it's helpful to constantly remind children of their past. Having signed a letterbox agreement after adopting Megan, I keep up my end of the bargain by writing to her birth parents twice a year, sending the letter via the local authority adoption team for onward forwarding. I also include Megan in the process, asking her whether she'd like to draw a picture for her birth parents.

She usually does so happily without asking many questions, a relief, since they never respond or send anything back. It's often a day or two later that she begins to press me on the details:

What shop did my first mum sell me in?
Was I on a shelf with the toys?
What shop did you buy Emily and Jamie from?
Why did Christina not want me? Is it because I'm bad/stupid/deaf?

'But if everyone has a daddy, why doesn't *my* daddy want to see me?' she asks now as she works on a picture of a unicorn for him.

My throat tightens. 'I expect he would very much like to see you,' I say carefully, 'but the judge, you know, the –'

'Yeah, yeah,' she cuts me off a touch impatiently, having heard about the wise man who makes important decisions on behalf of children many times before. 'I know the judge said I can't see him 'til I'm older, but *he* doesn't have to know. We could contact my dad secretly and then he can see what a big girl I'm grown into.'

'And he'd be very proud of you, darling,' I say, trying to keep a light-hearted tone. 'But what's most important is that we keep you safe. When you're older, you can decide whether you want to see him.'

She looks up sharply. 'I definitely will! I definitely will want to see him! I bet he misses me so much. He's probably sad.'

Her intensity whenever the subject of her birth father comes up always takes me by surprise, since she rarely shows much interest in Christina, her birth mother. Perhaps it's because she feels she has a mum, and although she has lots of positive male role models in her life, with Des and her grandad and uncles, she doesn't have a 'dad'.

'And you can, when you're older.' I take up a pencil and start copying her unicorn, then ask casually, 'What did you do at school today?'

She shrugs. 'Not much.'

'You're learning about families at the moment, aren't you?'

'Yeah.' She slams her pencil down and grabs another one. 'And it's stupid!'

I watch as she scratches the same spot over and over with the tip of the pencil, almost making a hole in the paper. 'It's stupid?'

'Yes. Because we're supposed to bring a picture of our mum *and* dad in tomorrow so everyone can decide who we take after.' She scribbles all over the picture she's drawn, then hurls the pencil across the room. Half a second later, the tears come.

'Oh, Megs.' I move around to her side of the table and lift her into my arms, then quickly sit down to take the weight of her onto my lap. 'You've got so many people who love you, sweetheart.'

'No one loves me,' she sobs, burrowing her damp face into my neck.

'Oh that's not true!' I cry, matching her intensity with my own. I run through our family members, listing them as 'Megan adorer number one', 'Megan adorer number two' and so on, to make her laugh. It works, and then suddenly she wipes her sleeve across her eyes and looks at me.

'Does Des love me?'

'Absolutely, he does, sweetheart, he adores you.'

She pauses, thinking, then looks at me again. 'And he sort of does dad-type things, doesn't he, like taking me to the park and fixing my bike and tipping me upside down.'

'He certainly does,' I say, laughing.

Her expression turns hopeful. 'So can I – can I take a photo of Des into school tomorrow?'

'Oh, sweetie,' I say, hugging her tight and telling her that Des would be chuffed to bits to hear that she wants to. 'Trouble is,' I say, pulling back and peering at her with an exaggerated expression, 'everyone will be asking why you haven't got his mad curly hair.'

She gasps then clamps her hand over her mouth to muffle her chuckles, as if we've shared an extremely cheeky joke.

After reading Megan a bedtime story, I text Des to tell him what Megan said.

You should see the chuffed grin on my face, his reply reads, followed by a smiling emoji and a heart.

Chapter Sixteen

When I collect Megan from school the next day she charges over to Louis, her enthusiasm restored. 'This is my brother, Louis,' she tells her school friends proudly, even though barely a week has passed since she first heard of the toddler's existence. 'Well, he's definitely my foster brother,' she corrects herself, after a tiny glance at my raised brows.

She's even more excited when I tell her we're picking Caitlin and Bartley up from school. She chatters away to Louis as we drive towards Millfield Primary, and I can't resist taking a snap of them from behind as they walk into the playground hand in hand. They look so sweet.

'Over here, guys,' I tell them as they gravitate towards the brightly coloured trim trail on the other side of the playground. The children from Caitlin's class are starting to emerge from the far side of the building so I guide them in that direction first.

'Where is she?' Megan says, standing on tiptoes. 'I can't see her!'

'She'll be out soon,' I soothe, although the number of children coming from the classroom has slowed down to a trickle. I'm keen to see that she's all right after her sleepover in her grandfather's lorry, but there's still no sign of her.

'I'm Rosie,' I tell the young teacher at the front of the line, when most of the children have been dismissed. He can't be much older than Jamie, but as soon as I ask for Caitlin he seems to age before my eyes, his smooth forehead creasing with anxiety. 'She's gone,' he says, flushing. 'I got a call from reception. They said she was to go with her brother. S-she went over an hour ago.'

My mind rummages around, trying to replay the conversation I had with Julie about collecting the children today. It was all very last minute, with Julie scrambling around for some nappies and overnight things for Louis, but I distinctly remember her asking me to cover the school pick-up. 'Did their grandmother collect them?'

'No, their father. Well, no, yes, I mean Bartley's dad. Bartley had a dentist appointment and had to leave early, so –' he pauses, asking the teaching assistant to wait with the remaining children, '– so Caitlin went at the same time.' He searches my face as I dial Julie's number. It goes straight to voicemail. When I end the call and shake my head, all the colour drains from his face. 'Oh heck, I'm starting to doubt myself now.'

'We've just got our wires crossed, I expect,' I reassure him, although I'm simultaneously wondering why Bartley's father would be picking Caitlin up at all. But it's when the teacher breaks into a jog that my heart leaps into my throat.

'All the protocols were followed, I can assure you, Mr Broker,' the white-haired receptionist says in a defensive tone. She peers at her computer screen to check her notes and then back at the flustered-looking teacher. 'Yes, their grandfather called to confirm the arrangements. And Bartley's father gave the correct password for both of them, otherwise Caitlin would certainly not have been passed into his care.'

Mr Broker's face reddens again. 'What about Ethan?' he asks, looking between me and the receptionist. 'Are you collecting him today?'

I nod. 'I'm supposed to be.'

'Ethan wasn't in school today,' the receptionist informs us briskly. 'His grandmother telephoned this morning to tell us that he's unwell, and that Mrs Lewis would be collecting the others. It's all here,' she says, tilting her head towards her screen. 'The call from Mrs Chambers, then her husband's later rearrangements. Everything is meticulously logged.'

'I don't doubt it,' I say, apologising to both of them. 'Just a misunderstanding.'

But when I call Julie again on the way back to our car, the long pause that follows tells me that she knew nothing about the changed plans. 'Ethan's been off with earache so I – I, well,' she stutters, though there's a thread of irritation in her voice as well.

I open the door to let Megan in, then lift Louis into his car seat. 'It's okay, as long as they're both all right.' There's another pause during which all I can hear is the sound of Ethan screeching. An image of the scruffy-looking man leaving Bonnie's house when I first met the children rises up in my mind again. 'Julie, they *are* all right, aren't they? Is it usual for Bartley's dad to take the others out?'

Silenced

Louis slaps me on the head as I lean over him to secure his seat belt. He screeches with laughter when I let out a low wail. All of the children except Caitlin seem boldly confident, on the face of it. I can't help but wonder how the haphazard contact arrangements might impact on an introverted child like her.

'Doesn't happen often,' Julie says, her tone regaining its usual forthrightness. 'I'll have a word with Ryan and make sure he leaves the arrangements to me from now on. So is young Louis behaving himself?'

I climb into the car and peer into the back, where Louis and Megan are holding hands. 'Good as gold,' I say. 'Right, I'll get them home, give them some tea and I'll drop Louis back to you about six-thirty.'

I'm about to end the call when Julie says, 'Before you go, did you get my message yesterday?'

'Message?'

'Yes, the nature article. You didn't respond.'

'Ah yes, yes I did,' is all I say, at a loss as to how to respond. After a long pause, all I can come up with is, 'Interesting. Thanks, Julie.'

Nothing is mentioned about the mix-up over school pick-up when I drop Louis off, and although I have the children most days after school for the next week and a half, I barely exchange more than a few words on the doorstep with Julie and Ryan.

It's later in the week, on the third Thursday in March, that Julie texts me about an upcoming sleepover at the weekend. Unfortunately, I have no idea what she's talking about. Having been invited to a wedding involving an overnight stay in a hotel, Julie apparently asked 'Rob' if all the children could have a two-night stay at mine. According to Julie, the social worker had agreed.

I stare at the message for a full two minutes before replying. It's not that I don't want the children to stay. It's the presumption on the part of Robert that irks me, the fact that he'd confirmed the sleepover without even consulting me. He'd also blanked my email letting him know about the haphazard pick-up arrangements for the children. I can't help but feel that a quick acknowledgement isn't too much to ask.

'What is it about people these days?' Julie says on Friday, when I arrive to collect the children. It's just over two weeks since first meeting the family, but it feels like much longer.

'Weddings used to be all about family,' Julie complains, after planting a lipstick-coated kiss on Caitlin's cheek. The grandmother's forehead is lined with strain in spite of the Botox and her cheeks are pale under a heavy coating of foundation. 'Now you can't even take kids to most of them. Ridiculous,' she adds, bestowing hugs on each of the other children in turn.

'And how are you feeling, lovey?' I ask Ethan when he bounds down the stairs and wraps his arms around me.

He gives me a blank look.

'Your earache? It's better now?'

Julie shakes her head at him and rolls her eyes affectionately. 'He's fine now, aren't you, babe.'

'Good. They'll have fun, don't worry,' I say, directing my words to the children as well as their grandmother.

* * *

Silenced

Megan is so excited when we get home with all four children that she charges around the house pulling toys out of the cupboards to show them, and bringing random items down from her room.

When I suggest a bouncing competition on the trampoline, even Bartley agrees. Stowing his phone in its box on the mantelpiece, he grabs Ethan by the collar of his jumper and practically drags him into the garden. It's an unseasonably mild day so I set out some Play-Doh on a low table by the patio doors for Louis. That way I can get on with preparing dinner and still keep an eye on him. I manage to peel three carrots before Megan comes charging across the garden. 'Bartley says there's not enough room for Caitlin. That's not fair, is it?!'

Peering through the kitchen window, I can see Caitlin skirting around the edge of the garden while the boys perform somersaults over each other on the trampoline.

'You must let the girls join in, Bartley,' I call out as I make my way down the garden. Peeler still in hand, I lift the protective netting surrounding the trampoline and wave Megan and Caitlin over.

'Do you mind not threatening me with that,' Bartley snaps.

'What?'

'That knife. No need to get violent.'

I look at the potato peeler and laugh, but it seems that Bartley is deadly serious. He glowers at me as Megan throws herself through the gap, then jerks his head towards Caitlin. 'I never said Megan couldn't stay on. It's that moron over there that's banned.'

'Everyone is allowed to bounce,' I say with a pointed look at Caitlin.

'No, she'll break it,' Ethan pipes up. As Bartley's foot soldier, Ethan is always more than willing to do his older brother's bidding. When I insist on Caitlin being included, the nine-year-old ventures warily over to the trampoline as if it might explode at any moment. It seems that all the children have grown used to casting Caitlin aside, but with so many adults involved in their lives, it's difficult to know who they're modelling themselves on.

'Come on, Ethan, there's suddenly a bad stink around here,' Bartley snarls, as soon as his sister climbs in. Grabbing Ethan by the collar again, he drags him across the jumping mat then down onto the grass.

I'm so busy refereeing scuffles between the boys, and policing them to keep Caitlin safe from unprovoked physical attacks, that Louis is the only one I've managed to feed and it's already 7 p.m. The cottage pie I'd planned for the rest of us still consists of three now slightly brown carrots and a bag of unpeeled potatoes. 'Don't worry, Mum,' Emily says when she gets in from work. 'I'll treat us to a takeaway.'

'Really? Oh thanks, love, that's a nice idea.'

Louis keeps saying, 'Again, again!' when I read him a story, so it's another half an hour before I get him settled in his cot. I'm still smiling as I come back down and pull our Game of Life out of the cupboard. I enjoy having young children around, but it's also lovely now Emily and Jamie are older, and it's a special treat when they give me a night off cooking.

Silenced

As soon as I open the box, Bartley sits at the table and slyly stuffs a few of the player tokens up his sleeve so that there are only enough cars for himself, Ethan, Megan and me. 'Ah, shame, there aren't enough pieces for all of us, but it isn't a problem,' I tell them cheerfully. 'We'll use Monopoly tokens instead.' I give Caitlin first dibs on which piece she'd like, much to Bartley's disgust. When she chooses the T-Rex, he looks like he's going to throttle her. Red-faced, he glares at his sister then throws himself on the sofa, claiming that he can't join in because 'the smell is rank'.

When Jamie decides to join us after his gig is cancelled, however, Bartley sidles back to the table and quietly chooses the top hat. For a boy who allegedly has no concept of mathematics, he also manages some rapid calculations at the end of the game, to prove that Caitlin has lost.

Inexplicably, he claims it's his sister's fault when the Uber delivery driver gets delayed and the food turns up lukewarm. The others tuck in excitedly, but Bartley won't let it go.

'Quit gaslighting, bro,' Jamie tells him through a mouthful of cheeseburger.

Bartley flushes and Caitlin gets a bit of a reprieve. When the Wi-Fi fails in the middle of downloading a film less than half an hour later, however, she's taken to task by Ethan who seems convinced the faulty connection is his sister's fault.

For the umpteenth time I find myself having to jump to the nine-year-old's defence. Caitlin is unmistakably the scapegoat of the family. And I can't help wondering who is responsible for putting her in that unenviable position.

Chapter Seventeen

It's a pattern that continues into Saturday, Caitlin being squeezed out of every game and Ethan being dragged around by Bartley like a shop-window mannequin. Unlike his sister, the six-year-old feels he has the right to fight back, which proves to be a double-edged sword. When he isn't kickboxing with Bartley, he's practising his moves on the doors, skirting boards, the legs of the table.

With his dimples and his cheeky nature, he's an angelic-looking child and easy to like, but I stiffen at the tone he uses every time he speaks to his older sister.

It's upsetting to see siblings so divided, but what makes my heart ache most of all is Caitlin's reaction to the rejection. No doubt used the being left out, she withdraws into herself at every harsh word and draws ever more intricate fractals in her sketchbook.

Even little Louis seems to have been recruited as Bartley's mule. When I gently remind him to use the crayons I've given him on paper, not on my walls, he gathers them up, pushes himself to his feet and deliberately crosses the room. Recognising Caitlin as the family whipping girl, he bypasses all of us and flings them in her face.

Despite being engrossed with the game on his phone, Bartley notices. 'Ha! Nice one, Lou!' he jeers from the sofa, holding his hand out to high-five the toddler.

'Right, time for a group activity!' I announce, swallowing down the urge to tear Bartley off a strip. Mindful of the tightrope I need to walk in caring for children who are still under the guardianship of their birth family, I'd been avoiding laying down the law. But they're in my care for the whole weekend now, and I know I can't stand by and allow Caitlin to be bullied until I drop them back on Sunday evening.

'It's called the democracy game,' I tell them, after retrieving a dusty old storage box from the yellow room, along with three wicker baskets. Having used the 'game' a year or so ago, when caring for a teenager whose addiction to unpleasant online clubs had left him deeply resentful and scathing of women, each basket was already tagged with its own sign:

NO LONGER TOLERATE
NEGOTIATE
IGNORE

'Jesus fucking wept,' Bartley moans from the sofa. 'Doesn't look like much of a game to me.'

'Congratulations, Bartley! You've come up with the first thing we will no longer tolerate!' I scribble down the word 'SWEARING' on a piece of paper and drop it into the 'NO LONGER TOLERATE' basket.

Megan, having played the game before with a number of children, enthusiastically grabs a piece of paper and writes 'NO MOR HITIN KAYTLIN'. Spelling the words by sound, Megan's writing can be difficult to decipher sometimes, but I usually manage to get the gist.

'No more saying mean things to her either!' she announces, getting straight to the heart of the matter with another page of scrawl that she proudly drops into the 'NO LONGER TOLERATE' basket.

'See what you cause,' Bartley growls at Caitlin. 'This is your fucking fault.'

'Mummy, that's two bad basket things he's done already,' Megan points out. 'You're really bad at the amocrity game, Bartley!'

'Like I care,' he jeers again, although as the paper rapidly fills up in the first basket (mainly courtesy of Megan, who is very robust about the enforcement of rules) he begins to look slightly less nonchalant. He tries to focus on his phone, but after a minute or so he turns his head to look at me. 'What happens if someone does one of those things?' he mumbles, jerking his head towards the first basket.

'Sank-shooms,' Megan announces gleefully.

'That's right, Megs. We impose sanctions whenever a rule is violated, Bartley.'

'What the heck does that mean?'

'A sanction is just another word for a consequence. What I'll do is go through each piece of paper and write the consequence on it. And there will also be rewards for good deeds. It's the democratic way.'

Having learned more about the impact of trauma on the brain in recent years, I tend to rely on visual displays to get my message across these days. That way, all of the children I care for, including those with neuro-disabilities, know exactly where they stand, and I don't have to feel like I'm constantly nagging.

It sounds silly, but I find the baskets help me too. Instead of floundering around helplessly when a child flies off the handle and threatens violence, having a system in place helps me take a firm stance against them. It also reminds me how to help them redirect their destructive behaviours, when my adrenaline levels are raised and my own mind is in a state of fight/flight/freeze.

Violence between romantic partners is a widely discussed and oft-featured storyline in novels, TV dramas and soaps, but child-to-parent violence is rarely spoken about, despite estimates that at least ten per cent of families are affected by it. Sadly, it's a phenomenon that seems to be on the increase, and one that is often ignored when reported by desperate parents, since social workers are keen to avoid taking difficult-to-place children into care. The issue has been complicated in recent years by parents who are fearful of defending themselves robustly, in case professionals accuse them of child abuse.

It's easy to get drawn into conflict with a dysregulated child. Years ago, before learning non-violent resistance techniques, I looked after a gang-affiliated teenager called Amy who vented her anger by screaming at me and smashing up our TV. Even though I'm generally mild-mannered, I sometimes found myself being swept along with the drama of her outbursts, jointly escalating the row by raising my voice to match hers. Amy then ratcheted up her aggression to outdo mine, the result being that both of us became more furious with every interaction.

Even parents who try their hardest to avoid conflict can inadvertently escalate domestic abuse by giving in. I've seen it happen many times during contact sessions – a child makes an unreasonable demand, their parent initially refuses but then capitulates if the resulting tantrum proves too difficult to contain, thereby reinforcing the child's belief that violence is an effective and acceptable tool to get their own way.

'So come on then,' Bartley says with a yawn. Swinging his legs off the sofa, he chucks his phone onto a cushion and rubs his eyes. 'Tell me what stuff I'm allowed to get away with.'

'Write some things down then.' I hand him some paper and a pen. 'And I'll see what I can bear to put in the "IGNORE" basket. If I can't decide, we'll pop it in the middle basket, for further discussion.'

Bartley sets to work immediately. A couple of minutes later he hands me a pile of papers with a smirk on his face.

The main object of the 'game' is to identify one or two of a child's most challenging behaviours so that a red line can be drawn under them. Less troubling issues are put aside, to be tackled when day-to-day life gets a little bit easier to cope with. With this in mind, I drop Bartley's 'belching', 'farting' and 'refusing to shower' straight into the 'IGNORE' basket, much to Ethan's amusement, and then deposit 'staying up all night', 'eating chocolate all day' and 'ten-hour phone marathons' into the one marked 'NEGOTIATE', to be tabled for discussion at a later date.

'Now get them to sign a contract, Mummy!' Megan cries, eager to formalise the agreement. She scribbles a note and asks everyone to sign and date it, even getting Louis to mark his own name in crayon.

'What's the date, then, numbskull?' Bartley says when she reaches him. Thankfully, he seems to have a soft spot for her. Whenever she mishears him, he repeats himself patiently, without the trace of a sneer. Yesterday, when she called spaghetti 'spoofetti', he patted her head and called her a cutie.

'What's the date, Mummy?' Megan says, pen poised like a mini-PA.

'The fifteenth.'

'It's her birthday tomorrow, then,' Bartley says disinterestedly, after scribbling his signature on Megan's pad. 'Thank fuck her dad can't come sniffing around any more. Oh Jesus,' he adds, clapping a hand to his mouth when he realises he's sworn.

'I'll let you off this time, Mr Potty Mouth, but from now on, three swear words and your phone goes in the box for the rest of the day, got it?'

He curls his top lip in acknowledgement. I turn to Caitlin, wondering whether she'd like to be asked about her father. It could be an opportunity she rarely gets to indulge. The look of pain on her face tells me it might be wise to shelve my questions, however. It's an unlikely topic to coax her out of her silence. Clearly the man isn't popular with Bartley. I'm keen to find out why, but I don't want to upset Caitlin more than she already is.

'Is it really your birthday tomorrow, sweetheart?' I ask instead, surprised that Julie hadn't thought to say anything.

She nods and gives me a shy smile. 'Well, I'm very glad you told me, Bartley. Well done for remembering,' I compliment him quickly, before he renders the one nice thing he's done for his sister all weekend invalid by abusive name calling or a physical assault.

Bartley, it seems, isn't used to being praised. When a child is working hard to make themselves unlikeable, it's easy to forget that they're as vulnerable as those whose fragility is easy to spot.

The ten-year-old shrugs and grabs his phone, but his cheeks flush pink. And when I tell him that he's earned first dibs on choosing tonight's pudding he tries his best to thumb-scroll his screen with nonchalance, but he can't help a broad, proud grin breaking out on his face.

Chapter Eighteen

Feeling like a child on Christmas Eve, I shower early on Sunday 17 March and make myself a coffee, resisting the urge to wake everyone up. Mungo, picking up on the excitement, runs circles around my feet as I take my drink to the sofa and pick up a magazine to distract myself.

It's not long before I hear footsteps on the stairs. Knowing it's Caitlin from the lightness of their patter, I go into the hallway to watch her face as she takes in the decorations and balloons I'd hastily hung around the place after everyone went to bed. Flushing a deep red, she stares around with a look of wide-eyed wonder. When I pass over the envelope containing her gift, she bursts into tears.

'Happy tears, I hope?' I put my hand on her shoulder, giving it a light rub when she doesn't pull away.

She nods, cries again and hugs the envelope to her chest. I'd managed to get hold of last-minute tickets for the Discovery Space Centre and, as luck would have it, there's a special programme of events planned for children this weekend. 'I've booked you in for a craft session and the zero-gravity experience, and there's a guest speaker from NASA there today.'

She goggles at me for a few seconds, then flings herself into my arms. My heart leaps as I pat her back. 'Happy birthday, sweetheart.'

Predictably hostile to the idea of Caitlin enjoying herself, Bartley manages to express his disgust without falling foul of the 'NO LONGER TOLERATE' basket. 'For the love of God and all that's holy,' he groans, when I tell him where we're going. 'Stinking boring lectures all day? Is Jamie coming?'

'No, honey, he's working.'

He blows out his cheeks. 'For hoot's sake, it's gonna be worse than school.'

The creative cursing intensifies when he finds out that the space centre is a 90-minute train ride away. When we round the corner from the train station and the rocket tower and the huge domed roof of the planetarium come into view, however, his intrigued expression brings me a glimmer of hope that the day might work out well. Captivated by the sight, Ethan stops making annoying noises for the first time since waking up.

Unfortunately, when someone is as tightly coiled as Bartley, it doesn't take much to trigger the spring. As we're filing through the wide gate intended for buggies, someone accidentally steps on Bartley's foot.

'What the hell you doing?!' he explodes, flailing his arms about. The look of fear on the face of the toddler-carrying mother responsible for the outrage emboldens him. He goes right up to her face and jerks his head as if he's going to head-butt her.

'I'm so sorry,' I say, dragging him away and gesturing for her to go ahead of us in the queue. She scurries past, but not before giving me a quick glance of disbelief. Like the parting of the Red Sea, the people in front of us shuffle aside and wave her through, out of harm's way. One gentleman tuts and gives me a slow blink of disgust, clearly of the opinion that I'm raising a monster.

'My trainers are ripped to fuck!' Bartley yells, exacting proxy revenge with a hard punch on Caitlin's arm. Ethan immediately copies him. If Louis hadn't been strapped into the buggy, he probably would have piled in as well.

Even wrapped up in a warm coat, I can see Caitlin's bony shoulders drooping. There's no complaint there, just a resigned disappointment that, yet again, she's the target of other people's frustration.

'Bartley, Ethan, use your hands gently please,' I say through gritted teeth. The crowd behind us disperses. Some hurry ahead to squeeze through the gate, others give us a wide berth and tag onto the end of other queues. Letting go of Louis's buggy with one hand, I give Caitlin's arm a rub. 'Right, shall we do the planetarium first? We're booked in to see "The Night Sky" show at half eleven so we could have a quick look round –'

Caitlin's eyes light up but Ethan pats my arm. 'I'm starving,' he says, bobbing on his toes.

'I wouldn't mind a bite to eat either,' Bartley says with an unashamed yawn, as if the assault on his sister were a trifling matter that's long forgotten.

Bearing the principles of HALT in mind (never attempt a constructive discussion with a child who is hungry, angry, lonely or tired) I decide that a visit to the café might not be a bad idea before expecting a child with ADHD traits to sit and watch a show. Everyone, apart from Caitlin, ate a decent breakfast and snacked on fruit on the train, but the merest hint of hunger in a child whose nervous system is easily overwhelmed can trigger a meltdown.

As is often the case with children under the radar of social services, however, Bartley and Ethan misread the hollow feeling inside of them as hunger. A few bites into their baguettes, they begin to lose interest. Ethan starts pulling out the contents of his ham and tomato roll. Bartley decides to leave his intact and use it as a missile. Breaking off a lump, he lobs it straight into his sister's face. Pumping the air with his fist, Ethan screeches with laughter. Caitlin, who had been sipping a milkshake, rears back in surprise, taking half of her drink with her.

'Bartley!' I gasp, mopping Caitlin's coat and the table with all the napkins I can lay my hands on.

'Wasn't me.'

'It *was* you!' Megan tells him categorically. 'Mummy, it was him. I saw him with mine own eyes!'

I pat her hand, trying to keep her out of it in case he decides to spray her with pepper or something. 'Bartley, let's not get silly.'

'Jesus! I always get the blame. I've done nothing.'

'We saw you do it, Bartley.'

'So *you* say. But you've got it in for me.'

'Get me some more napkins please,' I say firmly. 'This milkshake is about to run all over the floor.'

'Sounds like a YOU problem,' he retorts, breaking off another piece of roll and chucking it across the table at Ethan. The six-year-old lets out a shriek of shock which turns to delight. He retaliates with a fistful of ham and tomato. The gooey roux lands squarely on Louis's head and plops onto his highchair tray. Bellowing with shock, the toddler holds his arms out to me.

Taking him onto my lap, I level my gaze on Bartley. 'Five seconds to get me some napkins, or your phone goes in the box for the rest of the weekend.'

'Fine,' he growls, throwing himself back so violently that his chair upends and clatters on the wooden floor. Silence descends over the café, the eyes of every visitor and member of staff squarely focused on us.

'Thank you,' I manage in a controlled tone, when Bartley slaps a huge pile of napkins on our table.

'Fuck you,' he spits, then storms off towards an empty table on the far side of the café, pausing only long enough to show a dignified, elderly woman his middle finger. Her jaw drops. She gives me a shame-inducing look and then leans close to her elegantly dressed friend, whispering. Flushing, I lift a hand in apology. They hastily turn away, their mouths working in disgust.

Ethan heads over to join his brother. Able to keep them in my line of sight, I don't object, especially since a smartly dressed man with a grim expression is making his way over to our table.

'I'm so sorry,' I say, joggling my knee to soothe Louis, whose wails have softened into quiet sobs. *Julie*, I think to myself, *you're an absolute saint*.

'If you need any assistance,' the man says, disguising his

disapproval under a veil of politeness. His eyes drift over to the boys. They're presently grabbing at each other's clothes, seemingly intent on pulling each other off their chairs. 'I'm Guy, manager of the café.'

'They're naughty boys,' Megan pipes up, before I get the chance to speak. 'They're not mine brothers,' she adds, rapidly disowning them with a shake of her head. 'Well, these two are mine sort of brother and sister, but not the noisy boys over there,' she clarifies, patting Caitlin's arm and nodding at Louis. Caitlin, who had looked close to tears, can't help but smile.

Disarmed, the man grins and asks their names. 'I'm Megan,' she pats herself on the chest, then points at Caitlin. 'That's Caitlin. She's ten today but don't ask her anything, she can't talk. Well, Mummy says she can talk, she just doesn't know us well yet. And this is Louis.' She pokes her finger into the now quiet toddler's chest. 'Don't ask him anything either, cos he only knows swears.'

'I see,' Guy laughs, then he looks at me. 'Child minder?'

'Foster carer,' I say quietly.

'Ah,' he nods with a knowing look. His gaze drifts back across the café and settles on the boys. Clasped in a headlock by his older brother, Ethan is presently careening blindly into adjacent tables and screaming his head off. 'I see.'

'I'm so sorry about this.' Gathering up our bags, I call the boys over then deposit Louis back into his buggy and strap him in. The girls grab their coats.

Most people soften when they realise that the children creating chaos in their midst are in foster care. Guy is no exception. 'Hey, no rush,' he says kindly. 'Please, take your time.'

Demeanour transformed, the manager bestows a handful of large lollipops on me as we make our way out. 'It was lovely to meet you all,' he says, with a wink at Megan, then he holds the door for me so I can push the buggy through. 'Nothing but admiration for you,' he says with a nod, when I thank him.

The wind picks up as we cross the courtyard that separates the café from the planetarium. My heart sinks. I know from experience that windy weather and ADHD are a toxic combination. Sure enough, Ethan starts screeching and running in manic circles around the buggy. Seizing the opportunity, Bartley sticks his foot out and sends his brother flying.

Fragments of leaves whirl in the cold air, whipping our faces as I give Ethan a hug. Then, a swarm of starlings appears out of nowhere, darkening the sky and making us jump.

I try to hold onto my earlier optimism, but it's hard not to feel it's a portent that the day is about to get a whole lot worse.

Chapter Nineteen

I suppress a sigh at the sight of a queue for the theatre. Then I remember the lollipops. Knowing that sucking and crunching can soothe frayed nerves, I hand out the lollipops and join the end of the line. It works. Bartley and Ethan trudge peaceably forward with serene expressions on their faces. Until we reach the front of the line, that is.

'No food or drink allowed, I'm afraid,' one of the ushers at the doors tells us. She's chewing gum, an inconsistency that Bartley is quick to point out.

'Gum isn't food,' the young woman says with an affronted look. 'And I'm not *in* the auditorium.'

'Bartley, I know you'd like to finish your lolly,' I begin, getting in early to try and disarm him before a full explosion detonates. 'But it's the same rule for everyone, no food and drink allowed.'

He shakes his head. He's not going to give up that easily.

'I know it's annoying, but we can't take it in, so let's save it for after the show.' With the ACE technique followed to the letter (A, acknowledge the child's wishes, C provide context, i.e. explain the reason for your decision/request, E empathise), all that's left for me to do is hold out the wrappers.

Megan obediently pops the half-finished lollipop in one of the wrappers and rapidly chews the piece still in her mouth. Ethan does the same and sticks his tongue out afterwards, bush-tucker trial style, to show that he's swallowed every last shard.

'Bartley,' I say warningly, aware of a shuffling of feet behind us, the rest of the ticket holders eager to get to their seats before the performance starts.

'It's one stupid lolly,' he snaps, striding past the woman without so much as a glance in her direction, as if the rules don't apply to him. Ethan follows. The usher on the other side of the doors, a middle-aged woman with a pure-white bob and a badge marked 'JEAN', hurries to block their path. She looks at me expectantly, waiting for me to take charge.

'Boys, outside please.'

Ethan comes back to me but Bartley spreads his legs. 'No way. I need to dibs the best seats and I've been queuing for ages.'

Leaving the buggy in the doorway, I venture a few steps into the theatre. 'Get the fuck away from me,' Bartley yells, throwing out his arm and almost knocking Jean sideways. There's a collective gasp from those already in their seats, and one from Megan, who begins to choke on the residue of her lolly.

I'm so busy attending to Megan that the commotion around me fades to a low hum. After she recovers with a sip of drink and a tearful blow of her nose, the outside world begins to swim into focus again.

The first thing I notice is that the general hostility from everyone around me has softened. One or two of the audience members smile at me kindly. Then I realise why.

The manager from the café, armed with several sunflower lanyards, has taken the older usher to one side. After a quiet word, he takes the wind out of Bartley's sails by handing Ethan one of the lanyards and guiding him to a seat at the front of the auditorium. I'd heard about the Hidden Disabilities Scheme a year ago – a system designed to discreetly signal to others that the wearer has a hidden disability that may affect their behaviour – but hadn't made use of it before.

Bartley, eager not to miss out, holds his hand out expectantly. 'I hope I've done the right thing?' Guy says, looking at me. 'I just thought these might help your day go a bit more smoothly.'

'It's a brilliant idea,' I tell him gratefully, handing Bartley his lolly wrapper. 'Thank you so much.'

Bartley dutifully spits his lolly into the wrapper and bows compliantly so that Guy can slip the brightly coloured lanyard over his head. 'Not a problem. Give me a shout if you need any help. Enjoy the performance.'

'I'll sit nearby,' Jean tells me, eager to help us as well. 'If you need to slip out with one of them, I'll wait with the others so they don't miss out.'

'You're so kind, thank you.' The old adage 'it takes a village to raise a child' seems particularly apt at times like this.

Years ago, I fostered a young boy sporting a crew cut

and an ear-ring that his birth mother insisted he must wear at all times. Shocked to be on the receiving end of openly disapproving stares, a tiny part of me felt a glimmer of satisfaction when the little lad told gawpers in no uncertain terms to 'F off'. The softening of attitudes over the years and the greater acceptance of differences can only be helped by the Hidden Disabilities Scheme.

With children of all ages and temperaments in the audience, the presenters of 'The Night Sky' no doubt come to work in the knowledge that they'll be entertaining a tough crowd, but today they're really earning their pay. Thankfully, their passion for their subject and the domed screen upon which a beautiful representation of the night sky is projected hold all the children, even Louis, captivated. The next half an hour passes without a hitch.

Carrot sticks keep Bartley regulated as we line up for the Zero Gravity Experience. With Caitlin looking after Ethan and Louis in the adjacent soft play area that I can see from my position in the queue, I decide to revisit Bartley's earlier comment about Caitlin's father. 'So,' I say casually, 'Caitlin's dad used to see her on her birthday?'

'He used to, the creep. But not any more.'

'Creep? Why do you say that?'

He snorts. 'Because he is.'

I hand him another carrot stick. 'In what way is he creepy?'

He takes a large bite and speaks around it. 'Always fussing round her, bringing her new trainers and stuff.'

'Always?' I probe, realising that he's using 'creepy' to mean 'grovelling', rather than something more sinister.

'Every birthday,' Bartley answers, his lips tinged with orange. 'Sometimes at Christmas too. The dick. He's not right in the head. But that ship has sailed now.'

It's a phrase that doesn't strike me as a Bartley-ism. Not for the first time, I suspect he's repeating someone else's words.

The fact that he considers Caitlin spoiled because she used to see her father twice a year makes my heart ache for both of them. It makes me all the more determined to give them a good time while they're with me. After the Zero Gravity Experience, which they all love, I pay extra for them to have a go on a simulator of a launch-pad acceleration.

'You can choose something for your birthday, honey,' I tell Caitlin in the gift shop afterwards. She turns from a poster of the solar system that she'd been staring at longingly, and looks at me as if she can't quite believe her ears. 'You can have the poster, if you'd like? The rest of you –'

'That's not fair!' Bartley cuts me off. 'What an effing spoilt princess. She's ruined the vibe all day, now she gets rewarded for it.' He kicks out at a wooden barrel with delicate-looking glass models of planets and stars displayed on top. Ethan copies. There's a clinking noise as they rattle against each other. Thankfully none of them smash or fall off the sides.

The attendant raises his eyebrows at me. Probably thanks to the sunflower lanyards, when I apologise he smiles and says mildly, 'No harm done.'

'If you'll let me finish, Bartley, I was about to say that it's Caitlin's birthday so she can choose a present for herself, but the rest of you can have a little souvenir as well.'

Bartley blinks slowly, his cheeks reddening, then grabs a giant chocolate bar and persuades Ethan to do the same.

'That's not really a souvenir.'

'Yeah it is.' He points to the paper wrapper which has the name of the space centre on it surrounded by stars.

'Okay, okay, you've got me there. Pick up an extra one to take home with you,' I add, rolling my eyes as I grab a small bar of chocolate for Louis to snack on while we wait for the train. 'We don't want to leave Linzi out.'

The idea strikes me as soon as Megan sits next to me on the train and Caitlin slips into the booth directly behind. 'Well, what a nice day that was,' I say, pulling Louis's buggy close to clear a path for the boys. They shove each other as they cross the aisle and take the seats adjacent to ours. 'I've learned so much.'

'Me too! Me too!' Megan bounces up and down in her seat as the doors squeak to a close and the train jerks into motion.

'Oh good.' I mop smears of chocolate from Louis's face. He grins at me as I pass him a sippy cup of water. 'Like what, Megs?'

'Like you should never eat a lolly too fast.'

I laugh and ruffle her hair. 'Well, I've learned that Mercury is the hottest planet,' I blither, looking casually out the window.

It's after six and the darkening sky has rendered the glass so reflective that I can make out Caitlin's face. 'Makes sense I suppose, since it's nearest the sun, but I hadn't really thought about that before, and no one really teaches that stuff in school. At least, not when I was in school back in the seventies.'

I rattle on, aware of Caitlin's increasingly agitated expression. She looks fit to burst, especially when I come out with some nonsense about the moon. 'I don't think that astronaut from NASA was right about another moon landing. I don't think we'll ever go back. *If* we were ever there in the first place.'

Finally triggered to a degree she can't ignore, Caitlin makes a noise of disbelief and then bursts out, 'Oh, Rosie, of c-course, of course we went there!'

Meg's head swivels round, her eyes goggling in shock.

'Are you sure about that?' I say mildly, resisting the urge to punch the air. Through the reflection in the window, I can see my daughter staring at me in astonishment. When I don't react, she frowns and fiddles with her hearing aid, as if it might have been playing tricks on her. Then she peers through the gap in the seats. A small shake of my head has the desired effect when she opens her mouth to say something. I look back out the window. Thankfully, Megan gets the message.

'Absolutely, d-definitely,' Caitlin stutters, her sweet voice croaky through lack of use. 'Neil Armstrong landed on the moon in 1969. He planted a flag there! And Rosie, Mercury isn't the hottest planet,' she carries on. 'V-venus is! I know Mercury is the closest to the sun but it doesn't have an atmosphere so it can't trap the heat.'

'Ah, I see,' I say, quickly scrolling through my phone to draw up one of Jamie's recent messages. I've lost count of the number of breakthrough moments that have taken place over the years while travelling. There's something about the dynamic of motion and lack of eye contact in a car, train or bus that helps children feel less intimidated.

'Oh damnation, shut it, misfit,' Bartley growls at her. 'You're the –'

'Have you seen this meme, Bartley?' I interrupt. Leaning across the aisle, I hand him my phone to show him the latest meme Jamie sent me. Highly amused by the fact that I never find them funny, Emily and Jamie are forever texting memes to me.

It takes Caitlin a second or two to recover from Bartley's interruption, but when she does there's no stopping her. As if making up for lost time, she fills the next hour with talk about black holes, warp drives and the possibility for time travel almost without drawing breath. 'I'm going to work for Elon Musk one day, Rosie,' she tells me wistfully. 'I'm going to fly to Mars with SpaceX.'

'Excellent,' Bartley says, as I take back my phone and gather our rucksacks. 'It'll be a one-way ticket. We'll never have to set eyes on your bloated face again.'

'It *is* a one-way ticket, Rosie,' Caitlin whispers, as we stand and wait for the doors to open. 'Once I leave, I can never come back. Everyone will be so happy. It'll be like I've died.'

Chapter Twenty

The next hour is spent packing up the children's bags and passes peaceably enough, with Bartley only falling foul of the 'NO LONGER TOLERATE' basket a couple of times. Back from work, Emily offers to put Megan to bed while I drop the children back to their grandparents.

As we drive through the dark streets, Bartley manages to keep his hands to himself. While we're filing across the Chambers' driveway, however, the security light flicks on and illuminates Bartley as he flicks Caitlin inexplicably in the face with his finger.

'Don't start, Bartley, you've done so well,' I say, although there's not much I can do about it on his own turf, a situation I'm sure he's determined to milk. Sure enough, as we wait for our knocks to be answered, he and Ethan take turns stamping on Caitlin's toes. 'Stop that right now,' I snap, pressing a hand into Bartley's chest to separate him from his sister.

Ryan frowns when he opens the door. There's a patchwork of steri-strips running from the corner of his right eye to his hairline. His other eye is swollen and bruised and there's a deep gash in the middle of his bottom lip that's still glistening with spots of fresh blood. 'Had a bit of a tête-à-tête with a prop-forward at weekend,' he says, gingerly dabbing his lip with three strapped-up fingers.

'Ouch, broken fingers as well?' I say as we troop into the house.

He winces. 'The other guy came off a lot worse though, believe me.'

'What's all this?' Julie says as she comes down the stairs. She runs her eyes over the children, then settles her gaze on Caitlin's poster. A little break was clearly what she needed. She looks far more relaxed than when I left her on Friday.

Caitlin unfurls the poster and holds it up. 'Rosie got it for me.'

Julie starts at the sound of granddaughter's voice and gives me a wide-eyed look of surprise. Hoping not to bring too much attention to Caitlin, I hand Louis over to his grandmother and update her on what he's eaten over the weekend.

'Put it away, Caitlin,' Ryan says roughly, as Julie fusses over her youngest grandchild. Her face crumples. Without another word, she rolls the poster up, crams the end into her rucksack and dashes upstairs.

'Make sure you keep it over your side, loser,' Bartley says as he and Ethan run up the stairs after her.

Julie gives Ryan a look. 'You off to work soon?'

He nods and pecks her on the cheek. 'See you later, darlin'.' With a nod in my direction, he grabs his coat and lets himself out. Julie closes her eyes and breathes out slowly, then smiles at me.

'Here's a little something for Linzi.' I hand her the chocolate. 'We didn't want to leave her out.'

'Oh, that's so nice of you. She's still at her sleepover. Must have cost you a fortune, taking all of them out.'

As a foster carer on the Mockingbird scheme, I'm paid a weekly fostering allowance equivalent to caring for one child, no matter how many children I have in my hub. Consequently, I'd already spent my entire allowance for this week. As long as I can just about manage, however, I don't mind.

'Well,' I say, looking at her, 'we wanted to do something special for Caitlin's birthday.'

Julie gasps and clamps a hand over her mouth. 'What's the date today?'

'The seventeenth.'

A shadow falls across her face. 'Oh, poor Caitlin.' Her eyes grow shiny. 'God, I feel awful.'

I squeeze her arm. 'You've had a lot going on.'

She nods, sniffs. 'I'll make it up to her. Stay for a cuppa?'

'Okay, just a quick one then.' She potters around the kitchen and I sit myself at the breakfast bar. 'Good weekend? You're looking well.'

'It was lovely, I have to say. I know I complained about not being able to take the kids with us, but actually it was nice to let my hair down and not have to worry about getting back or anything.'

'Ryan doesn't look quite so rested.'

She laughs and joins me at the bar. 'It was one of *those* weddings,' she says, handing me a mug of tea. 'He's never happy unless it ends in a punch-up. There's a song about that, isn't there?'

I frown. 'Oh, Ryan said it was a rugby injury.'

'Did he? Probably embarrassed, silly sod.' She sips her drink and then looks at me. 'Still, this weekend has been good for us. Sometimes it's like walking on eggshells. When he's stressed it feels like I can't do anything right. Nothing like a punch-up and a weekend of sex to release some of the tension, eh?' She laughs again, then her eyes sweep over my face. 'Did you give the Botox and fillers any more thought? Honestly, you'll never look back once you've taken the plunge.'

'No,' I say firmly, wishing to draw an end to the discussion. 'I'll stick to a dab of Nivea before bed.'

'Oh,' she says, running her eyes over my crow's feet and softening chin with barely concealed disappointment. 'I'll WhatsApp you the details just in case you change your mind. I reckon if you did that and got your hair straightened, you'd knock ten years off. Got to keep the men happy, eh?'

'Mm,' I mumble, non-committal. It's not as if I don't appreciate forthrightness – a particularly outspoken social worker called Peggy, whom we all love, springs to mind. But Julie takes bluntness to a whole new level. Personally, I'd rather put my energies into making sure the children are happy than fighting a losing battle with gravity, but I manage to avoid getting any deeper into that particular conversation by telling her about the three baskets games we 'played' with Bartley.

'What a wonderful idea. There's plenty I could put in the "NO LONGER TOLERATE" pile, I tell you that. In fact,' she says with a sardonic smile, 'I might see if I can find a basket big enough for my husband.'

When my mobile rings before 8 o'clock the next morning, I expect to hear Joan's voice telling me that Millie has gone AWOL again. Instead, it's Robert. 'You're early for a Monday morning,' I say, putting a bowl of Weetabix in front of Megan.

'Yes, well, I was going to wait until the TAC meeting, but that's a few weeks away and this really needs addressing now.'

Team Around the Child or TAC meetings as they're called for short bring together all the different agencies responsible for making plans for a child. Besides sharing relevant information, the purpose of the meeting is to set goals and form a strategy about how they can be reached. Services can then be targeted in a co-ordinated way so that timescales are adhered to, avoiding what is commonly known as 'drift' – the tendency for months, and sometimes even years, to pass with nothing much happening on a child's case.

There's a grim undercurrent to the social worker's tone, one that makes my stomach tighten. 'What is it, Robert?'

'There's been a complaint, from Linzi Chambers.'

'Oh that,' I say, half-laughing with relief. The knot in my stomach loosens. 'That's been dealt with.'

'You say that, but I don't think we cover ourselves in glory by dismissing the voice of a child so quickly.'

I'm so taken aback that a social worker whose caseload is no doubt teetering under its own weight is wasting time on a complaint about a game of UNO that I struggle to find my voice for a moment. 'You're not serious?'

Robert clears his throat. 'Lorraine copied me into her email, so I know how she sees it. I'm merely letting you know that Linzi has requested an audience to hear her out, so I'll be going along this afternoon.'

'That's utterly ridiculous,' I reply, realising as I say it how like my mother I sound.

'As I say,' Robert responds pompously, 'we've got a TAC meeting coming up. You'll get a chance to air any views you have there. *If* you're still visiting the family at that stage.' He pauses. 'I've been speaking to Julie. The children have adjusted to their new circumstances quite nicely and the couple's assessments are nearing completion. I see no reason to extend your involvement beyond a couple of weeks or so.'

I end the call with a creeping sensation of nausea in my stomach.

There's a secret lurking at the heart of the family, I'm sure of it. And now I only have two weeks to find out what it is.

Chapter Twenty-One

It's mid-week before I see the children again, and then only briefly. As planned by text with Julie on Monday evening, I arrive at Millfield on Wednesday to pick them up, stunned to see the grandmother pulling up in her BMW. She parks on the yellow zig-zags adjacent to the school gate (directly opposite a 'STRICTLY NO PARKING' sign). Bartley, it seems, isn't the only one in the family who believes that rules apply to others but not himself.

'Julie?' I lean down as she opens the offside window. Louis grins at me from his car seat. When I say hello he presses his nose up against the rear window and lets out a snorty squeal, kicking his legs excitedly at the funny faces I'm pulling. I turn to Julie. 'I thought I was having them this afternoon?'

'No need,' she says airily, as if nothing's been arranged. 'We've got *family* coming over this afternoon.' It's not unusual for people to close ranks if they sense they're under threat from an outsider, and I can't help but notice a slight emphasis on the word 'family'. 'Tell you what though, you could grab them for me, save me the palaver of getting Louis out.'

A bit put out, I'm tempted to refuse. 'Of course,' I say after a moment's hesitation, politeness getting the better of me.

Caitlin's face lights up when she sees me and Ethan rushes over and throws his arms around my hips, burying his head inside my coat. Even Bartley looks relatively pleased. Their faces fall when I tell them they won't be coming to me. Megan makes her feelings known when they climb into Julie's car as well, and she's still pouting and frowning and chuntering as we walk back to our own.

I double-check with Julie when Robert asks me to have the two eldest children to stay at the weekend, and so on Friday afternoon Megan skips beside me as we cross their driveway, excited at the prospect of spending the weekend with Bartley and Caitlin.

'But that's not fair!' she blurts out, when Julie tells us that they aren't feeling very well.

'Aw, what a sweetheart.' Julie hunkers down so that she's level with Megan. 'You enjoy having my brood over then,' she says with a smile.

Megan nods. 'I love it.'

'Well, I would have texted Mummy to let her know,' Julie tells Megan out of the corner of her mouth, as if she's letting her into a secret, 'only I'm not sure she likes me messaging her.'

Megan frowns up at me. Julie rises to her feet and squeezes my forearm. 'I'm only teasing. To be honest I was hoping they'd be better by this afternoon. Were you –' she stops abruptly as Ryan appears behind her. 'For God's sake,

Ryan,' she complains as he jostles Caitlin past her, 'you nearly had me over. What are you doing?!'

'She's all right to go,' he says roughly, giving Caitlin a little shove in the middle of her back. The ten-year-old stumbles down the step, almost colliding into us.

'Yay!' Megan cheers, giving the solemn-looking child a hug.

'Just a minute, Megs.' I look from Caitlin to Julie, whose mouth is stretched into a thin line. 'This okay with you?'

'Course it's okay, she's right as rain, aren't you, Caitlin?' Ryan answers on Julie's behalf. She sighs and just about manages to blow Caitlin a kiss before her husband chucks a pink rucksack at us. Sweeping Julie out of the way with a tattooed arm, he then slams the door.

It's as I'm performing a three-point turn outside their house that I catch sight of Caitlin's space poster. Rather than taking pride of place in the middle of her bedroom, I'm taken aback to see it sticking up out of their green recycling bin, its tattered ends draped forlornly over the sides.

Caitlin remains silent throughout the journey to our house, despite Megan's best efforts to get her talking. It makes me sad to see the progress she made last weekend undone, but a plan comes together in my mind as I make dinner. When the plates are cleared away, I tell the girls about it.

'We're going camping?!' Megan cheers, looking between Caitlin and me with widened eyes. 'It's freezing, but o-kay!'

I laugh, pleased to see an expression of intrigue on Caitlin's face. 'Not camping, exactly. We'll be using sleeping bags to keep us warm, that's all. We won't be spending the whole night outside.'

In that slightly unsettling way Google has of displaying advertisements related to something you've recently spoken about, a pop-up about a new stargazing app had appeared on the screen of my mobile a couple of days ago. With Jamie's help and an evening under the stars in mind, I'd downloaded it.

'This is going to be the best night ever!' Caitlin says in a husky voice. She runs off with Megan to grab some of the camping gear from the airing cupboard. Mungo sets off in pursuit and waits for them at the foot of the stairs.

'We'll need a ground sheet, Megs,' I shout up. Stroking Mungo's soft ears, I'm delighted to hear Caitlin relaying the message when Megan doesn't hear. Arms loaded with lanterns and sleeping bags and blankets, they hobble down the stairs as quickly as they can manage, looking every bit like two excited school friends planning a sleepover.

It's 8 p.m. by the time we venture outside. I'm pleased to see that the sky is clear, but the lack of cloud cover means that the temperature has dipped at least five degrees since school pick-up. I'm guessing it's close to zero. 'Quick, tuck up,' I tell the girls, after spreading a ground sheet and sleeping mats over the icy grass. Already bundled up in coats, hats and gloves, they dive, giggling, into their sleeping bags. Within a couple of minutes, after a few sips of warm milk, both of them start stripping off their outer layers. 'I'm too hot,' Megan complains, kicking off her sleeping bag and attempting to pull off her coat.

'Here we go.' I quickly pull up the app to distract her from stripping off to her vest and knickers, and hand Caitlin the phone.

The air fills with an otherworldly melody as the app identifies the constellations above us.

'Rosie, this is so cool!' Caitlin cries. 'There's Mars over there! I'm going to live there one day, Megs. And there's a star cluster, look!'

My heart swells to see her so animated, and to hear the passion in her voice. She's still raving on about it as I return the equipment to the airing cupboard an hour later. Exhausted after a warm bath, Megan is fast asleep, her soft snores reaching us through her open door.

'Thank you, Rosie,' Caitlin says quietly. 'For the awesome evening, I mean.'

'You're very welcome, darling. Right, I'll run a fresh bath for you.'

Her expression darkens. 'No, I don't want one.'

'You should, sweetheart.' The pair of them were bundled up in hats and coats but they still got covered in mud.

'Please, I really don't want one.' Her body has gone completely rigid, utter panic on her face.

'Okay, sweetheart, what about a shower then?'

She looks slightly less petrified. 'Can I do it myself?'

'Of course. I'll set it running, though – it can be a bit glitchy.' A sense of dread fills my chest as I warm a towel on the radiator and get the water just right. Past experience has taught me to view a child's horror at the mention of undressing or having a bath as a red flag moment. Still, I remind myself, every case is different.

Pink-cheeked but still pensive, Caitlin comes down to say goodnight to me 20 minutes later.

'Goodnight, sweetheart.' I hand her a glass of water. 'Oh, hang on, before you go up.' She turns on the first stair and looks at me expectantly. 'I couldn't help noticing your poster in the recycling at Nan's house,' I venture as matter-of-factly as I can manage. Caitlin goes very still. 'I know how pleased you were with it, so I'm guessing *you* didn't put it there.'

'No, I – it wasn't,' she pauses and swallows, then drops her gaze. Her fingers play restlessly with the banister. 'I mean –' she stops again, her lower lip trembling, and then she glances up at me with such an agonised expression that I feel the need to help her out and move the subject on.

'I hope you were okay earlier, when Grandad …' I pause. I'm still not sure how she feels about Ryan. It's not my place to speak about family members in a negative way, but after seeing the way he shoved her out of the house, what I really want to ask is if he's prone to treating her roughly.

'He didn't hurt me,' she splutters, cheeks flushing a deeper red as she rushes to defend him.

'That's good. You like spending time with your grandad?'

She smiles uncertainly. 'I … m-miss him when he goes away.'

'But sometimes he takes you with him.'

Her smile fades. 'Sometimes. But sometimes Bartley gets to go instead.' There's a thread of dismay in her voice, as if she genuinely resents her brother taking her place. I stay at the bottom of the stairs when she says goodnight, wondering whether she has a form of Stockholm syndrome, a trauma bond that keeps her locked in co-dependency with someone abusive.

Mungo watches me closely, then tilts his head in a way that makes me feel as if he's reading my mind. 'You're right,' I whisper, crouching down and cupping his hairy face. 'I should get you some dinner and stop jumping to conclusions.'

By the morning of Sunday 24 March, Caitlin is almost as full of life as Megan. The pair of them dart in and out of the garden, Caitlin pausing only briefly to offer to help me peel some carrots. Rosy-cheeked, she looks pleased when I tell her to run off and enjoy herself. It's a surprise when she pops back in after a minute on the trampoline, and stands quietly at my side.

'Thirsty? It's hard work, all that jumping.'

'No, I just, I wondered … I wondered how Mummy is. Do you know?'

'Oh, sweetie.' I stop what I'm doing and look at her. 'I haven't heard. Have you asked Nanny? She's been visiting the hospital, hasn't she?'

Caitlin nods. 'She doesn't say much. It's okay though.'

I watch as she dashes off down the garden back to Megan, wondering why Julie hasn't told the children how their mother is getting on. Then again, if Bonnie is still in a bad way, perhaps she thinks they're better off being kept in the dark.

When babies come into care, it's usual for them to have daily contact with their birth mother. Older children generally get booked in for two or three sessions a week. If all parties agree and it's safe to do so, contact can take place in the foster home. In most instances, the meetings take place in a local authority contact centre, however, where trained support workers are available to supervise and take notes.

Contact is only suspended if it can't be carried out safely, or if birth parents let the children down with repeated 'no-shows'. It could be that Bonnie is still so overwrought that it would be upsetting for the children to see her. I make a mental note to ask Robert if he's able to arrange something. It's clear that Caitlin is keen to see her mum.

With bright sunlight glinting on the worktops and the sound of the girls' laughter drifting through the open door, it's easy to reassure myself that my worries about Caitlin were overblown, and possibly even entirely in my own head.

There's little point in dwelling on disclosures that might never come, I reason, forcing myself to relax and enjoy the relative peace of the day.

But when Des arrives later for dinner, with my mother in tow, I get the sense that the day might not pass entirely stress-free. 'What's wrong?' I demand immediately, having taken one look at my mum's strained expression. My mother's inability to hide her disapproval is infamous in our family. Today proves to be no exception.

'I'm fine,' she says firmly, although her reproachful glance in Des's direction doesn't escape my notice.

Des raises his eyebrows at me and blows out his cheeks, but when Mum nips upstairs to the bathroom he claims not to know what I'm talking about. 'I'm not silly, Des. You could cut the tension between you with a blunt spoon.'

One bushy eyebrow lifts higher than the other as he tries to arrange his face into an oblivious expression. 'I think I heard your phone go off,' he says, scratching his beard.

'My goodness, she's proactive,' I say, after checking my texts and finding one from Julie. Apparently, her beauty therapist is offering a 20 per cent discount at the moment.

'Who's proactive?' Mum asks, joining us in the dining area. Jamie, who yet again has arrived at the perfect time for dinner, drapes his arm casually around his grandmother's shoulder, high-fives Des and looks at me expectantly.

'Oh, it's just a message from Caitlin's gran.' I look from one to the other of them. 'Do you think I need Botox, or filler, or something?'

There's a pause while they gather their responses. Des and Jamie look at each other as if they'd like to confer before committing themselves. When Des finally opens his mouth, my mother cuts him off. 'I'd say,' she says, running her eyes scathingly over his face, 'that he's ill-equipped to offer an opinion on the matter.'

Jamie cackles. 'Ooh, that's such a burn, Nan!'

She smiles. Des chuckles along, but there's definitely something off between them. Megan picks up on it when we sit down for dinner. 'Why's everyone so quiet today?'

Despite being the youngest, she's often the first to detect the subtle changes in atmosphere that usually go over Jamie and Emily's heads. 'I know!' she cries with a twinkle in her eye. 'Let's talk about Brexit!'

'Noooo!' Jamie and I howl in unison. Megan giggles, the cheeky so-and-so. She may not entirely understand what Brexit is, but she knows it's likely to rouse a strong reaction among grown-ups. Mum and Des both smile at her, but in a restrained way. It's a gift for the pair of them

– the perfect opportunity for a bit of leg pulling and one they'd never usually pass up, but they keep their eyes on Megan, carefully avoiding each other's gaze.

'Are you sure you two haven't had a row?' I whisper in the kitchen, while Mum gets her coat on in the hall. I'd barely cleared the table before Des suggested giving her a lift home.

'Course not,' he says, giving me a brief peck on the cheek.

In the hallway, when I ask Mum if everything's okay, she gives Des a sharp look. 'What's he been saying now?'

Des holds his hands up. 'Nothing!' He attempts a smile, but there's a dull quality to his eyes that I recognise from years earlier, when he kept his trip to the US from me. My stomach turns over. The first I heard about his plan to work overseas was from one of my fostering friends. Could it be that he's told my mum that he's leaving again, and he hasn't got round to telling me?

As usual when fostering, there isn't much time to spare for introspection, or to ponder anything other than the tasks at hand. Des and Caitlin compete for my thoughts as I settle myself down to read for the evening, however. Unable to concentrate, I flick through some recipe books instead, making a note of some meals that Caitlin and Megan can make themselves. I even find one for a nut roast that requires lots of battering with a mallet. I turn the corner of the page. Bartley might well be enticed by that one.

It's a struggle to drop off, but soon after I do, my phone goes off. 'I'm sorry, Rosie,' Joan croaks. 'Millie's been arrested. I didn't even know she'd left her bed. I've left a message with the duty social worker but they haven't got back to me yet.'

'Okay, Joan, don't worry, I'm on my way,' I tell her as I gather my clothes. With Jamie at home, I'm free to leave the house.

Whatever's going on with Des, I haven't got the time or energy to worry about it at the moment.

Chapter Twenty-Two

'Whatever were you thinking, honey?' I say in a hushed tone, keeping my voice down so that the uniformed officers passing the detention room door won't hear our conversation. Under Police Codes of Practice, Millie has the right to eight hours' uninterrupted sleep before being interviewed. It might be 3 a.m., but from the way she's striding from one end of the cell to the other, I'm guessing it will be some time before exhaustion forces her to collapse onto the narrow bed I'm sitting on.

'Doing what I was told, weren't I?'

'What you were told?' I couldn't recall Judge Symonds telling her to shove six designer tracksuits into her rucksack after school, or to venture out late evening when Joan thought she was in bed, brazenly trying to sell her wares in the nearest public house. Local authorities provide children in the care system with a generous weekly clothing allowance these days, so it would strain credulity to claim that desperation drove her to stealing.

'The judge told me to leave old Mr Braces alone.' She stops mid-pace and grins at me. 'So I found something else to do with my time.'

'I think the judge had something else in mind than shop-lifting, lovey.' According to the custody sergeant, Millie made no attempt to run when the bar manager called the police, although as soon as they turned up she kicked off, trying to evade arrest. The decision to remand her in custody overnight, rather than bail her to appear at a later date, had been made for her own protection, rather than a belief that she posed significant danger to anyone other than herself.

Millie shrugs, her bottom lip quivering. 'Come here, lovey,' I say, patting the plastic-covered mattress. When she sits down, I drape a blue blanket over her lap, tucking it in at the sides. Her eyelids instantly start to droop. She lets out a loud yawn.

'It can't be much fun, traipsing around the cold streets instead of being tucked up in bed.'

'Not much fun?' she repeats, blinking at me in incomprehension. 'It's the best. I love it.'

I give her a doubtful look. Could it be that she enjoys the blast of adrenaline that comes with avoiding capture, I wonder. Then again, her blatant behaviour in the pub suggests that she was crying out to be found out. 'Love what?' I glance at the door, where shadows flit across the small recessed window. 'Stealing?'

She blushes and drops her gaze. 'Not that, no.' There's a pause, then she turns to me. 'I didn't even want the stuff I nicked, not really. But I had to do something and I couldn't risk stalking Mr Braces no more, could I, cos old Symonds threatened to send me away if I carried on.'

'But why did you have to do anything at all? Why not tuck down in your lovely bed and read a good book? Or watch something on Netflix?'

'I wanted to get myself arrested, didn't I.'

'You *wanted* to get arrested?'

She nods.

'Why on earth would you want to be arrested?' As soon as the words are out of my mouth I answer my own question, presuming that getting a record offers her some sort of kudos among her peers, or perhaps protection from gangs. But when she next speaks, she floors me with her honesty.

'Because if you resist, they have to restrain you. They pull you towards them and hold you tight.' She wraps her arms around herself and swings softly from side to side. 'Oh, Rosie, it feels so warm and safe when they do that, almost as if they're taking you in their arms and dancing.' She smiles at me without a trace of self-pity, as if what she's saying isn't utterly heartbreaking. 'It feels like the biggest cuddle. Honestly, you should try it sometime.'

The most awful thing about Millie's confession is that there's sound reasoning behind it. Moved by tenderness, I shuffle across the mattress until I'm close enough to put my arm around her.

Exhausted, she rests her head on my shoulder. Her breaths soon become shallow. Within a minute or so, she's sound asleep.

I make it back home in time to greet the girls when they wake up, and after dropping them off at their respective schools I head straight to the magistrates' court. Arriving in the car park half an hour early, I pull a blanket from the back seat and tuck it around my lap before dialling Robert's number on my mobile. The sky is overcast and the temperature is cool for the first week of spring. The warmth from the woolly blanket spreads to my toes as the call connects.

I haven't spoken to Robert for over a week and I'm fully expecting the call to switch to voicemail, so it's a surprise when I hear his voice. 'Rosie, I've been meaning to call you about the Easter holidays.'

'Ah, you saw my email then, about us going away?' When my friend offered us the use of one of her semi-renovated cottages in Whitby, I jumped at the chance of a low-cost fortnight away.

Millie's social worker would need to arrange for someone to cover any late-night jaunts to the police station, depending on what happens at court later today, but all the other families in my Mockingbird hub will be able to manage with telephone support only during the holiday period.

There's Dionne, a foster carer who's looking after siblings with sickle cell. A spell of cold weather is sometimes all it takes to send the children into a crisis that needs hospital care, but with both children having been well for almost a month, Dionne is braving a fortnight in the Isle of Wight over Easter.

Sharon, a young mother whose isolation led to depression after her three-year-old daughter was diagnosed with leukaemia, depends on a long chat a few times a week to keep her feeling connected to the world, but we often communicate over the phone, and I can do that from anywhere.

And finally there's Jade, a care leaver who gave birth soon after completing a twenty-six-week sentence for assault. With no parents or extended family in her network, and very few friends, the nineteen-year-old relies on advice to help her care for her young baby. Again, a quick phone call is often all it takes to reassure Jade that she's doing the right thing. Google has its place, but there's nothing quite like being able to pick up the phone to a mother figure when you're worrying at 2 a.m., about whether it's normal for a baby to sleep with their face planted in the mattress and their bottom in the air.

'Any chance they could go with you?' Robert says. 'I know I said the Powell children would be off your books well before Easter, but Jules and Ryan need to complete the "Who's in Charge?" parenting course before we can sign them off the system. It's booked solid for the next couple of months but the local authority is hosting a supplementary course for grandparents over the holidays. I'm keen to get the Chambers on it. Linzi's going to holiday club. We could consider financing holiday club places for the others, but it would be better if they could go with you.'

'That would be fine, as long as you're okay with them sharing a bedroom.'

'Not an issue with me.'

'I don't see why not, then.' I'm not entirely sure how my mum will feel when she hears that the children will be joining us on holiday. She usually loves the hurly-burly commotion that young children bring, but she's not Bartley's greatest fan.

'Great. Thanks, Rosie.'

'Oh, Robert, a couple of things before you go. If I'm to spend a fortnight with the children,' I venture, gathering my thoughts as I go, 'I'll need to spend a whole day at the Chambers so I can fully grasp their usual routines.'

Perhaps persuaded by the use of 'social worker speak', Robert doesn't hesitate to agree. 'Excellent idea. As a matter of fact, a full day's observation of the family would be helpful in demonstrating that they meet all the necessary requirements to ensure they're a viable option for the children. Thank you for being so proactive, Rosie.'

'Not a problem,' I say with a smile. 'And also, I was wondering whether Bonnie is up to having contact with the children. Caitlin's desperately keen to see her mum and –'

'We mustn't fixate on one child, Rosie,' Robert says, suddenly frosty.

'I'm sorry?'

'Julie mentioned that you seem to be favouring the girl. The others will pick up on it, you know.'

Almost speechless, I stare across the car park to the court, where suited barristers and court personnel are filing in through the entrance. 'Robert, I'm asking on behalf of all the children,' I say, my eyes on the journalists waiting outside the building, their heads craned over their phones. 'I mentioned Caitlin because she's the one who's been asking after her mum.'

'I think we can leave that side of it to Julie. She's visiting Bonnie regularly and feels strongly that she's not up to contact with the children at this stage in proceedings. I'm sure she's keeping them in the loop. I will check when she's free for you to spend a day at theirs, though. I'll let you know what she says.'

A strange sense of foreboding overtakes me as I cross the car park towards the court. From the way Robert talks, it's as if Julie is the one leading the management of the children's case instead of him.

Judge Symonds smiles at Millie with weary familiarity an hour later, after confirming that the CPS have recommended a charge of theft against the teenager. 'You need to understand that shoplifting is a serious offence,' he delivers in a monotone, no doubt suspecting that his words will fall on deaf ears.

Having accompanied Millie through her police interview, I know how sympathetic officers were to her plight, particularly after I'd made them aware of Millie's confession that she 'enjoyed' being arrested. The interviewing detective sergeant's eyes had grown misty after I'd had a quiet word. 'Poor kid,' she said, 'but we can't just let this go.'

Whilst their gentle words of advice and genuine sympathy were a credit to their compassionate professionalism, it was also a fact that had encouraged the affection-starved teenager's fixation on them.

The same cannot be said for Millie's feelings towards those in the court system. Her lip curls as the judge reads out the charges against her. Hostility seeps from her pores. 'Dunno,' she says, when asked why she turned to shoplifting, having never been arrested for that particular crime before. Forewarned of Millie's history of abuse and her disclosure to me when in police custody, the judge touches on the subject, suggesting gently that she may have a craving for attention rather than for the material goods she stole. 'There are significant mitigations,' he says, eyeing her sympathetically over the top of his glasses. 'One can see that.'

Millie rolls her eyes exaggeratedly and lets out a loud burp.

The judge blinks. He picks up a sheet of paper and studies it. 'The prosecution have grave misgivings about the wisdom of releasing you back to your current foster placement. Having considered your case and the charges against you, I concur that these are not entirely unfounded. In light of your persistent offending, I've decided to make an order for your relocation to semi-independent provision. There is an excellent facility in Cornwall and I believe they have a room waiting for you.'

Millie's look of disgust vanishes. She stares at the judge with wide eyes, her jaw slack with shock. 'Cornwall? Bloody Cornwall?! But that's hundreds of miles away!'

'Exactly,' Judge Symonds declares, keeping his eyes focused on his notes because it's probably easier than witnessing the pain of his decision playing out across the teenager's face. 'You deserve a fresh start, somewhere new. Your liberty will not be infringed upon, my dear. But you will be closely monitored. You're merely being offered an opportunity to explore constructive activities, and to find out what you're interested in. That doesn't sound bad now, does it?'

Millie looks at me and bursts into tears. My heart squeezes as I take in her stricken expression.

'Now, now,' the judge says in an even gentler tone. He goes on to explain that the move will allow her to make new, more positive associations.

As I pull her into a hug, I can't help but feel a little resentful towards the system. While I can understand the rationale behind moving her away from the orthodontist, it seems extreme to relocate her to the other end of the country. It's not as if she's gang-affiliated, and they still have orthodontists in Cornwall. Millie will take her problems with her, wherever she goes, so the move in itself isn't a solution.

Being sent to semi-independent provision is a bit of a lottery as well. I'd heard varying reports over the years; some supervised homes are excellent; while others are run by people who see the business as a bit of a cash cow. It all depends on who's at the top, holding the purse strings.

I swallow down the lump in my throat as Millie sobs on my shoulder. Joan will be very upset as well, when she hears the news. My eyes drift back to the judge as he continues with words of encouragement, wondering whether he struggles with sleepless nights at the end of a day making impossible decisions. Perhaps, like me, he feels utterly deflated, frustrated by the system and with the sad truth that, despite your best efforts, you can't help everyone.

'You can stay in touch,' I tell Millie later, as we drive towards Joan's. She has 24 hours to pack up her things. Tomorrow she'll be escorted on the long journey down to her new home.

Joan's waiting at the door when we pull up outside. 'I'll be thinking of you, sweetheart,' I tell the tearful teen, giving her another hug.

'Thanks for all you've done for me,' she croaks before rushing off to the foster carer. Joan, who must be close to 70 now, tries her best to give Millie a cuddle while supporting a wailing baby in her arms.

* * *

After putting Megan to bed, I sit on the floor of my bedroom with my back against the wall and weep. They aren't really my tears to cry, especially when I've been so fortunate in the lottery of life, what with my wonderful family and comfortable home. But I can't help thinking about all the children besides Millie who go to sleep in an unfamiliar place, knowing that the pillow they wake up on in the morning might not be the same one they'll rest their head on at night.

I take a deep breath and dab my eyes on the cuff of my sleeve, hoping fervently that my intervention with the Powells is more effective than my attempt to improve Millie's life.

Chapter Twenty-Three

When I pull up outside the Chambers' house on Tuesday 26 March, I spot Ryan hanging around further up the street. Brow creasing, he starts moving towards me as soon as I cut my engine. My heart picks up pace. It's almost as if he's been waiting for me. 'Ryan, hello,' I say with a smile, commandeering my lightest tone.

'What d'you think you're playing at?' he seethes, coming so close that I can feel his breath on my face.

'I'm sorry?' With the principles of non-violent resistance in mind, I lower my gaze and fold my arms tightly around my coat.

Ryan's jaw juts out in exactly the same way as Bartley's when he's angry. Despite the decades separating them and the fact that they're not biologically related, they look remarkably alike. For some reason, the resemblance unexpectedly warms him to me. 'Don't play the innocent with me. I know it was you what reported me for taking the kids in the lorry. Don't bother denying it. And it was you kicking up a stink about Bart's dad picking Cait up from school. What business is it of yours, eh? Tell me that.'

So, Robert may not have acknowledged my email, but he must have had words with the Chambers. 'I'm asking you why you think it's anything to do with you,' he rants, his teeth bared with rage. 'I could lose my HGV licence if the social gets onto my firm – did you even give that a second thought?'

'I hope that doesn't happen. But I'm obliged to report anything that might affect the children,' I say firmly. 'It's nothing personal.'

He looks skyward, as if exasperated. 'Ryan, I want to support your family in the best way I can. That's all I'm trying to do.'

He settles his gaze back on me. 'Love, I'm not being funny but you don't know nothing about this family.' With a tiny shake of his head, he turns and walks back up the road.

My heart is still thumping hard against my ribcage when I cross the Chambers' drive. My hand trembles as I reach out for the doorbell, partly through fear – there's little doubt that Ryan is an intimidating man – but there's a small part of me that feels a little ashamed as well, almost as if I've been caught out telling tales.

Looking at it from Ryan's perspective, it's hardly surprising that he feels aggrieved. I've relayed information to outsiders that I only became privy to because I embedded myself in his home. Information that might even put his job at risk. In my own defence, it would have been made clear to the Chambers when they agreed to become a satellite family in the Mockingbird scheme that the foster carer coming into their home would be obliged to report relevant information to the authorities.

What choice did I have, I reason, but it's hard to shake the feeling of being a cuckoo in the nest, as Julie opens the door and lets me in.

With the older children at school and Ryan at work, the next couple of hours pass smoothly enough, although I can't help but get the feeling that Julie feels a whole day's visit is a bit of an imposition. 'No, not at all, it's my pleasure,' she insists when I thank her for putting up with me, but her voice is high and tight, and her smile a little too fixed.

She relaxes when I ask about her past, however, and now, perched on the arm of the sofa as I play with Louis on the floor, she seems to be enjoying herself. 'Twenty years in the police force, I did, before Bonnie's babies came along.'

'I had no idea,' I say, as Louis drives small Matchbox cars up and down my arms. 'Although now I know, I can visualise you giving street stragglers what for on a Saturday night.'

She laughs. 'I did have a knack of keeping the locals in line. That's why it's so frustrating that they're insisting I go through this two-week parenting course. I mean, there's not much anyone can tell me about discipline and bringing up kids that I don't already know. Twenty years in the force and managing Bon's children as well as Linzi, practically single-handed I might add, should tell them all they need to know about my ability to cope.'

'I suppose it's an equitable system,' I say, wondering how she squares Bartley's violence towards his sister with the claim that she has a handle on how the children behave.

'Everyone has to jump through the same hoops so that the relevant boxes can be ticked.'

Our chat helps improve the atmosphere and I'm on my third cup of tea when Julie offers me some lunch. 'Thanks very much, but I've got a cheese sandwich in my bag.' Not wanting to put on her any more than I have to, I made sure I got up early enough to make a packed lunch for myself.

'A boring old cheese sandwich? Bin it,' Julie says firmly. 'You'll have the same as me.' She hums under her breath as she potters around the kitchen, pulling pans out of the cupboards and vegetables from the fridge. It's a relief to have worked through the bad vibes, but still I check my watch several times over the next half an hour, longing to get through the day so that I can get back to my own territory.

It's a valuable insight into how adopters must feel during the handover period, a ten-day marathon of increasingly long periods spent first in the foster carer's home, and then in their own, with the foster carer supervising the transition. Having managed several moves onto adoption, I can attest to the fact that it's an intense period for foster carers, but it's even more arduous for adopters. Beside the fears that all new parents experience, there's the pressure of feeling like they're being watched and the emotional upset of witnessing the slow severing of the bond between the foster carer and their much-longed-for child.

'Wow, he's got a sophisticated palette.' I smile at Louis from the breakfast bar as he digs his fork into the bowl of chicken yakisoba noodles on his highchair tray. Our lunch is delicious and I'm grateful to Julie for including me, but even I'm struggling with the strength of the chilli in the recipe. With beads of perspiration gathering on my brow, I stop every couple of mouthfuls to take a few sips of cooling water.

As soon as Louis touches a mouthful to his lips, however, his whole body shudders. 'Oh dear, I think I may have spoken too soon.'

'He does like it, he's had it before,' Julie says through a mouthful of noodles. She makes encouraging 'Yum-yum' noises at him, but Louis still hasn't touched anything by the time we've cleared the plates, and he's beginning to whinge.

Rules around mealtimes are deeply personal to some people, so even though I'm tempted to ask if I can cobble together a quick sandwich for Louis, I busy myself with stacking the dishwasher. By the time I've cleared the worktops of bowls, cups and plates, however, the two-year-old's whines are beginning to turn into cries.

It's an effort not to sweep him up into my arms as he looks at me mournfully through his long fringe. 'Aw, that sounds like a tired cry,' I say instead, smiling at him as I wipe down the worktops.

'Finish your lunch then, mate,' Julie tells him. 'Then you can go down for a nap.' Twirling his fork to gather up some noodles, she tries to tempt him by tapping it on his bottom lip. Louis turns his head away with a wail. 'Okay, okay,' Julie says. She doesn't force him, but something in the way she stands over him feels uncomfortably coercive.

'Mine were always like that,' I say lightly, rinsing my hands under the tap. 'Once tiredness set in they couldn't eat, no matter how hungry they were.' It's a light-hearted attempt to get Louis off the hook without causing any friction between us, but Julie's having none of it.

We lock eyes. 'Did you see that newspaper article the other day about the children who only eat crisps? That's what you get when you indulge fussy eating. Their preferences get more and more narrow and, before you know it, they're refusing everything but Haribo.' She laughs, but there's not much amusement in her tone. 'Right, would you like another tea?'

'I couldn't at the moment,' I say, my gaze returning to Louis. Lunch churns in my stomach as his miserable howls fill the kitchen. There's nothing outrightly abusive about Julie's behaviour towards him, but it's close to it.

She chatters on about her days in uniform and the commendations she's won as I help fold the newly washed clothes from the washing machine, but I'm so focused on Louis that my responses are perhaps a little less enthusiastic than she expects.

'Did you hear, Rosie? I was saying, I was all set for promotion when Bonnie fell off the wagon the first time. I would have made inspector by now, that's worst case. I probably would have gone a lot further than that.'

'I see, gosh, how about that. Um, Julie,' I suggest, when all the washing is folded, 'I'm wondering if Louis might like some warm milk before his nap.' His little head is beginning to nod, his lips sucking rhythmically in imitation of his new-born self. His eyelids droop, then fall closed. Every time his baby-plump chin hits his chest he startles, then whimpers again.

Julie shakes her head stiffly. 'I'll offer him a bit of fruit when he wakes up,' she says tersely, finally lifting the exhausted toddler from his high chair. My shoulders sag with relief at the sight of him clasped to her hip. His little head bobs on her shoulder as she turns towards the stairs, and I can't help but wonder how long she might have left him sitting there had she been alone.

'Offering alternatives is a sure-fire way to create pickiness and I can't be doing with that,' she says when she comes back down and puts the kettle on.

And after Louis's nap the sickening battle of wills continues.

Chapter Twenty-Four

'Oh, I didn't realise you were potty training,' I say, watching in dismay as Julie plants Louis onto a blue plastic potty in the living area. Still groggy with sleep, he looks like he needs a cuddle more than anything else.

'He's two so it needs doing,' Julie trills. 'Bonnie left the others until they were gone three but I can't bear to see kids that age in nappies. Turns my stomach.'

'Have you only just started training? I wouldn't expect you to change your routine for me but we've got the holiday coming up. I'm not sure how easy it'll be to keep up potty training while we're away.' I'm already picturing frequent stops on motorway laybys as we travel up to Whitby. 'It might be easier if he stays in nappies until we get back.'

Julie smiles thinly. 'Easier? For you, you mean.'

'Well, yes. And for all of us.'

She snorts, and when Louis makes a move to climb off the potty, she grasps his shoulders and plonks him back down again. 'You sit until you've done something, matey.'

Silenced

The atmosphere, already tense, becomes super-charged. I sit on the sofa and pull out my phone in an attempt to take some of the heat out of the situation. Hopefully, Louis will relax and produce something, then he'll be free to have a banana or something, the poor little love. The minutes tick by, Louis looking increasingly miserable, but the potty remains empty.

'P'raps he doesn't have much in his tummy,' I say pointedly. It's almost time for me to leave to pick the older children up and I can't bear the thought of Louis being stuck here for the duration. 'He hasn't eaten since I arrived.'

'He had a large breakfast,' Julie snaps, making no attempt to maintain the appearance of civility. 'No,' she barks, when Louis looks at me and puts his arms out. 'Wee-wee first, then you can get up.'

Her behaviour towards him is repulsive and shocking, and it's making me feel quite sick.

Feeling nauseous as I drive towards Millfield Primary, I suck on a mint and try to take my mind off what might be going on at the Chambers. Arriving with ten minutes to spare before the gates open, I call Robert's number and concentrate on breathing slowly as the call connects. Emotionally churned up by what I've witnessed, it's an effort not to gabble when he picks up the phone. Taking my time, I calmly recount the events of the day.

Robert sighs. 'She encouraged him to eat his lunch, you say.' His tone suggests that I'm being oversensitive.

I take my time to conjure a response. How can I put into words the uncomfortable feeling of dread in my stomach when I left Louis in the house with Julie, without sounding too emotional about it? 'It was mistreatment, Robert, virtually right under my nose.'

'Mistreatment? Sounds a bit extreme.'

An image of Louis's desperate expression flashes into my mind, but Robert's disbelieving tone makes me doubt my take on events. Could it be that I simply caught Julie on a bad day? Might she merely be an overwhelmed grandmother who's got too much on her plate? After a pause I say, 'It was unkind, at the very least.'

'But she didn't *force* him to eat?'

'Not exactly. But he was tired and hungry and was made to sit there for ages. It was upsetting to watch.'

'I suppose families have different rules around eating.'

'This seemed to be all about control, Robert. She wasn't going to let Louis get the better of her, and she wanted to let me know it too.' When I relay the potty incident to him, he's equally dismissive.

'With the greatest respect, you're contradicting yourself, Rosie. You'd have me believe she was withholding food one minute, but in the next breath you're telling me she was encouraging the child to eat.' He pauses. 'Look, it's not unusual for a clash of heads to occur when two women are involved in the care of the same child. Try to remember you're there to support Julie, not take over.'

I try not to seethe at the suggestion that my problem with Julie has something to do with a clash of personalities.

Taking a breath, I summon some social worker speak to try and get through to him. 'I'm concerned that the care the Chambers are offering falls short of good-enough parenting, Robert. We can't leave the children there. It would be irresponsible.'

Robert lets out a humourless guffaw. 'Do you know how many families I've got on my caseload whose care falls below the required standard, Rosie? The Chambers are going through a rigorous assessment process, of which you are part, and we're holding a professionals' meeting in the next few days to make sure everything is on track.'

'Ah, okay, do I need to come along?' A meeting sounds like the perfect opportunity to explain exactly how concerned I am about the family.

'No, no,' Robert says airily. 'It's just professionals at this stage.'

Professionals' meetings are held to gather input from other agencies besides social services and sometimes involve police, healthcare and education. Foster carers are generally excluded from the invite list even though we're the ones most heavily invested with the family. We usually know more about the children being discussed than anyone apart from their birth family. Being brushed off, especially when I feel I have important things to say, is frustrating to say the least.

'You've got two weeks with the children coming up and we have the TAC meeting a couple of days after you get back. I suggest you log everything meticulously and voice any reservations you still have when we're all sat around the table together. We'll take a view on your continued involvement with the family then.'

Julie starts on Caitlin as soon as we walk through the door. 'Look at that long face. What's up with you?' It's the clearest case of projecting negative feelings onto someone else that I've ever witnessed – despite Bartley's attempts to sabotage her mood, Caitlin had spent the journey home cheerily enthusing about a water-cycle project they were working on at school.

The ten-year-old's face immediately falls, bolstering Julie's claim that she's sulking. Squatting in front of the washing machine, Julie shoves a duvet cover inside then studies her granddaughter as she removes her coat and shoes. 'Someone upset the little princess again, I suppose?'

A single tear traces a path down Caitlin's cheek. 'Oh Jesus, here we go with the waterworks.' Julie sounds tired, but there's malice simmering beneath the surface.

'Always bringing down the vibe,' Bartley mutters, sounding remarkably like his grandmother in tone.

Red in the face, Caitlin's breaths come fast. Her chest puffs out with indignation and I can't help silently cheering her on. 'What have I done?' she cries, her lips trembling with feeling. More tears spill down her cheeks as she flattens her palms and looks at me. 'I don't know what I've done!'

Julie straightens and stares at her, her jaw falling slack. She looks utterly dumbfounded for a few seconds, but then her gaze steadies, her icy stare almost daring Caitlin to risk the same reckless outburst again.

In stark contrast to the melodramatic strop from Linzi that Julie kowtowed to three weeks earlier, Caitlin's feeble attempt to defend herself seems to be considered beyond the pale. Hopping nervously from one foot to the other, the child chokes back her bold protest in a wobbly stutter. 'I'm sorry, Nan, it's just I, I don't know, h-how I've upset you.'

Apparently reassured by the return of Caitlin's habitual timidity, Julie's shoulders relax. 'Think about it,' is all she says. It's a simple sentence tying the fear of delayed punishment with the unequivocal message that the ten-year-old is entirely and solely to blame. It's so utterly unfair, so unjust, that Caitlin can't bear to listen any more.

With one last despairing glance at me, she scuttles up the stairs. Ethan sighs, rolls his eyes at me and trudges up after her. Bartley, who pulled his phone out of his schoolbag the second he came out of school, throws himself on the sofa with a look of nonchalance, apparently entirely immune to the tension in the house.

'What's *she* doing here?' Linzi sneers when she walks through the front door half a second later.

Acid from our spicy lunch twists in my stomach at the sound of Caitlin's distant sobbing. 'Hello, Linzi,' I manage pleasantly.

'Don't start, Linz, I'm having a day of it,' Julie warns her from the kitchen. Linzi shoots me a dirty look before disappearing upstairs, as if I'm responsible for her mother's foul mood. On this occasion, she's probably right. As I join the grandmother in the kitchen, I begin to suspect that she can only cope with projecting a pleasant, bubbly air for a couple of hours or so. After that, her true colours begin to emerge.

'I told Robert I'd stay until five, so not much longer until I'm out of your way.'

She closes her eyes and breathes out slowly. 'What us women have to go through, hey? I don't know about you, but *certain* people try me more than others. I get tired of always being the bad guy, know what I mean?' She raises her eyebrows meaningfully, trying to draw me in, and rests her hand on my arm in a comradely way. All I can see in my mind's eye is the venom in her gaze when she looked at Caitlin. 'Fancy a glass of something? I think we could both do with it.'

'Nothing for me, thank you. I'm driving. I'll keep Louis occupied for a while.'

'Cheers,' she says, tilting a wine glass in my direction and then opening a bottle. Grateful that Megan is back at Maya's for tea again, I try to shake the feeling of being an interloper and determine to let whatever usually happens in the Chambers' home unfold before my eyes.

The celebrities on *Big Brother* claim that they forget the cameras are there after only a short period in the house, and as I hunker down in the living room and play quietly at Louis's side I can well believe it. 'Fuck it,' Julie growls, when the tea towel she's holding catches on one of the spice-rack hooks. There follows a series of low mutters, and at the sound of a key in the door she swears again. 'What are you doing back?'

'They gave me a short run instead,' comes Ryan's reply. 'I'm not on 'til tomorrow morning now.'

Doing my best to blend into the background as I pass toys back and forth to Louis, I watch Ryan walk slowly into the kitchen. 'Can I help with dinner?'

She gives him a scathing look. 'You haven't even washed your hands yet.'

Louis lets out a loud screech as he lifts the car he's holding up to my face. Ryan spins round and looks at us. 'Oh, you're still here,' he says in a flat tone.

'I'll be out of your way soon.' There's a sinking sensation in my stomach. I had been hoping to observe the dynamics between the couple, but the next ten minutes pass with them moving mechanically, and almost completely silently, round each other. As soon as the boys reappear, however, jostling each other and breaking out into the occasional fight, I become part of the furniture again.

'Move out of the kitchen, boys,' Julie says mildly, when they crash into an open cupboard door. She waves them away then peers at her husband, who's examining a long plastic-wrapped packet. 'What's the issue, Ryan? It's a French stick, for fuck's sake. Just an ordinary, everyday French stick.'

'I thought it might be one of those you have to bake in the oven, that's all.'

Pink-faced, Julie exhales a long breath. 'All I wanted was a hand getting tea ready. Is that too much to ask? God knows there are limits to your capabilities, Ryan, but –' she stops, her expression transforming as Linzi walks into the kitchen. 'Hello, my poppet.'

'What's *he* doing back?' She shoots her grandfather a look of disgust.

Ryan tears into the packet with his teeth then speaks to his daughter without looking at her. 'Don't you have homework to do?'

Linzi reddens then turns and flounces back up the hall. Unexpectedly, my heart goes out to her. Overlooking all the preening and prancing and stomping, she's a young girl whose life changed overnight. Accustomed to being the centre of attention, she suddenly became one of five children. It wouldn't be surprising for any child to kick back against that.

Julie regards her husband coolly. 'Happy now?'

Casting the stick of bread down on the worktop, he mutters, 'That kid deserves a good hiding.'

'For God's sake, try being the grown-up for once.' When he doesn't respond she turns to him with her hands on her hips. 'And what about me, Ryan? What about what I deserve?'

'I'm getting too old for all this shit.' Snatching up his keys from the worktop, Ryan stalks into the hall and bellows up the stairs for Caitlin to come down. Almost immediately, I hear the light tread of footsteps. Practically skidding down the last two stairs, Caitlin thrusts her feet into her shoes and hobbles out the door after her grandfather, without even pausing to strap them up.

By five o'clock, Julie is all smiles again. 'I'll WhatsApp you the yakisoba recipe when I get a minute,' she says, as she walks with me down the hall. 'Thanks for your company. I don't have many friends, so it's been nice having you around.'

'I'll see you next week, Julie.' A small wisp of sympathy winds its way around my chest as I walk to the car.

Julie and Ryan have a stormy relationship but so what, I reason. So do millions of other couples across the country. Adding a sectioned daughter, four extra children and a social worker into the mix is hardly going to help them stay on an even keel.

Nevertheless, after putting Megan to bed I email Robert again. I suspect that he'll explain away Julie's treatment of Caitlin, so I copy the fostering team manager and the manager of children's services, Alison Castle, into the message.

Silenced

I know I may be overstepping the mark, but I also suggest that the information should be passed on to the medical team treating the children's mother. If there's one person who knows exactly what it's like to be parented by the Chambers, it's Bonnie Powell.

Chapter Twenty-Five

Julie and Caitlin are already on the driveway when I pull into the Chambers' road to collect the children a week later. It's Saturday 6 April, the first day of the Easter break, and as I park up I notice that they're having an animated conversation. For the first time since leaving home, Megan falls silent. She cranes her neck, watching them through narrowed eyes.

'Rosie, hi,' the grandmother smiles warmly as I climb out of the car. There's no sign of the tension of a week ago. The prospect of a fortnight free from the usual responsibilities is no doubt working its spell on her already. 'This is so good of you, they're all very excited.' She squeezes Caitlin's shoulder. 'This one's a bit anxious about being away, but we know you'll take good care of her.' As Emily helps to load the children's suitcases into the boot, Julie pulls Caitlin into a hug. 'Chin up, poppet, remember what I said, okay.'

Tearful, Caitlin clings on long after her grandmother releases her. 'Go on, silly sausage,' Julie says, planting a final kiss on the ten-year-old's forehead. 'You be good now.'

Silenced

Caitlin bows her head as she passes me and climbs silently into the car. 'Wow!' Bartley shouts, dragging a wheeled suitcase behind him. My heart sinks at the sight of the mobile phone in his other hand. 'You got a new car?!'

'Not new, it's only on loan.' Jenny, who had recently moved a toddler on to adoption, booked herself a fortnight in Spain to recover from the trauma of parting with him, and very kindly offered me use of her Ford Tourneo while she's away. 'Bartley, maybe you should leave your phone at home. I don't want to risk you losing it and there might not be any Wi-Fi where we're going.'

'S'all right, I got data,' he shrugs.

Mungo lets out a howl of excitement from inside the car as the boys jostle over who's going to sit where and Emily straps Louis's car seat in.

'I did try to dissuade him,' Julie grimaces in solidarity. 'But you know what boys are like with their toys.'

I roll my eyes. 'We'll see you in two weeks, Julie. Good luck with the course. And have a good rest.'

'Right,' I say to my mum, who's sitting in the passenger seat. 'Here we go.'

With Des appointed by Megan as chief rabbit carer and my other Mockingbird families primed to expect telephone support over the next two weeks, I'm free to concentrate on making sure everyone, including my somewhat subdued mother, has a good time. I'm determined to get to the bottom of her fall-out with Des while we're away. I'm also hoping to get the children, and Caitlin in particular, talking.

I've learned over the years that if you want to draw out information from someone, there's little point in bombarding probative questions at them. Dragging a child's past out of them is not the role of a foster carer, and any disclosures elicited through leading questions are inadmissible in court anyway. But if a happy, relaxed holiday provides them with the time and space to open up about their troubles, that's all to the good.

With this in mind, when we arrive at our destination – a sprawling property with its own gates that I would describe as a mansion rather than a cottage – the first thing I unload from the car is the worry hook.

Bartley sniggers when I offer it to him. Megan, unusually quiet for most of the journey, comes to life when her feet land on the drive and snatches at Bartley's empty hands. 'I'll hang it up if you don't want to,' she shouts, running towards the wide front door.

'I can't believe it!' Emily says, as we unload the cases. 'What a beautiful place. Jenny's so kind.'

I nod. 'Shame Jamie couldn't join us. We haven't seen inside yet, though. Jenny said it's not ready to let out officially yet.' But when I input the code into the key safe and open the door, there's a collective gasp from all of us.

Bartley shoves Ethan aside so that he's first into the wide hall. 'Jesus fucking Christ, it's unbelievable.'

'Did you bring the three baskets with you, Mummy?' Megan pipes up. She mimes hanging the worry hook by the door, bless her, then points at Bartley. 'Because he just did a "NO LONGER TOLERATE" whoopsie.'

My mum kisses Megan's head. 'Bless you, my darling.' She grabs her suitcase. 'I think I'll go up and get unpacked, Rosie, love. Where shall I put myself –' she gasps, almost losing her footing as Bartley, who had been darting in and out of the rooms off the hall, barges past her to get to the stairs first. Wincing, she lets out a long breath.

My mother has joined us for most of our holidays over the years. With a thirst for exploring new places, a sense of adventure and a love of children, she's usually the ideal travelling companion, but her look of frustration as she clutches her side says it all. How are we going to get through two weeks of *this*?

'Somewhat fraught' is a polite description of the next couple of hours. My mother stays out of the way for the entire afternoon, only venturing downstairs when I suggest that we take a walk to the pub for an evening meal. Bartley, whose behaviour continued in the same vein all afternoon, is now at top volume, with Ethan a close second.

Since holidays and trips away are the ultimate routine disrupter, they almost always trigger a downturn in behaviour in children prone to anxiousness. Social stories – a visual representation of all the activities planned – are the recommended antidote. They're helpful for children who may have autistic traits or those who panic about the unknown, because they provide a concrete idea of what's coming next. The social story I'd cobbled together soon after we'd arrived did little to calm Bartley, however.

The cosiness of the pub, with its roaring log fire and muted lighting, only seems to ramp up his tension.

'Can't be arsed,' he says, when I ask if he'd like to play hangman while we wait for the food to arrive. I pop a couple of bread sticks on Louis's high-chair tray, so that at least he's happy. Perhaps not quite recovered from the yakisoba episode, he picks one up and examines it warily before pushing it into his mouth. Mum watches him, smiling in a distant way.

'I'll play,' Megan and Caitlin chime in unison.

'Course you will, fucking mentalists,' Bartley goads. Megan looks at me aghast. Caitlin doesn't turn a hair so he ups the ante, determined to get a reaction. No matter how much I try to distract him, he simply can't leave his sister alone.

And then, after five minutes of almost continual tormenting, he punches her on the shoulder. 'Right, that's it.' I hold out my hand. A showdown the like of which we went through at home when I confiscated his phone won't be pleasant for the other diners to witness, but there's only so much I can choose to ignore. 'Bartley, hand your phone over, please.'

'For what?'

'For continually aggravating Caitlin. And then hitting her.'

He spreads his hands and looks at his brother. 'I never touched her, did I, Ethan?'

Ethan hesitates, then shakes his head. 'Bartley, don't encourage your brother to lie. I saw you do it.'

'So *you* say.'

'You damn rotter,' Mum cuts in with an exasperated tone. She'd been doing her best to ignore his behaviour, twisting the rings on her fingers and staring around the restaurant, but he's clearly tested the limits of her restraint. 'I saw you do it as well.'

'Saw wrong then, didn't you.'

Mum wags her finger at him. 'That sort of cheek cuts little mustard with me, young man.'

'Like I care,' he snaps back quickly, then he prods Caitlin nastily in the shoulder again. 'Snitch.'

Mum's shoulders sag. She turns her head, her lips stretching into a thin line. She looks drained, utterly exhausted with it all. My throat tightens. Perhaps it had been a mistake to expect her to cope with all this at her age.

'Who wants to play I-spy?' Emily asks cheerfully. She'd strategically placed herself between the boys and her grandmother on arrival, but now she shuffles along the bench on the other side of the table until she's next to Bartley.

'I'm not six years old,' Bartley sneers, but the invitation works as a distraction because he slaps his phone into my hand with a heavy sigh. Never one to turn down an opportunity to tear Caitlin down a peg or two, he also uses it as ammunition. When Caitlin has her turn, with something beginning with 'S', and Megan guesses 'sky', his venom reappears with fresh vigour.

'You're so obsessed! *Sky* this, *universe* that. You're starting to look like an alien, you know that? That's why you're, like, properly ugly. Soon your eyes'll start to bulge out your head even more than they do now, then they'll pop out and dangle on your chest like a big fat pair of –'

'Bartley!' my mum snaps. 'I'll do you a mischief in a minute.'

'Ignore him, Mum,' I say soothingly.

She takes off her glasses tiredly and pinches the bridge of her nose. Thankfully, the food arrives.

Bartley proves that it's difficult, but not impossible, to spew toxic hate while tucking into hot chocolate fudge cake. 'Make peace with your god, space face,' he says, peppering the table with slimy brown crumbs. 'You're gonna get it later for snitching on me.'

Even the fifty-yard walk home isn't without issue. 'Oi, face ache, get out my line of sight can't you? You're gonna make my dinner come up if I have to keep looking at your mush all evening.'

'Be quiet, you idiot,' Meg snaps, reaching up on tiptoes as she walks along, so she can put her arm around Caitlin's shoulders. 'You're always making her sad.'

'Well that just goes to show what a weak, pathetic loser she is.'

'You spoil EVERYTHING!' Megan growls.

The sniping is still going on after I get down from putting Louis to bed. 'I've had enough,' Mum says apologetically. 'I'll swing for him if I have to listen to much more.'

I kiss her soft cheek. 'Sorry, Mum.'

'Not your fault, love.'

Guilt narrows my throat as she grasps her handbag and trudges heavily up the stairs, but part of me is puzzled as well. We've cared for lots of children in the past with issues more complex than Bartley's, and although my mum has always despaired of what she refers to as my lily-livered approach, she's always helped me to see the funny side too. I've never known a child to trigger her the way that Bartley seems to.

Still awake at 3 a.m., I decide that since we're going to be spending a whole two weeks together, I need to switch into classic fostering mode. When the children were only staying with me for short periods it made no sense to impose our rules on them, only for them to be undone as soon as they got back to Julie's. But I don't need to walk the tight-rope between two homes for the next fortnight. And if we carry on as we are, all of us are going to have a miserable time.

With my mind made up, the whole cottage seems a little brighter when I get up on Sunday morning. I know that nothing has changed as I switch on the swish coffee maker in the kitchen and choose the latte option, but I feel like I'm back on solid ground.

When a child's perception that the world is an unjust place and people aren't to be trusted is challenged, it's unsettling for them. Some even find it infuriating. They scream and cry and rage. Others, like Bartley, lash out. But eventually … eventually firm and loving persistence shows them that all that they've known is not all that there is.

With a cool, salty morning breeze drifting in through the open patio doors, I sit in the large conservatory and sip my cinnamon-flavoured latte contemplatively.

I almost can't wait for Bartley to get up.

Chapter Twenty-Six

It doesn't take long for the drama to kick off.

As soon as I remind Bartley that he forfeited his mobile phone for 24 hours as a consequence of hitting Caitlin in the restaurant, he swings the sweatshirt he's holding high above his head and flings it across the room. 'Ouch!' Megan squeals, as the zip fastening catches her at the side of one eye.

'I think that was an accident,' I say, rushing to hug Megan. Blinking through her tears, she eyes Bartley resentfully, waiting for an apology. I prompt him. 'Wasn't it, Bartley?'

'Yep, I meant to get space-face,' he says, jerking his chin towards his sister. Quietly sketching in her pad at the dining-room table, Caitlin looks up at Megan and apologises.

'It's not your fault, sweetie,' I tell her, then I look at Bartley. 'It's good manners to apologise when you've hurt someone, even when it's an accident. Look at Megan, you've really hurt her.'

'Ah well, every cloud …' he says with a shrug, before slumping down on the large corner sofa.

'Right, after breakfast we're going to pack up for a day at the beach. And just so you know,' I say, looking round so that my focus isn't directed at anyone in particular, 'if anyone falls foul of the "NO LONGER TOLERATE" basket, they'll be spending the day here with me. No TV, no gadgets, no screens. Clear?'

Megan swings around and glares pointedly at Bartley. 'Let's get ready then!' Emily says, with a meaningful smile at me. Ethan and Megan cheer and dash off to grab their swimming costumes. Bartley tries his best to show disinterest as he slopes slowly after them, but I know he's keen to swim in the sea because he'd already told me he'd never done it before.

When the online groceries I ordered a few days ago arrive, I put Louis in his high chair and scatter some soldiers of toast and pieces of fruit on his tray so that I'm free to unpack. Hopeful that Bartley's keenness for the beach will help him stay on the straight and narrow, I get to work on a picnic large enough for all of us. Mungo flits between Louis's high chair and my feet, hoovering up the crumbs.

But when the picnic is almost packed, Megan comes flying down the stairs. Bartley, it seems, has reverted to his stock in trade and punched his sister in the neck. 'Caitlin can't breathe,' Megan blurts out breathlessly as she tugs on my hand.

Mungo gives chase as she scoots down the hall. I hurry after them, my heart in my mouth. Relief washes over me at the sound of Emily's calm voice. 'She's all right, Mum, just a bit shaken up.' The pair of them appear at the top of the stairs, Emily with her arms around the pale and shaky ten-year-old. Coughing intermittently, Caitlin clutches at her throat like a victim of strangulation as she comes downstairs, her eyes red and bulging.

'Let's do what we agreed,' Emily says quietly, referring to a conversation I had with her before the others got up. 'I'm happy to take Louis as well. I'll be fine with four.'

'No, it's okay,' I say, giving Caitlin a cuddle. 'I'll keep Louis here, you take Meggie, Caitlin and Ethan. As long as you're sure?'

'Course. Without Bartley, those three'll be a cinch.'

It seems to me that Emily has hit the nail on the head. Even in the last 24 hours I had noticed a change in Ethan. He seems calmer somehow. Away from Bartley, I'm confident he'll be even more chilled. 'Thanks, Ems. Nan will probably go with you since his nibs is staying here.'

I rub Caitlin's shoulder, then give Emily a rueful look. 'Right, I'll grab Louis, then I'll break the news to Bartley.'

'Good luck,' Emily whispers as she puts her arm around Caitlin again.

'You're keeping me prisoner?' Bartley gasps, after I tell him that we'll be staying in together.

Distancing a child who may have a history of trauma or rejection can be counter-productive, so using 'time out' as a tool for managing behaviour isn't recommended these days. As an advocate of therapeutic or gentle parenting, as it's sometimes known, I'm keen to present our day together as 'time in' rather than 'time out', an opportunity to work towards finding a solution to manage his violent outbursts.

'Of course not, honey,' I say, swapping Louis to my other hip. 'Today isn't a punishment, we're just going to spend some time together, that's all.'

Bartley's having none of it. Sprawled out on his bed, he props himself up on his elbow and looks at me. 'Sounds like a punishment to me.'

From his open doorway, I can hear the sound of receding footsteps as Emily, my mum and the children head off to the beach. Bartley's gaze drifts over my shoulder as their excited chatter drifts through the open window in the hall. A crestfallen expression replaces his sneer. He sits up sharply. 'They're *really* going without us?'

'I did give you a warning, honey. When you lash out it makes everyone feel unsafe. We need to find a solution.'

'You can't keep me locked up! I'm calling Nan!'

'No one is locking anyone up, Bartley. We're simply solution-finding. That means spending some quality time together and working through our difficulties so that we can find a way forward. I'm happy to stay up here with you, or I can leave you alone, if that's what you prefer.'

'Go do one, you uptight piece of shit.'

'Shit!' Louis shouts cheerfully. 'Shit, shit, shit.'

I give Bartley a congenial nod, accepting that, with him involved, 'time in' is a technique that might take some finessing. 'I'll be nearby if you need me. Would you like your door left open?'

'Fuck off.'

I hum to myself as I unpack the rest of Louis's small case, partly to lighten the atmosphere and convey a sense of wellbeing to Bartley, but also because I'm feeling more in charge of the situation than at any point since meeting the family almost six weeks earlier. No matter how trying the circumstances, having a plan of action always make me feel reassured. And making children feel safe is my bread and butter.

Louis potters around after me, pulling his small vests, nappies, T-shirts and shorts out of drawers after I've neatly folded them and put them away. 'You rascal,' I say, much to his delight. He shrieks a giggle when I grab him and lift him high in the air, then wriggles to get down so he can run through the entire routine again.

In the kitchen, I get to work on a nice meal – mildly spiced potato wedges and chicken Kiev, which I put in the fridge to chill until everyone comes back.

An hour later, at 11 a.m., there's still no sign of movement upstairs. After frying some bacon and making up some sandwiches, I slip Louis in his high chair and give him some water, then take a drink and sandwich upstairs.

Lying prone on his mattress, Bartley turns his head sideways and eyes me resentfully when I tap on his door. On sight of the snack, however, he heaves himself up.

'Can I come in?'

'I s'pose,' he shrugs, no doubt softened by the scent of bacon.

'Have you come up with a solution yet?' I say as I slip the plate onto his bedside cabinet.

'Solution?! I'll give you a fucking solution. How about taking your fat arse back downstairs and leaving me alone.'

I can still hear him whingeing about 'false allegations' trumped up by his 'lying bitch' of a sister when I reach the kitchen. 'She's got a fucking vendetta against me,' he screams, emphatically insisting that he's being unjustly held against his will. I'm pleased to hear that his next rants are muffled by the sound of chewing as he tucks into his bacon sandwich. Considering how much he loves his food, a hunger strike was unlikely, but it's reassuring to know that he's eaten. Having a full tummy might improve his mood and open the doorway to a productive round of negotiations.

I leave it another hour or so, then carry Louis upstairs for a nap. He grizzles when I lay him in his cot so I stroke his hair and tuck the blankets up under his chin so that he feels warm and safe. There's something deeply rewarding about putting a tired, pink-cheeked child to bed, especially one that may not always have been given the fuss that most children enjoy.

I wait until his breathing slows then tiptoe across the room and pause for a moment in the doorway. Through the bars of the cot, I can just make out the tendrils of his long dark fringe and the curve of a ruddy cheek. The boisterousness of toddlerhood temporarily tamed. He seems much smaller and more vulnerable in sleep, and the sight brings to mind something Des once said about the children who come into the care system being the Baby Ps who didn't die.

I always try to bear those words in mind when a child's behaviour tests me to my limits. It's something at the forefront of my thoughts as I venture down the hall towards Bartley's room.

Chapter Twenty-Seven

'Are you ready to discuss a way forward, honey?'

'I never done nothing wrong!' Bartley shouts indignantly. 'Why don't you lock that twisted streak of piss up instead of me? She's the one that caused all this!'

Children are prone to playing up when they feel out of control. It's my job to make Bartley realise that, no matter how challenging his behaviour, I will still take care of his needs and keep him safe. Sit-ins might not necessarily work on children who aren't neurotypical, but I've found them to be effective in most cases, even with children who have a diagnosis of oppositional defiant disorder, or ODD.

Most children challenge authority figures at some point during their development, especially during the toddler and teenage years, but ODD is characterised by an extreme aversion to authority figures and an almost pathological need to avoid complying with any request. Children with ODD frequently argue with their caregivers and violently oppose instructions, even those that are clearly in their own best interests.

Silenced

I've cared for lots of children who've displayed characteristics of ODD to varying degrees, although one girl in particular stands out in my mind. Ten-year-old Skye arrived as an emergency placement after witnessing her mother being brutally beaten by her drug-addled partner. As soon as I caught sight of Skye's scowling expression at our garden gate, and her social worker's look of exasperation, I suspected I may have a case of ODD on my hands.

'She refused to wear her coat,' the young woman told me as she waved Skye over, trying to coax her in. 'Took her shoes off in the car and threw her socks out the window. She hasn't eaten since coming into police protection hours ago so I know she's hungry, but she threw the sausage roll I bought her in my face.'

Recognising the signs of what my mother might have called 'bloody-mindedness', I made up my mind there and then not to get drawn into a power struggle. After a bit of persuading, the social worker agreed to conduct the Placement Information Meeting in the hall with the front door open, so that I could keep an eye on Skye without making any demands on her.

Thankfully it was a warm summer's evening but the ten-year-old was still at the gate, bare-footed, as the sun was going down. 'Good luck,' the social worker whispered with a sympathetic glance, before heading off down the darkening path.

Jamie still remembers every painful detail of Skye's first couple of weeks with us; the way she would deliberately annoy everyone in the house, then blame him for it. Torpedoing our every attempt to include her, she'd sit on the floor in the hall when we watched a film. She'd go without meals, even though she was clearly hungry.

ODD can be caused by genetic factors, but in Skye's case I think it was simply that she'd never met anyone she could trust. Abused by her step-father and ignored by her mother when she tried to tell her what was going on, the behaviour was a natural reaction to the harsh realities of her world, a defence mechanism constructed to keep herself safe. Beneath all the bluster and the stubborn refusals and the verbal abuse, she was just a young girl crying out for someone to love her.

Suspecting that years of trauma lay at the heart of her behaviour, I went out of my way to reduce the number of demands on her while staying firm, clear and consistent about the expectations I wasn't prepared to let go. When she refused to go to bed, I gave her a sleeping bag and pillow and let her hunker down in the hall. Instead of insisting that she sat with us at meal times, I served everything in large dishes, set them down in the middle of the table and gave everyone an empty plate so that they could serve themselves.

It took weeks, but eventually Skye's need to control everything around her slowly reduced.

Still refusing to engage, I remind Bartley that I'm ready to talk whenever he is, and then take myself back downstairs. Just as I'm stirring a cup of milky coffee, I hear him calling me. 'How's it going?' I say mildly, peering around his doorway. Lying on his side in the foetal position with one hand tucked under one cheek, he looks younger than usual.

'I feel like smacking someone in the face, that's how it's going.' He sits up with a sigh. 'Where's Caitlin when I need her?' He grins at me as if he's momentarily forgotten who I am and thinks that I'll find the tasteless joke funny.

I lift a brow. His smile evaporates. 'Ready to talk, sweetheart?'

'But you won't listen,' he complains, a scowl replacing his look of utter boredom. 'You're always on Caitlin's side.'

I take a few steps into the room. It's saddening to hear that he feels disregarded. Instinct tells me that his aggression is a fear response, a learned survival mechanism masking deep shame or dissatisfaction. It's my job to honour and acknowledge his inner life, and to teach him how to express himself in a fair, balanced and calm way, so that the people around him can listen without their own flight/fight response being triggered. I want him to know that his feelings are important, and that he has licence to tell me exactly what he thinks of me.

'But we need to tell each other how we feel in a respectful way, Bartley,' I say, kneeling a couple of feet from his bed. 'I really want to help you manage your feelings. And I know exactly how to do it, if you'll let me. There are lots of strategies I can teach you that work, but you need to agree them with me.'

'See!' he shouts, flinging his arm out so that his fingertips brush against my nose. 'You automatically blame me! It's Caitlin what starts it. If you'd only listen, I could tell *you* a solution.'

'Okay. Tell me what you need from me.'

No doubt expecting a lecture, he looks up at me in surprise. 'I need you to listen.'

'I will listen. Tell me your solution.'

'I bet you won't.'

'I promise you, I want to hear your ideas. You have a full two minutes. I won't interrupt once.'

He takes a deep breath and spreads his hands. 'Okay, so you tell Caitlin to shut up about space and the universe and all that crap, and tell her to keep her fat face out of my sight and get her to stop trying to muscle in on everything, yeah? You tell her that, and I'll stop whacking her.' He looks at me. 'Okay?'

I give my head a little shake and get to my feet. 'That's not a workable solution, I'm afraid. I'll come back when you're ready to talk again.'

'You stinking useless tub of lard!' he shouts as I creep along the hall to check on Louis. Somehow, the toddler has slept through the uproar. His low and steady breaths drift through the half-open door.

'You're the worst foster carer in the world, you know that?! And you're the ugliest. I pity the poor kids who get stuck with you.'

I've long since learned not to take abuse from wound-up children and teenagers personally. Fostering is not a personality contest. I'd like Bartley to realise that I'm firmly on his side, but my main objective is to make him feel safe and cared for. I don't need to be his friend.

Half an hour later, I try again.

'What's the point?! You won't listen to me.'

'Bartley.' I kneel again, keeping a couple of feet away in case he lashes out again. 'We all feel angry and upset sometimes and that's okay. It's what we do when we feel that way that matters. Shall I tell you about some ways –'

'There you go again!' he cries, his top lip wobbling. He looks close to tears. 'Blaming me! Everyone hates me.'

'Everyone hates you?' I repeat, to show him that I'm listening. It's tempting to disagree and insist that everyone loves him, but I want him to feel listened to instead of disregarded. 'Why do you say that?'

'Because they do! Grandad especially, but Nan does too, and Caitlin, and all my teachers. They just want rid of me.'

'Why do you think Grandad hates you?'

He stiffens. 'You won't believe me if I tell you.'

His words give me a strange chill. 'I will, honey.'

'You'll just say I'm being mean to Caitlin again.'

I level my gaze. 'Give me a chance, Bartley. I truly want to help you.'

He pulls his sleeve across his nose and sniffs, then looks at me. 'Okay. So it's Caitlin's fault that Grandad hates me. He's got this weird thing about her. Some obsession or something, always taking her out all the time. He hardly ever takes me in the lorry, no matter how much I keep on about it.'

I shuffle forward on my knees and rest my hand on his leg. 'Thank you for telling me how you feel,' I venture slowly, my mind puzzling again over the strange relationship between Caitlin and her grandfather. Could it be that Bartley has somehow intuited something unnatural between them, something that repulses him? I wonder if an unconscious revulsion is what's driving his hateful behaviour towards his sister. 'It makes me sad to think of you feeling that way. You're such a smart boy, and you're fun to be around. I don't know why anyone would dislike you.'

'They hate me because I'm a bully,' he shouts, his cheeks turning puce. 'You'd hate someone who hits you all the time, wouldn't you? Only I don't have a choice.' He sniffs loudly and then lifts his arm up to hide his watery eyes. Without warning, he punches himself in the side of the head. Leaping to my feet, I grab his wrists as he tries to pummel himself again. He uses so much force that I almost fall over.

'I won't let you hurt yourself, honey,' I say breathlessly, tightening my grip on his wrists. He flails around, roaring and cursing, but half a minute later all the fight goes out of him. Dropping his hands to his lap, he leans his head against my midriff and bursts into tears.

'I hate everyone,' he howls into my jumper. 'Everyone hates me and I hate them!' I wrap my arms around him and make soothing noises, and gradually his shouts turn to sobs.

'It's okay,' I say after a few minutes, when his sobs subside. I rub the back of his hair, smoothing it down, then sit myself back on the floor.

'I'm such an idiot,' he mumbles after drying his eyes on his sleeves.

'You're so hard on yourself! You're not an idiot! We all have wobbles.'

'Yeah, well, you would have wobbles,' he says, scrambling to maintain some dignity with a scornful bark of laughter. 'Cos you're so damn fat.'

There's a small groan from along the hall as Louis begins to stir. I give Bartley a rueful smile and get to my feet, but I don't reply. It's possible that he hasn't had a say in anything that's happened to him in his short life. Feeling powerless, it's not surprising that he lashes out. I decide that letting him save face by having the last word is the least I can do.

It's almost five when Emily and my mum come back. They exchange surprised glances when they see Bartley helping me in the kitchen. Wisely, they don't say anything. I suspect they've already warned the children not to harp on too much about the fun they've had, because despite their bright eyes and rosy cheeks, Caitlin and Ethan give muted responses when I ask them how they are.

Megan breaks rank, however, running over with a big excited grin on her face. 'Nanny did amazing on the grabber machines, Mummy!' she says, waving a bright orange and black striped tiger cub in the air. 'We all got a cuddly, even Emily!'

Bartley, who had been spearing cheese and sausages onto cocktail sticks, pauses and looks at them with a defeated expression. My throat tightens. 'She got one for you too, Bartley!' Megan announces, running over to her grandmother to fetch the lion cub that she's pulling out of her handbag.

'I hope you like it, Bartley,' Mum says, smiling. 'I know you're probably past cuddly toys, but this is an American football mascot, the sort Jamie likes.'

Bartley takes the soft toy from Megan with a grin, then mumbles a soft thank you in Mum's direction. She gives me a small smile and a wink when he sits the mascot on the worktop, but she doesn't say anything. Her quietly thoughtful gestures of support have helped me more than she could ever realise over the years. I make a mental note to tell her just how much they mean to me later, when Bartley's out of earshot.

Chapter Twenty-Eight

I wake the next morning, Monday 8 April, with plans to broker a truce between Bartley and Caitlin running through my mind.

The idea develops as I cobble together some chocolate pancakes in the kitchen, Radio 2 in the background, Louis squatting at my side and running his cars over my feet. Life should have been easier a week ago, when only one or two of the Powell children were visiting us at any one time. In reality, I'd been chasing my own tail. I'm back on familiar ground with a house full, and in a better position to help everyone get along.

Bartley breathes out heavily and hands me his phone when it's time to sit down for breakfast. 'I'd like to take Bartley to the amusements today since he missed out yesterday,' Mum says quickly, rewarding him for voluntarily surrendering his device.

The ten-year-old's head spins round to look at her, his jaw hanging slack. 'Sounds like a plan,' I say, setting a platter of pancakes in the middle of the table along with some maple syrup and strawberries. 'What do you think, Bartley?'

'Cool.' He doesn't look at Mum, but his eyes shine as he reaches for a plate.

'That's what we'll do then,' I say, as I take a seat opposite Bartley. 'We'll spend the day at the beach, and this evening we're having a competition.'

The prospect of another beach day prompts a round of cheers from Ethan, Megan and Caitlin. Louis parrots them, cheering and punching the air from his high chair. Honing in on my mention of a competition, Bartley's eyes fix on my face. 'What competition?'

'Wait and see.' I tap the side of my nose. 'I think you'll like it.'

It's a cloudy day, not quite 19 degrees, but that doesn't stop the children stripping off and getting into their costumes as soon as we hit the beach. They empty the bags of spades, buckets and beach toys, and I sort through the rest of the paraphernalia: blankets, beach chairs and a windbreaker.

Bartley and my mum are gone almost the entire morning. It's almost midday when I spot them, a pink-cheeked Bartley holding out his arm chivalrously to support Mum over the larger pebbles that are tricky for her to manage.

It's so pleasing to see them forging a relationship that my eyes fill with tears. 'Sorry we've been gone so long, lovey,' Mum says breathlessly when they reach us. 'We went on the amusements and then this one spotted a little steam train. We had to have a go, didn't we, lad?' She looks at Bartley with a smile, her voice relaxed and free from the strained quality of the last few weeks.

'You said you needed a sit down,' Bartley corrects, grinning at her. 'Then we saw this bloke doing portraits,' he says excitedly as he unfurls a roll of paper. 'Nan said I could get one done.' He looks so chuffed as he holds up the charcoal drawing of himself that I don't like to pull him up for referring to her as 'Nan'.

'What a likeness! That's lovely, Bartley.'

'He's been good as gold,' Mum says. 'He's an absolute pleasure to be with.'

Bartley grins again, basking in the compliment. His tongue appears at the corner of his mouth as he carefully rolls the drawing back up. After giving it to Mum for safe-keeping, he tears his top off and joins Emily and the others at the water's edge.

'I'm exhausted,' Mum says, sinking into a beach chair. She takes a proffered cup of tea from our flask with a heavy sigh. 'Oh thanks, lovey. He's walked me off my feet. Good as gold, though, he's been, like I say. Not even any outdoor language.' She looks at me. 'He did say something strange though.'

'Oh yes?' I draw up another chair and sit beside her.

'Well, as you know, he wanted his portrait done but there was a queue so we had a bit of a wait. There was a family ahead of us and the mother had a youngster with her. Babe in arms, only a little dot, couldn't have been more than a few weeks old.'

'O-kay,' I say, trying to encourage her to get to the point.

'Well, so the older ones sat for their portrait and their mum perched herself a few feet away from us. Of course, after a while the baby got the grizzles so Mum started breastfeeding. All under a blanket, she was quite discreet about it, but Bartley couldn't stop staring. Got quite embarrassing it did. I tried distracting him but it was no use. So I asked him outright what he thought he was playing at, and do you know what he said?' I shake my head and she pushes her glasses further onto her nose. 'He said, "That poor baby, I feel so sorry for it." I asked why and he said that he hates the taste of breast milk. "Don't be so daft," I said. "You can't possibly remember what it tastes like."

'He insisted he could, then he said that Louis went off it too. "That's why Nan gets so cross with him," he said, so I asked him why his nan would be upset about it, and he said that she said breast milk is good for them. I didn't like to press him on it but,' Mum pauses and looks at me again, 'it sounded to me like it's their nan who was feeding them, not their mum. And she wasn't happy when Louis rejected her.'

I frown, staring at her. 'Julie did say she was the one who had to see to them when they were young.' I turn away, watching Bartley and Ethan as they scramble over the shingle, chasing each other. Buckets in hand, Caitlin, Megan and little Louis pick up shells, rope and driftwood under Emily's watchful eye, Mungo trotting eagerly beside them. 'That does seem quite odd, doesn't it? I'll mention it to the social worker.'

She nods. 'Poor kids,' she says, with another deep sigh.

We sit for a while in silence, watching the children and sipping our tea. The sky parts, revealing a bright blue sky. 'Are you all right, Mum?' I ask, the sun bringing enough warmth for me to shrug off my cardigan.

Silenced

'Never better.'

'You've been a bit reserved the last few weeks.'

She scoffs a laugh, inclining her chin towards the water's edge. 'Can't get a word in edgeways with that lot around.'

I smile and pour us some more tea. 'I wonder how Des is getting on with the rabbits.'

'He'll cope,' is all she says. The salty air starts to prickle between us.

I leave it a while then look at her. 'What happened between you two?'

'What two?' she says vaguely, without taking her eyes off the children.

'You and Des. He's annoyed you in some way.'

She barks another laugh and lifts an eyebrow at me. 'No more than usual.'

I'm so busy analysing her reaction that I don't see Louis coming until his sodden swim shorts land on my lap. 'Oh my goodness!' I gasp, laughing. The shivering toddler stretches his arms around my middle, snuggling into me. After grasping a towel and wrapping it around him, I turn to her and try again. 'Is Des going away, Mum?'

'He's getting hungry, I expect.' Sidestepping the question, Mum starts to rifle through one of the picnic bags looking for a snack.

'Mum …'

'Look, Des hasn't told me anything,' she says, reaching under the towel and wiping Louis's hands over with a wet wipe. When she finishes, she chucks him under the chin and gives him a bread stick to munch on. 'Even if someone we love has to leave,' she says eventually, her gaze fixed out to sea, 'it doesn't mean we've lost them.' Her voice cracks, her thoughts no doubt with her recently deceased sister. 'They stay in our hearts. We just have to remember that.'

I smile sadly and rub her shoulder. 'Sorry, Mum.'

She gives my hand a short sharp squeeze, signalling the end of the conversation. 'Right,' she says briskly, 'are you going to get some chips to go with these sandwiches, or are me and Louis to waste away right here on the beach?'

Chapter Twenty-Nine

By the time we get back to the cottage, Louis is almost asleep in my arms. 'Just a very quick cat lick,' I say softly, balancing on the edge of the bath so I can wash the sand and sun cream off his skin.

He complains, but only mildly. As I tuck him up in the cot beside my bed, I think about the happy dreams that will hopefully run through his mind tonight. It's nice to imagine that memories of our holiday might overwrite any unpleasant ones that might otherwise be lurking there.

Bartley is waiting for me at the bottom of the stairs. 'Is it time yet?' He's been badgering me all day to find out what's in store for them, so while Emily grabs some pillows and blankets from upstairs, I lead them into the cottage garden. 'We're swimming?!' Bartley exclaims at the sight of the large paddling pool in the middle of the lawn.

'Not swimming, no. But we need to get into teams. I suggest that you team up with Caitlin, and Ethan can join Megan and –'

'Not happening,' Bartley says with disgust. 'I'm having Ethan on my team.' He high-fives his brother, who cheers in response and runs circles round the pool.

'Okay, if you're sure. Only, you don't know the rules of the game yet.' Emily returns with an armful of bedding and scatters quilts and throws inside the pool.

Bartley blinks, beginning to look doubtful, but then he recovers. 'Don't care what they are …' he says, jerking his chin towards Caitlin, 'I'm not being with her. She's useless.'

'Okay, so what we're doing,' I say, retrieving a box I'd stashed under the patio table earlier, 'is searching for constellations in the night sky – that means we're looking for groups of stars that form particular shapes. Whoever finds the most is the winner.' I shake the box of cardboard tubes that I'd prepared this morning, ignoring Bartley's expression of outrage. 'Each of these viewers has holes punched into the card taped to the end. The holes match the patterns of constellations. You're going to lay in the pool and search the sky, and you'll get a chocolate for each one you locate.'

'Wait, what?' Bartley cries, staring at his sister open-mouthed. 'That's not fair! She's obviously going to win!'

'Well, I suppose you could say her *team* has an advantage,' I say mildly.

'I'm on her side,' Bartley says, ditching his brother without a second's hesitation.

'Well, I don't know about that.' I chew my lip and try to look unpersuaded, a feat that requires significant acting skills. 'You've chosen Ethan now so …'

'Oh please, Rosie, you gotta let me be on Caitlin's team!' Bartley clutches his hands together in a position of prayer. 'I've been so good all day, haven't I? Ple-e-ease.'

'What do you think, Caitlin, are you prepared to accept him?' Bartley drops to his knees with a pleading expression, shaking his clasped hands at his sister in an over-the-top, comical display.

She grins, looking chuffed. 'Okay then.'

Ethan's eyes are so focused on the bowl of chocolates my mum brings to the table that he doesn't look too bothered about the unceremonious dumping.

'Yes-ss!' Bartley performs a fist punch and throws himself, stuntman style, into the now padded pool.

The others follow his lead, diving in and covering themselves up. Emily laughs. 'I used to love doing this. Where's your phone, Mum? I'll pull up Google Sky, it's better than the other app.'

'Found one!' Caitlin says after less than half a minute. 'It's Orion, look, up there.' Bartley leans towards her, squinting through her viewer in the direction she's pointing.

'Cool!' her brother cheers. 'You're going to boss this, Cait!'

It's the first time I've heard affection in his tone and I can't stop myself grinning as I watch them.

'Er, Mum,' Emily says, coming to my side.

'One point to Caitlin and Bartley's team then,' I say, only half-registering Emily's hesitant tone as I hand each of them a chocolate. It's a contrived situation designed to encourage co-operation between them, and it's working so well that they don't even complain when Ethan, Megan and I tuck into the sweets as well.

'Mum, you need to listen to this,' Emily hisses, drawing me towards the house. She taps a few buttons on the screen then holds the phone to my ear. After a few clicks, I hear a loud thump and then a tirade of screeching abuse.

Disorientated, I take hold of the phone and press it closer to my ear.

Emily watches my expression. Slowly, the voice computes in my mind. 'Julie?'

'She must have pocket-dialled you,' Emily whispers, glancing over at the children. 'She needs to go to the top of the waiting list for anger management. She's off the scale. Who's she having a go at? Her husband?'

I stare at Emily in shock as the verbal abuse intensifies in my ear. 'I have no idea. I'm guessing so. Thank goodness the children aren't there.'

According to a brief voice message from Robert soon after we arrived in Whitby, Julie's hospital visits had been suspended after my reports of her controlling behaviour were sent to the medical team caring for Bonnie. Knowing how incensed she's likely to be, I'm not relishing the thought of seeing her again.

'I can see hundreds of stars, Rosie!' Ethan calls out. He munches on another chocolate. 'I never see'd more than one or two before.'

'That's because there's lots of light pollution where we live,' I say distractedly, my heart thumping uncomfortably in my chest. Aggression always reduces me to jelly. That's why I sometimes find LAC reviews difficult – birth parents often explode when their abusive behaviour is detailed in front of strangers, their anger a shield against embarrassment and shame. The level of anger and hysteria in Julie's voice is making my knees go weak. I look at Emily again. 'I don't know what to do,' I say in a low voice, holding the phone speaker away from my mouth. 'Do I ignore it? Call someone and report it?'

'Don't worry, I'm recording it.' Emily takes the phone and rests it on the patio table. 'Just let it run. It'll pick everything up.'

'You clever thing.' I squeeze Emily's arm, grateful for her quick thinking. At least I'll have evidence of Julie's aggression to present to Robert when I see him.

Caitlin sits up and lowers her viewer. 'The longer you look, the more stars you'll see, Ethan. Although they might not even be stars any more. They might be black holes by now.'

'Course they're stars, stupid,' Bartley says dismissively. 'I can see them shining.'

Caitlin shakes her head. 'Some of them are so far away that their light takes years and years and years to reach us. We're actually time travelling. When we look up at the sky, we're seeing the past.' She looks over to me for confirmation.

'She's right, Bartley.' He flings his arms out and falls back onto one of the sleeping bags in a parody of shock.

Caitlin giggles. 'Did you know as well, Bartley, that only 12 people have ever been to the moon, and because there's no wind their footsteps are still there.'

There's such an earnest expression on her face that my stomach tightens, knowing that what she'll probably get in return is a sneer. 'That's so cool,' Bartley says half a second later. He unwraps another chocolate and stares appreciably up at the sky as he chews on it. Mum and I exchange glances and smile. It's been such a wonderful day.

* * *

Bartley turns 11 while we're away and chooses to spend the day on the beach. In the evening, when we return to the pub for a meal, I have a hushed word with the waiter. When he brings out a pudding topped with sparklers and a flaming candle, and everyone in the restaurant sings 'Happy Birthday', Bartley flushes a deep red and looks close to tears.

We return to the beach for the last day of our holiday. About 7.30 p.m., just as the light is fading and the hustle-bustle along the seafront begins to still, we pack up our bags and wade through the sand dunes towards our cottage. The route takes us through an ornamental garden and a spontaneous game of tag breaks out between the children as we pass a rusting old bandstand.

Louis, beginning to nod off in the buggy, shakes himself awake. Squirming around, he shouts for Emily to stop pushing and release him from the straps. He squeals when she sets him free to join in the fun.

Mum, Emily and I rest on a bench and watch them, listening to their hoots of laughter as they throw themselves up and down the wooden steps and duck out of each other's way.

But then my heart jumps into my mouth. Louis, who had been carefully pulling himself up one set of steps, almost collides with Caitlin, who's coming the other way. In an impressive reflex action, she manages to both dodge around him and grasp hold of his arm to stop him hurtling backwards, down the stairs. In doing so, she barges straight into Bartley, who promptly thwacks his head on one of the metal struts.

Caitlin gasps and freezes. Bartley yelps. There's a long pause in which I think all of us hold our breath. And then comes a collective sigh of relief as, after a vigorous rubbing of his head, Bartley tags his sister and shouts, 'You're it!' He dashes away and the manic circuits of the bandstand continue.

I feel a warm glow. I've learned to treasure timeless moments like this, when the trauma lurking in a child's past temporarily fades away and everyone seems happy and carefree. I know from experience that it may not last long.

I link arms with my mum as we set off for the cottage again. The children troop ahead of us. 'It's been nice, hasn't it, after all.'

'Lovely,' she says. 'I'm so glad I came.'

'I used to think you were a complete waste of space,' Bartley says to his sister when we reach the cottage. Nudging her gently with his elbow as they wait for me to unlock the door, he adds, 'Get it? A waste of *space*, lol.'

He doesn't follow it up with a compliment, but it's a victory of sorts. Caitlin giggles and nudges him back, and I perform a mental high-five, filled with gratitude towards Jenny. All the children needed was some time and space to reset their nervous systems after the stress of the last few weeks without their mum. That's what I tell myself as I shake the picnic blankets free of crumbs and wash the sand off Louis's toes.

It's a theory that proves difficult to maintain the next day, however, as we head back home.

Chapter Thirty

The closer we get to Julie's house, the sullener the children grow. And when we pull into their road, Bartley's animosity towards his sister returns with a vengeance. Not only that, but for the first time in almost a fortnight he strikes out physically, punching her on the thigh.

Mum twists in her seat and rubs Caitlin's knee, giving Bartley one long look of disapproval before turning back.

Julie must have heard us pull up because she appears on the drive before I even cut the engine. Ethan is the first out. He runs to his grandmother and throws his arms around her. 'Oh, I've missed you all so much!' She leans down and kisses the top of his head then holds out her arms as Caitlin and Bartley climb out. 'Come here, my babies!'

Emily unloads the cases from the boot. I'm just about to reach into the back for Louis, when Ryan appears. Silently, he lifts the sleeping toddler up and disappears into the house without a word. My heart rate picks up as I walk to the other side of the car to speak to Julie. 'We had a great time, didn't we, guys?'

Still in a group hug with their grandmother, Caitlin and Bartley's heads bob slightly. Enveloped in the middle of the fold, Ethan makes a muted noise of agreement. Presuming that Bartley was keeping his grandmother updated with regular texts, I'd only sent Julie a couple of messages while we were away, just to reassure her that the children were fine. I hadn't received any replies.

'How was the course, Julie?' I ask, when she releases the children. She crosses her arms over her chest and finally meets my gaze.

'Bye, Rosie,' Ethan says. He gives me a brief hug and then he and Bartley scoot across the drive. I laugh. 'Bye, boys!'

Caitlin hovers, looking unsure.

'Can I give you a cuddle?' She nods and I wrap my arms around her. 'Thank you for being such lovely company.' She pauses when I release her and looks at me, then she follows her brothers into the house.

Julie gives me a frosty look when I turn back to her. 'Are you okay, Julie?'

'Fine. I'll see you at the meeting next week no doubt.'

'She's so mean,' Megan says as we pull out of the Chambers' turning and onto the main road.

'She?' I glance in the rear-view mirror, hoping that Megan hasn't been corrupted into following Bartley's tendency to blame his sister for everything.

'That lady. The nanny.'

'She's talking about Julie,' Mum says, looking at me. She turns with difficulty to look at Megan, who's sitting directly behind her. 'Is that who you mean? Their grandma.'

'Yes,' she says in a definite way. 'She's not a nice nanny like you, Nanny, she's a meanie.' Her words send a cold chill down the back of my neck.

Emily frowns. 'Why do you say that, Megs?'

'She says bad things to Caitlin.'

'How do you know? Did Caitlin tell you that?' It's often the case that birth children are the first to hear disclosures from foster children, particularly when they strike up close friendships, and the pair of them had spent a lot of time together while we were away.

Megan's expression clouds in the rear-view mirror. 'Sorry, Mummy. I didn't mean to. I saw them talking and accidentally did some pobbing.' She pauses, gauging my reaction. When she senses no disapproval, she screws up her face and twists her lips, deepening her voice. "You keep your fat mouth shut, you little bitch, you hear me?" That's what she said.'

'When, sweetie? When did she say it?'

'The day before the day before the day before last week. When we picked them up for holiday. It was weird, Mummy. That nanny looked like she was being nice on her face, but bad words were coming out of her mouth. Can I tell you them? I knowed them already from Connor at school.'

I glance at Mum, whose face has crumpled. I meet Emily's gaze in the rear-view mirror. She widens her eyes, lifting her brows.

My youngest daughter, it seems, has been honing her 'pobbing' skills to useful effect, confirming my suspicions that Julie is most definitely not the loving grandmother she makes herself out to be.

* * *

Silenced

What with an Easter egg hunt in the garden on Sunday 21 April and a trip to see relatives on Easter Monday, the long weekend passes in a flash. I'm glad of it, eager to get to the TAC meeting scheduled for Tuesday 23rd, when all the children return to school.

Walking into the local authority offices is like taking a trip into the past. Seventies fluorescent lights flicker overhead as the receptionist authorises the security lift to take me up to the fourth floor. The grey commercial carpet tiles feel slightly uneven beneath my feet as I step into the corridor. Cork display boards hang at odd angles on the walls. It's only the leaflets, curling at the edges, that give a clue as to the decade we're in; 'Ask for Angela' posters displayed alongside county lines warnings and sex-trafficking helplines.

I like its character and individuality though. It's as though the stories of the people passing through its doors over the last 50 years have been absorbed into the walls.

'Ah, Robert!' I call when he emerges from an office a few metres ahead of me. 'I was hoping to have a word with you.' Breathlessly, I hurry to catch him up.

'Rosie, good morning,' he says, shaking my hand. He pulls his phone from the pocket of his velvet jacket and glances at the screen. 'It's not quite ten but I think we're all here now.'

He takes a few steps towards the meeting room. 'Robert, please – just a second. Before we go in … did you get my email?'

I'd summarised everything that had happened over the last two weeks when we got home on Saturday, including

Megan's account of Julie being abusive to Caitlin, Bartley's intimation that Julie was angry about Louis rejecting the breast and repeating my discomfort over the way the toddler was treated when I spent the day with her. 'I have serious concerns.'

'If your email summarised the worst of it, I'd say they're not doing too bad,' the social worker responds swiftly, as if he'd been anticipating our conversation.

I shake my head. 'Something's seriously off with the whole set-up, Robert. Ryan's obsession with a girl who isn't even his daughter. There's something very wrong there, and their marriage isn't in a good place either.'

The social worker smiles tolerantly. 'I daresay inheriting four children overnight hasn't done them any favours.'

I shake my head. 'It's more than that. Bartley managed to keep his hands to himself for almost two weeks while we were away, yet the second we head back to Julie's he starts attacking his sister again.'

Another wintry smile from Robert tells me I'm getting nowhere. My mind runs over all the incidents that have unsettled me in the last two months, since first meeting the family. 'Julie is extremely controlling,' I say in a steely tone.

When Robert asks for examples, the first thing that comes into my mind is the kangaroo text.

He stares at me as if he can't quite work out whether I'm being serious or not. Then he laughs. 'She sent you a text, you say.' He pauses for effect, as if he wants me to realise the triviality of it. 'About – a kangaroo?'

Frustration ties my tongue for a moment. A recurring theme from Serious Case Reviews held following the deaths of children already under the radar of social workers is the lack of joined-up thinking amongst professionals. A failure to zoom out and see the bigger picture. All of my reports about Julie may well seem trivial when viewed in isolation, but they add up to my overall sense that she's a controlling individual who can't bear to be disagreed with. I level my gaze, hoping to communicate how strongly I feel. 'What about the voice recording?'

He adjusts his cravat and gives me a slow blink. 'The one you wiped, you mean?'

'I didn't deliberately delete it!' I should have waited for Emily to help me but I'd been so keen to send the abusive voice recording to Robert that I'd tried to send it after she'd gone to bed on the night of our stargazing, and had accidentally erased the whole file.

Robert lifts a brow, as if he finds that hard to believe. My cheeks start to burn. It's almost as if he suspects me of making the whole thing up.

'Look, Rosie, I respect you as a foster carer. I've heard lots of excellent reports about your work, but it's clear that what we're dealing with here is a clash of personalities. Jules is a strong-willed woman, I'll concede –'

'Robert,' I cut him off, feeling livid. 'This has nothing whatsoever to do with Julie as a person. This is about her treatment of the children.'

'May I remind you that your role on Mockingbird is to support the family, not to record private conversations. Illegally, I might add.' In full stride now, his pink-shirted chest expands as he churns out some bureaucratic babble about my responsibilities to the family. 'Jules is under a lot of pressure at the moment. This is a very overwhelming situation for her and one she's taken on without a moment's complaint.'

Julie bestows a charming smile on him when he leads the way into the meeting room. The effect on Robert is instant, the furrows across his forehead instantly evaporating.

Her gaze slides over me without the slightest flicker of acknowledgement. She follows the snub up with an extravagant rub of Robert's arm, when he takes the seat next to hers.

Game face on, I make for the seat at the far end of the long oval table, recognising some faces as I squeeze past their chairs. There's Sophie, a student social worker I've met before, and a bearded secretary who has a laptop open in front of him, ready to take notes.

Diane Howell, an Independent Reviewing Officer (IRO), is seated at the centre of the table on the opposite side, two seats away from Robert. I've met her several times before. She's one of those people who never seems to age, the only sign of the passing years a few streaks of grey in her auburn hair. 'Nice to see you've joined Mockingbird, Rosie,' she says with a friendly smile, as I take a seat next to Clare Barnard from the children's school. 'I think you're perfect for it.'

'Thanks, Diane.'

'Right,' she says, turning to address the group, 'it's just gone ten. Shall we get started with the introductions, Robert? You've not had any further apologies?'

'Nothing from Ethan's father, no. Nor Louis's. I was hoping one of the children's teachers could make it, but they've sent their apologies, as well as Ryan, who has to work. We do have their SENCo here though.'

Clare inclines her head in acknowledgement. With everyone focused on her, she says, 'Shall I start then? I'm Clare Barnard, SENCo at Millfield.'

She turns to me and the introductions ripple around the group. The buck-toothed, ferrety-looking man I bumped into on my first visit to the family announces himself as Billy Harcourt, Bartley's dad. Two seats away from him sits Trevor Penrose, Caitlin's father.

I'm surprised and pleased that he's made the effort to come, but he looks as if he's wishing he hadn't. Twisting his hands, he barely glances up when he mumbles his name. Clearly uncomfortable, he grabs one of the paper cups from a pile in the centre of the table. The jug trembles in his nervous fingers as he pours himself some water.

My heart goes out to him. I'm not a fan of formal meetings myself, at least not when I can sense a confrontation brewing. It's not a problem when all I have to report is how the children are getting on in my care – I enjoy recounting little anecdotes that are revealing of their personalities, and making plans to support them while they're in placement – but today I have some uncomfortable truths to air, and I suspect that they won't go down too well.

'Lovely,' Diane says, ticking off an item on the agenda in front of her. 'So, the purpose of today's conference is to –'

'A-hem,' Robert, seated to her left, clears his throat. 'I prefer to call our get-together a "listening circle" if you don't mind. I believe it sets the right tone at the outset.'

He gives Julie a little smile. She nods approvingly. Diane stares at him, mouth open. 'As I was saying,' she says after a moment. 'Today is all about finding out what we can do to support the children while their mother is in hospital, and making sure we have parallel plans in place should they not be able to return to her care.

'We can start with you, Julie, if you'd like? I believe you found the "Who's in Charge?" course beneficial?'

Julie leans her elbows on the table and steeples her fingers, bringing them to her lips. 'I have to admit that I approached the course with a heavy heart. I've had two children of my own and practically brought up Bonnie's four as well, so to be prescribed a parenting course felt a little insulting.' She smiles graciously and blinks around the table. 'I hadn't banked on meeting some amazing people while I was there. Hearing their stories and the courage they've shown ...' she pauses, swallowing as if trying to rein in her emotions, 'was inspiring. I should have approached it with an open heart.' She glances sideways and flutters her lashes at Robert. 'And a little more humility.'

Robert, who had been nodding vigorously throughout, smiles at her. 'Powerful,' he says, his eyes shining admiringly.

'And how are you coping with the children?' Diane asks briskly, clearly not as sucked in by the emotional speech as Robert.

'They're great. As I said, I've been heavily involved since the year dot. I've had no choice. But I'm not one to complain. You just have to get on with it, don't you?'

Diane nods. 'Thank you, Julie. Rosie,' she turns to me, 'would you like to update us on your involvement? I believe you played some Voice of the Child games with the children?' She flicks through her notes and looks back at me. 'They clearly want to be with their grandmother. But are they missing their mum a lot? How has their behaviour been?'

My heart thuds. I take a deep breath and start by talking a bit about our holiday. 'That's incredible,' Clare adds, when I mention the temporary improvement in the relationship between Caitlin and Bartley. 'They avoid each other like the plague at school.'

'There seems to be a lot of animosity between them.' I pause, gathering myself before continuing. 'Bartley confided some of his worries while we were away.'

Diane sharpens her gaze. Billy sits forward in his seat and frowns. The atmosphere in the room intensifies. 'Bartley feels that everyone hates him, particularly his grandfather. He struggles to understand why Caitlin is always chosen to go out with Ryan. I think that's partly why he's so resentful of his sister.'

Julie snorts. 'You've known the family all of five minutes and now you're making sweeping statements about things you know nothing about.'

I look at Diane. 'I'm not sure how freely I'm allowed to speak with everyone here.'

She nods. 'Right, good point. How about we hear from Mr Harcourt and Mr Penrose now, and then they'll be free to leave.'

'Call me Billy. And no, I wanna know what the woman's on about before I say my piece,' he snaps. 'There's been too much sweeping stuff under the carpet far as I'm concerned. So come on,' he says, hooking a dirty finger at me, 'out with it.'

I glance at Diane. 'What do you mean by that, Billy?' the chairperson says calmly. 'What has been swept under the carpet?'

'Her,' he barks, jabbing his forefinger at Julie.

The grandmother reels back as if he's smacked her across the face and then blinks at Robert in shock. The social worker pats her arm protectively. Billy, in a rant peppered with a liberal amount of swear words, accuses her of allowing him to see Bartley one minute, and blocking him the next. 'If it was up to her, I'd never see Bart. S'only down to Ryan that I get to see him when I do. Except when it suits her of course, then I'm allowed to have the bloody lot of them.'

He thumps his fist down on the table so hard that one of the paper cups upends and douses Diane's files in water. 'Security please,' Robert gabbles into his mobile phone.

'I really don't think there's any need for that, Robert.' Diane lifts the sodden pile of papers up and shakes them gently. Next second, a beefy, uniformed security officer bounds into the room. Startled, Billy jumps to his feet. He spits out an expletive-laden rant as he's half-led, half-dragged from the room.

My legs start shaking. Being in close quarters with someone so out of control is intimidating in itself, but I have a feeling that the worst is yet to come.

Chapter Thirty-One

Julie bursts into tears. 'I despair of that man,' she says, pulling a tissue from her bag and dabbing her eyes. 'He's *so* unreliable, turning up when he's not expected, and when he does bother to make an arrangement he lets poor Bart down half the time.' She gulps, looking at Robert. 'All I've tried to do is protect them from' – she waves her tissue at the door – 'that sort of display, and I get demonised for it.'

Robert makes soothing noises like a parent to an upset child. Julie reaches into her bag for her vape.

Diane frowns. 'Er, no, sorry. No vaping –'

'But surely,' Robert interjects, 'we can make an exception?'

Julie slams the vape down and folds her arms when Diane shakes her head. Robert hastily pours a glass of water and places it in front of her but she pushes it away as much as to say, *If I can't have my e-cig, I'm not having anything.*

'Mr Penrose?' Diane says crisply, no doubt eager to get the meeting back on a professional footing. 'What would you like to contribute?'

Caitlin's father blinks, looking overwhelmed. 'I'd like access to my daughter. That's all I've wanted all along.'

Julie lets out a shrill laugh. 'Is it really, Trevor?' She gives him a triumphant sneer. 'Is that *really* all you wanted?'

Trevor's nervousness dissipates. A look of pure hatred replaces it.

'What are you implying, Julie?' Diane says, looking between them.

'Oh, just that Trevor isn't quite as dedicated to his daughter as he'd like you all to think.'

Trevor lowers his head, and once Clare has updated the meeting on the children's attainment at school and readies herself to leave, he shoots Julie a look of disgust before following the SENCo out the door.

'Goodbye to you too,' Julie says, with a despairing shake of her head. 'What a total waste of space they are.' Her face twists as she speaks and it becomes clear that Bartley picked up that particular scornful mannerism from her, as well as the turn of phrase.

Diane looks at me. 'Rosie, you can speak freely now.'

I nod, my stomach tightening with tension again. What I aim to do is present all the facts as succinctly as possible without coming across as accusatory or judgemental. It's a tough line to walk gracefully. 'I do have quite a few concerns about the children.' I keep my gaze focused on Diane, but I'm aware of Julie's eyes boring into me as I speak. 'Although it's Caitlin I'm most concerned about.'

Diane nods. 'Her SENCo mentioned her selective mutism.'

Julie barks a harsh laugh at that. I glance at her, then return my attention to Diane. 'Caitlin is stifled. She's not allowed to express any emotion. Her voice has been taken away.'

'Not allowed to express any emotion?!' Julie repeats, looking at Robert and shaking her head in disbelief. 'The girl bursts into tears at the drop of a hat.'

Offended on Caitlin's behalf, it's an effort not to leap to her defence by telling Julie exactly what I think of her. What I need to do, however, is present only the facts, and in a calm, professional way. 'Caitlin plucked up the courage to tell you how she was feeling a while ago, Julie,' I say, addressing her directly. 'But you immediately silenced her.'

The grandmother shakes her head at Robert again. 'I have absolutely no idea what she's talking about.'

I pull my notebook out of my bag and flick through it. 'It was the afternoon of Tuesday 26 March.'

Julie flounders for a moment, somewhat taken aback. I turn my attention back to Diane. 'I spent the whole day with Julie and wrote a detailed report afterwards because there were a number of issues that caused me concern.' I speak about Louis being forced to stay in his high chair, and then the protracted period of time on his potty. 'I could tell Julie was tense that day.'

'I felt under siege!' she snaps.

'Understandable. None of us enjoy being watched,' Robert pipes up. 'It can be especially intrusive in the home environment.'

'I agree,' I nod, 'but I believe Julie's treatment of Louis and Caitlin went beyond the awkwardness of feeling observed.'

Julie's mouth drops open. Diane scribbles something

on her pad and then looks at me. 'Okay, I think this needs unpacking. Can you give us some more examples, Rosie?'

Feeling uncomfortable again, I start by going into detail about Julie's treatment of Caitlin when she came home from school, then move onto Bartley's comments while we were on holiday, about Julie breastfeeding Louis and her fury at being refused.

'This is all so unfair,' Julie wails, growing teary again. 'You're dressing it up to sound weird, but there's nothing more natural than nurturing your daughter's children, especially when she isn't able to do it herself.' She takes a breath and tucks her hair behind her ear as she turns towards Robert. 'Bonnie wasn't in a fit state to meet the children's needs when they were little. I was feeding Linzi, so it made sense to nurse Bonnie's babies with my own milk when they came along. I just didn't have the time to make up bottles and sterilise them, especially since I was trying to hold down a full-time job as well.'

She sighs, following it up with a little hiccup. 'After all I've done for the family, taking early retirement and devoting myself to keeping them together, it's a bit rich to be criticised for it. Then again I suppose it's typical for the woman to get the blame for everything.' Her eyes flick over to me. 'But when it's another woman going on the attack, it's particularly galling.'

Diane taps her pen on the table. 'It's not unusual for some women to find it difficult when a baby they've nurtured wants to develop more independence.' The chairperson holds up her hands in response to a look of daggers from Julie. 'That's not an accusation. I'm just saying, it happens. Could it be that you felt a little rejected when Louis gave up the breast, Julie?'

Robert looks scandalised by the suggestion that Julie could be anything less than perfect.

'Not at all,' Julie says firmly. 'In fact, I've been keen to toilet train him so that he gains some more independence. It was Rosie who told me not to bother. I believe she's going on the attack as a deflection tactic, to divert attention from her own obvious shortcomings.'

Like a moth to a flame, Robert shuffles his chair an inch or two towards her, unconsciously, perhaps, moving further away from me. Clever and beguiling, Julie is so gifted at twisting the truth and making it appear as if everyone around her is at fault that it's no wonder Caitlin was rendered silent by her behaviour.

'Examples?' Diane says, narrowing her eyes. She uses a non-committal tone and I just hope she's known me long enough not to fall under Julie's spell as well.

'Rosie uses terms I find offensive, for a start.'

I gape at her. 'I'm sorry?'

'Old-fashioned terms that have no place in modern society.' Gobsmacked, I do nothing but stare at her. 'It's not just the microaggressions and the use of outdated terms, though,' continues Julie. 'It's your whole attitude, Rosie. Allowing your daughter to call Louis her brother. Your mother insisting that Bartley calls her *Nan*.'

Robert's head spins round at that. He stares at me, flabbergasted. 'She's unreliable, turning up late, or not at all, then blaming me for it. And when she does turn up, she stuffs the children full of chocolate. While they were away she used sweets as prizes, giving them entirely the wrong message about healthy foods.

'But it's the aggression that most concerns me,' Julie declares when I open my mouth to speak. Wrinkling her brow, she pauses to maximise the effect, then looks at Robert. 'She threatened poor Bartley with a knife,' she says, delivering the killer blow with a tremor in her voice. 'How can that be classed as safe care? Answer me that!'

A small gasp escapes someone's lips. I'm so shocked, and so fixated on Julie's face, that I can't tell if it's Diane, or the secretary or student social worker. Julie watches me carefully with pinkening cheeks, thoroughly enjoying my discomfort. 'I mean, I know he can be a handful but that's just not acceptable.'

Hardly able to tear my eyes away from her, it's about 30 seconds before I find my voice. 'It was a potato peeler,' I say weakly.

The accusation is so farcical, I'm almost tempted to laugh. I risk a glance at Diane and notice her lip twitching. Does she recognise the absurdity of the claim? With everything that's happened I begin to worry that none of them can see what's really going on.

Julie's eyes shine as she recounts a number of other 'distressing incidents', including my mother making verbal threats towards Bartley and me holding him prisoner against his will. If she's like this with me, in front of a roomful of professionals, what on earth is she capable of behind closed doors, I wonder.

There's a silence as everyone absorbs Julie's words. My head swims. I feel giddy, and slightly sick. 'That's quite a list of allegations, Julie,' Diane says. 'Obviously Rosie should get the chance to present her recollections, as she sees them, but I wonder if you might clarify a few points first.'

'To be honest I don't see why I should,' Julie says, looking at Robert for support. The social worker's gaze shrinks away. Something in his demeanour tells me he's uncomfortable with the direction his 'listening circle' has taken. 'I've tried my best, but the relationship between us has broken down.'

'Now, let's not be too hasty,' Robert intervenes, taking me by surprise. His high colour has deepened, his complexion taking on a mildly purple hue. 'Rosie has established a good relationship with the children. I'd prefer not to unsettle them by introducing someone new at this stage in proceedings.'

Displeased by his audacity in disagreeing with her, Julie peers down her nose at him. 'I've tried, I really have, Rob, but I'm afraid I'm not prepared to work with her any more.'

A heavy weight settles in my stomach in anticipation of Robert's next words. He sighs. 'It's clear that the relationship between you and the family has broken down, Rosie. I'm afraid I have no choice but to terminate your involvement with immediate effect.'

He looks from me to Diane, who gives a curt nod. 'If that's what you've decided. These relationships don't always work to best advantage.'

I swallow, trying to absorb the shock. Basking in her triumph, Julie's eyes shine as she gives Robert a sad little smile. Infuriatingly, I know that if I make any sort of protest or rise to defend myself, I'll only confirm that Julie was right to label me aggressive. So I don't. Collecting my bag and my notebook, I nod to Diane and leave the room with as much dignity as I can muster.

As soon as I'm out of the building, I call Des. 'They wouldn't listen,' I say, my insides quivering at the thought of the children returning to Julie after their day at school. 'They're like lambs to the slaughter.'

Chapter Thirty-Two

Des is waiting for me on the doorstep when I get home.

'This is a nice surprise.' I smile tiredly, leaning into him for a hug. 'Staying for lunch?'

'Aye, if you're offering.'

In the kitchen, he listens quietly as I pull random items from the fridge and relay the events of the morning. He chuckles as I spread everything over the counter beside him. 'You're supposed to be knocking up a sandwich, not feeding the five thousand.'

I groan and rub a hand over my face. 'My head's all over the place at the moment. I just can't bear to think of what those children must go through at home, especially Caitlin.'

'Sweetheart,' he says soothingly, resting a steadying hand on my arm, 'you're tired after all the travelling over the weekend, and now this meeting has taken it out of you as well. Sit down and let *me* rustle something up.'

I pull away from him. 'Are you seriously using HALT techniques on me?!' I'm only half joking, my worries getting the better of me and making me tetchy.

'What? No, I –'

I frown at him. 'What went on between you and my mum?'

There's a pause, then he turns away and pulls a spoon out of the cutlery drawer.

'Ever since that day you came over for dinner three or four weeks ago, there's been something up between the two of you.'

He reaches for some mugs. Usually when making tea, he adds a teabag to some milk, fills the cup with some cold water and then shoves it in the microwave, a routine that horrifies my mum. Sometimes he doesn't even remove the bag before drinking, and he never bothers to stir. Today, he boils the kettle and repositions the mugs several times before pouring, then faffs around with the spoon, carefully squeezing the teabag against the sides.

'I can guess why you fell out,' I say quietly to his back. 'You're going away, aren't you, and Mum knows.'

He turns to face me with a heavy sigh. 'She'll roast me on a spit if she finds out I've told you.'

'Told me what?' I feel a bit sick. 'Des, please.'

He tugs on his beard, then looks down at me. 'She has some daft idea about protecting you by leaving it as long as possible before coming clean. She's not well. I tried convincing her to break it to you but … I just didn't feel it was my place to go against her wishes.'

With a sudden lurch of my stomach, I grab my keys from the side. 'Can you pick Megan up from school?'

I hadn't been aware of his hands holding mine, but when his grip loosens, I feel a chill. 'Of course, sweetheart.

Silenced

'I told her it was a terrible idea,' he calls as I fly out the door.

Half an hour later, Mum reaches across her sofa and hands me a tissue.

'We've had some laughs, haven't we?' she says after I've mopped my face. 'And lots of tears too. Remember how poorly Sarah was when you picked her up from hospital, poor little scrap. And Phoebe with her vomiting? I've never known anything like it in all my born days.' She chuckles croakily, then her eyes grow misty. 'I'd love to see them all again.'

It's the thought that she might not get the chance that undoes me again. 'Don't take against Des,' she says softly, when I've gathered myself a second time. 'He's been ever so good. Ferrying me back and forth to appointments, making sure I've got enough medication.'

'Careful,' I say, my voice wobbling at the thought of her being in pain. 'It almost sounds as if you like him.'

She chuckles again. 'He's a scruffy devil. Looks like the wild man of Borneo. And some of his political views are downright dangerous.' Still smiling, she meets my eye. 'But I do like him, yes. He's gentle and kind, and he thinks the world of you and the kids.

'Now,' she says, patting her hands on her knees, 'enough maudlin. I want to enjoy what time I've got left. That means carrying on as normal. So you go and pop the kettle on. I want to hear all about what's going on with the kiddies.'

My mum knows that I never break confidences. I share the bare minimum information about a child's past at the beginning of a placement and never discuss their birth family with anyone. As is often the way, however, she ends up knowing almost as much as I do because she develops such a strong relationship with the children that they open up to her.

When I return with a tea tray, her pink-rimmed eyes, translucent skin and sharply visible cheekbones seem to jump out at me, all clues that should have alerted me to the fact that the breast cancer she was treated for years earlier had returned. I marvel at the glaringly obvious things your conscious mind ignores, when acknowledging them would cause too much pain.

I'm reminded of a situational awareness course I attended last year in which the tutor explained that the human mind can easily be distracted, and so lost in thought that our natural ability to sense threat is compromised. We learned that it's particularly important for foster carers to be aware of their surroundings in view of the fact that some looked-after children may be at risk of being snatched by their birth family.

'How was the meeting?' my mum says, her canny eyes on me as I rest the tray on her coffee table and pour tea from the pot.

I tell her it was fine and try to steer her towards other subjects as I sit beside her again. She has enough to worry about, without me burdening her.

'Come on, I'm not daft. Besides, whatever it is will take my mind off my own troubles for a bit.'

There seems little point in pretending so I tell her as much as I can, without compromising the privacy of the family.

'Well, there's only one thing you can do,' she says when I've finished. She rests her cup on a side table and looks at me over the top of her glasses. 'You've got to set this Robert character straight.'

I pull a face. 'That's easier said than done. If I go in too hard, defending myself, I might end up confirming the grandmother's accusations.'

'She really accused *you* of being aggressive? I've never heard anything so ridiculous in all my days. Well, girl, you've got yourself in hot water plenty of times before with the likes of social services, but it's always worked out well in the end.'

I nod, remembering the times I've had to stand firm against individual social workers, sometimes going over their heads when they've refused to set much store by the words of a lowly foster carer.

Before I leave, I give her a gentle hug, hoping to communicate everything I feel without actually saying anything. I know she'll give me short shrift if I get sentimental and anyway the words are so jammed in my throat that it's all I can do to smile and tell her I'll see her tomorrow.

The battle to keep Megan looms large in my memory as I let myself back out into the cold. Megan's social worker, knowing how much we loved her and having seen how well she fitted into our family, encouraged me to throw my hat into the ring when the local authority began family finding. But Veronica Harper, the social worker on the adoption team responsible for matching, had her sights set on a different family, and dismissed my original application with a condescending scoff. '*If only I had a penny for every foster carer who wanted to adopt the baby they'd been minding …*' I seem to remember her saying.

Social workers are often reluctant to support foster carers in their applications to adopt, except in cases where the child would be extremely difficult to place elsewhere. It's understandable in some ways – adoption sometimes brings an end to a family's capacity to foster, especially when space is tight. The match Veronica was fixated on went ahead, only to disrupt a few months afterwards. It was then that I decided that Megan wasn't going to suffer any more upheaval. Standing strong against the might of social services had been daunting, but I couldn't imagine our lives now without her.

Mum's words go round and round my head as I hurry home. By hook or by crook, I know that I have to get someone in social services to listen to me.

Chapter Thirty-Three

Settling myself on the sofa after putting Megan to bed, I try to conjure nice thoughts to calm my whirring mind. Having left a message on Robert's mobile and emailed him as well, I resign myself to the fact that there's little more I can do until morning.

Images of warm sandy beaches and sun-dappled forests don't help me relax. I try staring into the low flames of the log fire instead, but all I can think about is Bartley's confusion when he told me about his feelings towards his sister and grandfather, and Caitlin's stricken face when we dropped her back home.

My dreams are plagued by rows of unfamiliar children, eyes wide with fear, their mouths bound up tightly with duct tape. As soon as I wake at 5 a.m., I'm up and out of bed, relieved that the night is over.

I head straight for the civic centre offices after dropping Megan at school. Bypassing the main receptionist, I follow a suited woman as she heads for the lifts at the far end of the space. She uses the security pass dangling on a lanyard around her neck to summon the lift. When it arrives, her eyes flick briefly in my direction. She looks vaguely familiar and doesn't challenge me when I duck in after her, perhaps because she recognises me too.

She exits at the second floor, but I ride on to the fourth. I've already left two messages for Robert on his mobile this morning but I call him again anyway. The answerphone bleeps as I step out of the lift. I leave another message telling him that I'm on the fourth floor and need to speak to him, then make myself comfortable on one of the benches at the far end of the corridor. Robert could be out on a call, or on annual leave for all I know, but there's every chance he's sitting at a desk on the other side of one of the nearby closed doors. At some point he's going to have to answer the call of nature, or visit the canteen for some lunch.

Two minutes later one of the doors along the corridor opens and a young woman pops her head out. She looks straight at me and ducks back in again. There's a low hum of voices, and then she emerges and comes over. 'Are you Rosie?'

I stand up and nod, trying my best not to look like an obsessive stalker. 'I'm afraid Robert can't see you right now.'

'That's okay,' I smile. 'I'll wait.'

'There's really no point. He's back-to-back with meetings all morning.'

I glance at her name badge and then level my gaze. 'I'm not leaving here until I speak to him, Toria.'

She raises her brows. If I'm not mistaken, she looks slightly impressed. 'O-kay,' she nods, then withdraws. I sit back down, prepared to wait all day if I have to. Megan has a two-hour session with Stagecoach after school today, so I have ages until pick-up. I pull out a novel and a flask of tea from my shoulder bag, and make myself comfortable. When it comes to sit-ins, I learned from the best, something I wrote about in *Torn*.

Taylor was ten years old when she came to stay with us. Determined to make herself as unlikeable as possible, she came up with some surprisingly creative ways to make my life difficult. One of her little exploits was to refuse to leave school at the end of the day. I'd turn up to get her with Jamie, Emily and Taylor's five-year-old brother, Reece, in tow, but she would simply refuse to leave the classroom.

Buoyed by her success – the other children getting ratty with tiredness and hunger and her usually serene teacher screechy with frustration – the sit-ins got longer and longer as each day passed. We were still in the classroom at six-thirty some days. During one interminable session, her teacher threatened to leave Taylor in the school alone overnight. It was futile. Taylor knew we would never abandon her, and she knew we couldn't physically remove her either. We were all hostage to Taylor's mood and powerless to do anything about it. She had us over the proverbial barrel.

Loud, bullish and brashly overconfident, it took time for me to recognise the fear and fragility driving Taylor's behaviour. Now a grown woman in her early twenties, Taylor stays in regular contact with our family and often teases me about those days early on in her placement.

I'm proud of the woman Taylor has become, and pleased that I can put what I learned from her past behaviour to good use.

I'm only halfway through my first cup of tea and a few pages into my novel when Robert makes an appearance. 'Rosie, an unexpected surprise,' he says evenly as I rise to my feet.

'We're supposed to be keeping them safe, Robert!' I say, battling to keep my voice from shaking.

'Rosie.'

He holds up a hand to stop me but I shake my head. 'No, Robert, I'm sorry, but this is too important to let go.' He spins on his heel and walks purposefully away from me. Abandoning my flask and novel where I left them, I grab my shoulder bag and jog to catch him up. 'That girl is terrified, Robert. It's fear that's making her silent, not the upset over her mum going into hospital. And Bartley seems like a tough kid but he's so confused. He's copying –'

My words dry up as the social worker comes to an abrupt halt outside the office of the Director of Children's Services, Alison Castle. My chest tightens with apprehension as he taps on the door. But then a fresh wave of determination surges through me. 'I won't be silenced, Robert, even if it means losing my job.'

When Ms Castle calls out, Robert strides in. Fully expecting him to close the door in my face, I'm surprised when he stands aside and holds it open. He waves me in with a twist of the hand and theatrical half-bow.

'Oh, Rosie,' she smiles at me as I take a few tentative steps closer to her desk. She gestures towards one of two seats across her desk. 'We've just been talking about you.'

I've only met Ms Castle a handful of times but I recall immediately warming to her because she'd remembered the names of the children I had in placement at the time, and asked after my own family as well.

My heart sinks when I sit down, however. On the top of the pile of papers on her desk, I can see that she has a printed copy of the UNO email from Linzi. My bravery temporarily escapes me and my stomach wobbles. Fostering is more than simply a job to me. It lies at the heart of our family. It's our way of life, something that provides meaning and purpose. My heart would break to have that taken away from me. 'You're here to protest about the Powell children being removed from your hub, so I'm told?' She glances at Robert who, grim-faced, takes the seat beside me.

My cheeks feel hot. My heart thumps hard. I swallow and gather myself. 'This isn't about me, Ms Castle.'

She waves a hand through the air. 'Please, call me Alison.'

I nod, feeling slightly surer of myself. If suspension were on the cards, I reason, she wouldn't dispense with formalities. 'This really isn't about me, Alison, I can assure you. If the Chambers feel they can't work with me any more, then of course I understand. But it shouldn't end like this. At the very least, the children should be given the opportunity to say a proper goodbye to me.'

Even when a placement breaks down, foster carers are encouraged to end their relationship with the child on a positive note. Severed attachments are difficult enough for children to process, but when they haven't been given the chance to say goodbye there's a high chance that they'll internalise the message that they're not worthy of even basic consideration.

'It's the Chambers' motivation for getting me out of the way that worries me most,' I continue. 'Attack is the best form of defence. I feel that Julie's accusations –' I pause, more heat rising to my cheeks at the thought of her claim that I'm aggressive, especially the allegation that I threatened Bartley. 'They were –'

'A smokescreen,' Alison completes my sentence. 'We don't doubt it.'

I frown, confused. 'Then why …' My eyes fall to the email from Linzi. Having reached the in-tray of the Director of Children's Services, someone must have flagged it up as important. But Alison tucks it out of sight in the drawer of her desk. 'Robert gave me a copy of the daughter's email to demonstrate the pressure he was under very early on to terminate your involvement with the family. We'll say no more about it.'

My shoulders sag with relief but then I frown again and turn to Robert. He clears his throat. 'I felt terrible yesterday,' he says, spreading his hands as he explains. 'But I really had no choice. It wouldn't have been fair to send you back into the family home when tensions were so high.'

'But it's okay to leave the children in that environment?'

He blows out his cheeks and looks at Alison.

'The Disclosure and Barring Service checks came back clear,' the director points out. 'But what we didn't realise was that there have been numerous call-outs to the Chambers' home address, and to Bonnie's house over the years, after reports of domestic violence from various neighbours. Normally, as you know, we'd receive a report after a DV call-out, but because Julie herself was a police officer, words of advice were given each time, but nothing was escalated. All this only came to light because Robert raised concerns yesterday after the TAC, and so more robust investigations were carried out.'

I shake my head, my stomach swooping at the thought of police officers risking the welfare of vulnerable children, simply because Julie was one of their own. 'How could they do that?'

'Julie, it seems, is a master at manipulation, Rosie. Every time, it was the same. Officers would visit the house after reports of disturbances by the neighbours, but of course, once they arrived, Julie and the children were absolutely fine. They had no idea that Ryan was the one under attack.'

I don't say anything for a moment as I absorb the shock of realising that all along Ryan was the victim. And then suddenly all the other jigsaw pieces fall into place – Ryan taking Caitlin out in his lorry, pushing her towards me when Julie claimed she wasn't feeling well. He was being protective, not abusive.

'We're conducting an unannounced welfare check on the Chambers,' Alison continues, tapping the mobile on her desk and peering at the time. 'Right about now, as it happens, and we're holding an Emergency Strategy Meeting this afternoon.'

'It was strange, the way she turned on you,' Robert adds quietly. 'It was like she was desperate to get you out of the way. I'm sorry I haven't answered your calls. I've been back-to-back, trying to get things arranged. I wanted to have something positive to tell you before we spoke again.'

I nod, relieved that I'm finally being listened to, and so grateful that the children are being checked on that my eyes well up. I blink several times, concentrating on Alison's voice so that I don't dissolve in a teary heap.

'The psychiatrist treating Bonnie wasn't able to attend the TAC meeting yesterday, but he sent a report over this morning. He paints rather a concerning picture of Julie Chambers, one that chimes with some of the things you've been saying, Rosie.'

My mouth goes dry. 'It took weeks of intense therapy to get to the point where Bonnie sees thing a bit clearly. It sounds like Julie's indoctrination was so deeply embedded in her psyche that she's still trying to untangle the addiction issues from the toxic hold that Julie holds over her. According to her psychiatrist, Julie was vindictive and abusive throughout Bonnie's childhood, but because she grew up with it she didn't recognise it as such. To her, it's just the way things were. It was once Julie's visits were suspended that Bonnie began discussing her childhood with her psychiatrist, and recognising her ordeals, and how severe they were.' Alison smiles sadly. 'And people think emotional abuse is the least damaging of all the cruelties parents can mete out on their children.

'Apparently Julie was genuinely helpful with Bonnie's children, taking care of them when she wasn't able to. But that was probably because she liked being in control. Her spite continued towards Bonnie, but when Bonnie went into hospital Caitlin became the new scapegoat.

'We're going to apply for an EPO if we can get an urgent hearing at court. Are you available to take them straight away, Rosie?'

If granted by the court, an Emergency Protection Order would allow social services to remove the children from the Chambers' care immediately. The enforced removal of children from their family home understandably evokes high emotions and so police officers usually attend to support social workers. If parents are obstructive, the EPO gives officers the power to force entry.

'Straight away? Today?'

'If we can't get a hearing, the police will take the children straight into emergency protective custody. So, yes, hopefully today. It might be very late, though.'

Chapter Thirty-Four

But when I pull up outside our house, Caitlin and Bartley are already on the doorstep.

Disorientated, I scan our front garden for a police officer or social worker. Then I realise they must have come alone. 'Please don't tell anyone, Rosie.' Caitlin leaps up from the step as soon as I climb out of the car. 'Please don't send us back!'

She collapses into my arms and sobs. I wrap my arms around her, glancing at Bartley over her shoulder. He's scowling, his face turned away. 'Honey, no one's sending you back,' I reassure her when she pulls away. I glance at my mobile to check the time. It's just before midday. 'You ran away from school?'

She takes a shaky breath, looking like she might burst into tears again. I can see the fear in her eyes. She's not a natural rebel.

Bartley gets to his feet and looks at me. 'We had to.'

'Well, I'm very glad you came here.' I put an arm around Caitlin's shoulder. Then another thought occurs to me. 'Where's Ethan?'

'Still at school,' they say in unison.

'And Louis is at home?'

They nod gloomily, their faces pale. 'Okay. It will be okay. Now come on, let's get you inside.'

'What you doing?' Bartley demands as I let them into the hall and lift the phone to my ear. He looks at Caitlin. 'She's telling! You said we could trust her! She's telling Nan we're here.'

'Bartley, it's okay. I need to let everyone know you're safe, that's all.'

He examines me for a moment, as if he's not sure whether to believe me. Caitlin's expression relaxes but her brother's remains guarded.

I could reiterate that they're both safe, but being told it doesn't mean they're going to feel it. Fear is a legitimate and natural response to the sort of experiences the children must have lived through. As child psychologists say, trauma in, trauma out. No matter how many times I reassure the children that they're safe, it's going to take time for the message to be encoded into their brains. In the meantime, I'm going to hand over as much control as I can, while ensuring they know that I'm ultimately in charge.

I dangle my keys in the air in front of him. 'Here, lock the door and keep the keys. It's the only set I have, so the only person who can open it is you.'

Bartley looks at me with wide eyes. He can't quite believe I'm handing over the reins, but then he snatches the keys from me and tries several in the lock, fumbling with shaking hands as if he's being pursued. At the sound of a heavy clunk as the lock slips into its housing, he pockets the bunch and sags against the wall. 'Come on,' I say, herding them down the hall. 'Go through to the kitchen. I've got some news for you, but you must let me make a couple of calls first, so everyone knows you're safe.'

'Thank goodness,' a voice I recognise says, when I duck into the yellow room and call the school office. It's the middle-aged, slightly uptight receptionist. 'We were about to call the police.' There's a muffled sound, as if she's slipped a hand over the mouthpiece, then I hear a hurried conversation with several urgent voices. After a click, she says, 'Are you bringing them back in?'

I know she's not going to like it when I tell her that I'll be taking advice from their social worker first. 'It doesn't matter what anyone says,' she responds primly. 'Within school hours, they need to be in school.'

'I'll keep you informed,' I say as pleasantly as possible before ending the call. Robert's line goes straight to voicemail so I leave him a hurried message telling him that the older children are with me, then I slip the phone in my pocket and walk into the kitchen. Caitlin and Bartley are pacing, their expressions anguished. They both look ready to bolt.

'It's okay, guys.' I relay a sanitised version of my meeting with the Director of Children's Services while preparing them a mug of hot chocolate each.

'We're staying here?!' Bartley exclaims, looking from me to Caitlin. 'You swear? All of us, Ethan as well? And Louis?'

'I'm not sure of the details yet, but I do know you won't be going back to your nan, not today anyway.'

Caitlin dissolves into tears again, presumably with relief. Her relationship with her grandparents is so complicated, it's hard to know for certain. I put my whisk down ready to put my arm around her, but Bartley gets to her first and pulls her into a clumsy, half-rough hug.

My heart swells at the sight. Caitlin lets out a little sob on her brother's shoulder. After a second, he pulls away. She gives him a grateful, watery smile. Embarrassed, he shoves his hands in the pockets of his trousers and kicks out at the bin.

In the living room, the siblings sit a foot apart on the sofa and clutch at their mugs as if holding on for dear life. As soon as I take the armchair, Caitlin looks at me. 'What if –' she stutters, 'what if Robert tells Nan we're here?'

The thought had already crossed my mind. The location of the foster home is usually kept under wraps for obvious reasons, but because Julie had voluntarily allowed the children to stay with me, she might have been given my address. In that case, there's every chance that the children won't be allowed to stay with me. No matter how unsettling it might be for them to move on to a carer they don't know, their safety is paramount and wouldn't be compromised. 'She won't be allowed to come anywhere near here, sweetheart,' I say with more confidence than I feel.

As I'd begun to suspect, their fears seem to be focused on Julie. There's been no mention of Ryan, no suggestion that there's any threat from him knowing their whereabouts. 'What happened?' I ask softly. 'What made you run?'

Bartley grabs Caitlin's hand. They look at each other. Caitlin nods and he takes a deep breath.

Chapter Thirty-Five

'Nan is mean to Caitlin,' he begins. 'I mean, really, really mean. All the time.'

Caitlin reddens as if she feels responsible for being singled out. 'Mean in what way?' I ask gently, when they both fall silent.

Bartley opens his mouth to speak again, but Caitlin thrusts her mug at him with a strangled wail. 'I feel really sick, Rosie,' she says, her face turning ashen.

She makes it to the kitchen sink seconds before throwing up. I rub her back and hand her a tissue. 'I'm really sorry,' she gasps, after a sip of water.

'Don't you worry, you poor thing.' I give the sink a quick rinse and spray some bleach around it. A proper clean can wait. I put my arm around her and guide her as she shuffles back to the sofa. 'Let's get you comfortable.'

Distraught, she sits shivering under a quilt. Bartley, in contrast, seems composed, but his eyes have glazed over. Knowing they're unlikely to have the energy to talk if they're hungry and tired, I offer them some lunch.

'I c-couldn't,' Caitlin stammers. 'I still feel really sick.'

Even Bartley shakes his head.

I decide to take a different tack to get them talking. 'We've all missed you these last few days. We had a lovely holiday, didn't we?'

They both nod sombrely. 'How was your weekend, after I dropped you home?'

Chewing on an already red and bloodied fingernail, Caitlin glances at her brother. He looks at me. 'You're sure we're not going back?' he demands. 'You swear on your life?'

It's tempting to offer them certainty, but I have to be honest with them. 'I can't say I'm one hundred per cent certain, Bartley, but it's highly unlikely, particularly if you have things to tell me that are concerning. All anyone wants is to make sure you're safe. If your nan's house isn't a safe place for you, you definitely won't be going back there. That's why it's important for you to summon your courage, and tell me what's been going on.'

A sob hiccoughs through Caitlin's chest and catches in her throat. Bartley takes over, telling me, tentatively at first, about his grandmother's rapidly changing moods. 'Everything can be fine, then all of a sudden she goes quiet and we know one of us has upset her.'

'Usually me,' Caitlin says quietly.

'Yep, usually her,' Bartley agrees, jerking his chin in his sister's direction. 'Nan might not do anything for days, but she has this look on her face and you know, you just know you're in for it.'

'Like the fish,' Caitlin adds ominously. She blows out a long slow breath and inhales deeply through her nostrils, trying hard to get on top of her nausea.

Bartley nods and looks at me. 'She poured bleach in the tank cos she didn't believe me when I said I'd cleaned my teeth.'

'She knew you lied,' Caitlin corrects him gently. She turns to me and explains. 'Bartley told Nan he'd got himself ready for bed but she'd already put the toothpaste on the brush earlier in the day. When she checked, it was all dried up on the brush, so she knew he hadn't done them.'

'Yeah, that don't mean she has a right to murder the fish, does it!' Bartley snaps angrily.

'Of course not.' I take a few shallow breaths, trying to chase away the nausea enveloping my own insides. 'None of this is your fault, guys. I know it's hard, but it's very good that you're telling me this. Keeping this sort of upset to yourselves doesn't do anyone any good.'

There's a pause in which they exchange glances, then Caitlin says, 'Shall we tell her what happened to Humphrey?' Her pale cheeks are tinged with green. I think the recollections are making her feel as light-headed as I'm beginning to feel.

'That was so bad.' Bartley shakes his head. Caitlin shudders.

Prickles of heat run across the back of my neck. I work hard to steady myself. They need to get everything off their chests, I know that, but I'm not sure I have the stomach to hear about more cruelty to pets. 'Nan got angry with Ethan cos he had a strop when Grandad took Caitlin to work instead of him, so she pulled Humphrey out of his tube, dragged him out by his back legs and swung him against the wall, over and over again.'

Silenced

It's an effort not to bury my face in my hands. I try hard to hide my shock but Caitlin must have noticed the horror on my face because she reaches out and pats my shoulder. 'Are you all right, Rosie? It's so awful, isn't it?'

'I went to Nan like, "How could you do that to Ethan?"' Bartley continues. 'But she just walks upstairs like nothing's happened. When Caitlin gets home she puts Humphrey back in his tube and pretends to Ethan that he'll get better.'

'I had to,' she jumps in. 'He was so upset he wet himself. I just wanted to make him all right.'

'Then a bit later Nan's like, "Have you kids done something to the hamster?"' Bartley continues. 'It was like she thought that if she acted like she hadn't done anything, then we'd believe her.'

Classic gaslighting, I think, as Bartley goes on. 'Same with the fish. Nan told Linzi I'd emptied the whole pot of food flakes in the tank but I never. She made it up.'

'Poor Ethan,' Caitlin says, fresh tears coursing down her cheeks. 'He was so scared about going back into school and facing everyone. Some of his friends were so mean about Humphrey. They thought it was his fault.'

I heave a heavy sigh. Poor Ethan indeed. Poor all of them.

'She wanted Smokey dead too,' Caitlin goes on. 'Only Grandad rescued him.'

I shake my head, trying to keep up. 'Smokey?'

'Our cat,' Caitlin nods, and then I remember the tabby she was petting when I first met her, the one Julie had referred to as Six Dinner Sid. 'Nan said he was a stray but he's not, he's ours. She just wanted him to die but Grandad sneaked to our house and got him without her knowing.'

'Where is he, then?' Bartley asks, clearly not party to the rescue mission.

'Grandad's keeping him in the lorry.'

'Cool,' Bartley says, looking unusually impressed. 'So anyway,' he carries on, his voice gathering pace, 'Nan was in an okay mood for a bit after you dropped us off on Saturday, but Caitlin kept joining in when we were telling her what we did while we were away, even after Grandad went out.'

'I was excited,' Caitlin mumbles.

'Yeah, but you made it so obvious you'd had a good time,' Bartley snaps. 'It was bound to set her off.' Caitlin's cheeks flush as if she'd committed some crime by expressing happiness. 'Like when we got back from the space centre. She was so mad about Caitlin's poster. She made me rip it up and stick it in the recycling.'

'It set her off because …' I prompt.

Bartley shrugs. 'Because she hates Caitlin, I guess. It got much worse when Mum went away. She tried to make me give Cait a cold bath the night we got back from Whitby. That always shuts her up.' He looks at me. 'But this time I said I wouldn't.'

'Oh, Caitlin. Your poor sweetheart.' The ten-year-old's head is bowed so I can't see her face but her trembling shoulders tell me she's crying again. 'But that must have been awful for you too, Bartley.'

He flushes and drops his gaze. 'I have to do what she says, otherwise she does it to me.' I suddenly remember his agonised expression in Whitby as he tried to express his frustration about lashing out … *I don't have a choice.*

My throat tightens with guilt. I'd completely misunderstood, assuming he meant that he struggled to contain his feelings of anger. Julie had been Bartley's puppet master, forcing him to mete out punishments on her behalf.

Abuse by proxy is a sickening act used by sadistic parents to protect themselves from allegations. Foster carers, teachers and others responsible for the welfare of children are trained to look out for signs of non-accidental injuries – multiple bruises in different stages of healing, particularly in unlikely, non-bony regions of the body, or on non-mobile babies, burns, bites or binding injuries, and implausible explanations for any of the above – but the picture becomes hazy if a child explains that their injuries were the result of an innocent tussle with siblings. It's the perfect cover story. Or it was, until professionals became wise to the tactic.

I'm guessing that our two weeks in Whitby had broken the habit Julie had indoctrinated Bartley into, and shown him another way.

'He was so brave this time, saying no to her.' Caitlin gives him a grateful glance. 'But she was so angry with him she … s-she hurt him with her straighteners. Show her, Bartley.'

Still keeping his gaze averted, Bartley cautiously eases up the sleeve of his blazer. I catch sight of a large red welt above his pale wrist and my hand flies to my mouth automatically, before I can stop it. Immediately, he drops his sleeve and covers it up. 'Bartley,' I say eventually, 'we need to get that arm dressed and bandaged.'

'It's fine, doesn't even hurt,' he says with a trace of his old swagger. His eyes, however, tell a different story. He looks traumatised, although bravely he goes on to tell me about how the day progressed. 'She's not usually this aggy with me.'

It's hard to believe that a child could possibly describe being burnt with a pair of straighteners as 'aggy'. Then again, it never ceases to amaze me how adept children are at normalising behaviour, however extreme. It reminds me of the metaphor of the boiling frog that Des always uses to explain why victims of domestic abuse often don't realise the dangerous situation they're in.

He says that if you drop a frog in a vat of hot water, it will do its best to jump out. If, however, it's swimming around a saucepan of tepid water that's put on a low heat, it slowly adjusts to its surroundings, never recognising that it's slowly being boiled to death.

'Nan hates it when we include Caitlin in anything,' Bartley explains, his own cheeks flushing with shame. 'I felt bad about it sometimes, but if I don't do what she says I end up getting shit done to me.'

'She's normally nice to Bartley and the others,' Caitlin adds with a puzzled expression. 'And sometimes she's even nice to me.'

My heart feels so heavy for them that it's a job to hold back my own tears. I suspect that Julie was nice to Caitlin on occasion to manipulate her emotions and confuse her even more. Or strategically, before handing her over to me, for example, or sweetening her up before sending her off to school, so that she'd be less likely to confide in a teacher. The hugs I watched Julie bestow on her granddaughter suddenly come to mind, followed by Caitlin's tears.

The picture I had been building in my mind since spending the day with Julie was a bed of roses compared to the actual reality. Life can be so unfair sometimes. Such lovely children deserve to be treasured, not ridiculed and terrorised. I move to the sofa. Sitting between them, I blot Caitlin's tears with a tissue and then pat Bartley's knee. 'You poor kids. I'm so sorry you had to go through all of that.'

My stomach cramps at the idea of the children having to endure such cruelty, and I suspect that today's disclosures are only the tip of the iceberg. It's clear that Caitlin had borne the brunt of Julie's aggression, but living with someone who was loving one minute and vicious the next would have been torturous and bewildering for all the children.

I recall sitting opposite Julie in her kitchen and chatting with her over a cup of tea. There was no hard edge to her smile. No cold and calculated stare. It wasn't until I'd spent a protracted amount of time in her company that alarm bells really started ringing. It's unsettling to know that, on first meeting the grandmother, I'd liked her.

I'm supposed to be attuned to the needs of children, yet the Powells had been suffering right under my nose and I simply hadn't had a clue. It's hard not to feel guilty about that.

But then again, snapshots of family life can be so misleading. I always think of the photographs of Victoria Climbié that were released after her death at the hands of a relative, with a beautiful beaming smile on her face.

'What about Grandad?' Gathering evidence against birth family members is way outside my remit as a foster carer. Apart from the risk of being accused of putting words into their mouths, children are prone to telling grown-ups what they think they'd like to hear. Asking open questions is a wiser way to get them talking.

'Grandad takes me out when things get really bad,' Caitlin says. 'But then I feel terrible because Nan takes it out on him.'

A picture of the cut above Ryan's eye when I first met him comes into my mind. His broken nose and taped-up fingers. All explained away as rugby injuries or fights down the pub. How could I not have realised it before?

'You mustn't feel bad about any of this,' I reiterate, though I know that emotional abuse is so ingrained and internalised that it will take time for the children to accept that they are not responsible, and that their grandmother is entirely at fault.

I have hope that it won't take too long. Those two short weeks in Whitby show how quickly children can adjust, given a calm atmosphere.

They both fall silent, looking exhausted.

'Time's getting on. Can I tempt you into some lunch now?'

'I could eat,' Bartley says, but Caitlin shudders.

'I can't face anything. I still feel so sick.'

Bartley tucks hungrily into a ham sandwich a few minutes later. When I hand Caitlin a plate with a few triangles of toast on it, she shakes her head. 'I don't think I can.'

'Maybe just have a bite or two, sweetie. It might help the nausea.'

Looking unconvinced, she nibbles on a crust tentatively and sips her drink. After a couple of minutes her colour restores. She eats some more. When she's finished, she takes a breath and gives me a brave smile.

'It took a lot of courage for you to come here and tell me all of this. I'm proud of you.' My voice cracks so I don't say any more for a moment or two. I've heard many disclosures from children over the years and my heart breaks every single time. I squeeze Bartley's hand. 'You've been very brave too, honey.'

'Victim of my own brilliance, aren't I?' he shrugs. After a second, he grins. 'Jamie says that.'

'Oh, Bartley.' I chuckle, wiping a finger under my eye. 'You do make me laugh.'

Chapter Thirty-Six

'I wasn't sure you'd come,' Des says as I approach the table in our local Italian restaurant. He smiles and gets to his feet, looking relieved. It's almost nine thirty. I'd usually be winding down and getting into my PJs by now, but Des was keen for us to talk away from the house. He cups my elbow and plants a kiss on my cheek. 'I wouldn't blame you if you'd stood me up,' he adds, as we sit opposite each other. I switch my mobile to silent and pop it on the table in case Emily needs me.

'Don't be daft. I just wanted to make sure the children were settled before I left them with Emily.' I trust my daughter completely. She's more than capable of dealing with any situation that might arise, whether it's a meltdown, tummy upset or a bad dream, but it didn't seem fair to leave the children before they were asleep, not after everything they'd been through in the last 24 hours.

Our GP, who has always been accommodating over the years, very kindly agreed to squeeze us in for an emergency appointment so that Bartley's burn could be checked. Dr Kenwick is a rotund, jolly character who did his best to put

Bartley at ease, but like most children who are worried about causing trouble for their family the 11-year-old closed down as soon as we stepped into the consulting room. It took a good deal of cajoling before he'd even roll up his sleeve. When he finally agreed, Dr Kenwick took one look, quickly covered it with a dressing and referred us on to Accident & Emergency.

On arrival at the hospital, I had a quiet word with the triage nurse. After substantiating our story with a call to social services, she filled in the medical staff before waving us in for treatment, so that Bartley wouldn't be subjected to dozens of uncomfortable questions. Still, his cheeks were puce as the consultant sought advice from the specialist burns team.

For all his bluster, the look of fear on his face as his wounds were tended to brought home to me just how young he still is. In full view, his injury looked as if someone had slipped a bangle a couple of inches thick over his forearm. The sight of his poor skin, swollen and puckered with blisters, brought tears to my eyes.

My rage at Julie was partly soothed when Robert called to say that the children had been booked in to see the police surgeon the next day, but I still don't have much of an appetite.

Des holds up his hand. 'You don't have to explain. I'm just happy I'm forgiven.' He looks at me. 'I *am* forgiven, aren't I?'

My throat tightens at the reminder of the difficult times ahead. I'd been so busy getting the children settled that I'd managed to push my worries about my mum to the back of my mind.

Misreading my hesitation, Des's expression crumples. 'Sweetheart, I'm so sorry. I didn't know what to do for the best.'

'Des, it's okay, really, I understand why you did it.'

He orders a shandy and glugs it down in one go. We get a chance to catch up on how his own caseload is holding up before ordering our meals, but then my phone buzzes. I slip outside to take the call. 'That was Jenny's nephew,' I explain, when I join Des again. 'He's a plumber. He's going to squeeze a loo in under the stairs.'

'After all my hard work building you a sensory cave?'

I pull a face. 'I know, I'm sorry.'

He fakes annoyance, but then he pats my hand. 'I'm kidding. For your mum, I'm guessing? She'll be moving in?'

I nod and take a sip of my fizzy elderflower water. I'd already spoken to our local hospice and the palliative care team had confirmed that they would be able to provide support at home as her disease progressed.

'And she's agreed to this?'

'I spoke to her earlier. She huffed and puffed, said she didn't want me going to all that trouble and what a lot of fuss and nonsense, you know her. But yes, she agreed. She sounded relieved actually.'

He smiles sadly. 'I'm glad. But where will she kip? You've already got a houseful.'

'It'll be a tight squeeze,' I smile, 'but it's nothing we haven't managed before.'

Emily had tearfully offered up her bedroom when I broke it to her that her nan was unwell. When working night shifts, she often stays at her colleague's flat around the corner from the hospital where she's far more likely to get a decent daytime sleep. She said she could do that every night, or sleep on the sofa at home. It was kind of her, but I'd already decided Mum would be better off in the yellow room, since it's downstairs.

I know that the weeks ahead will be hectic, but after making the arrangements I feel like a weight has been lifted. Having my mum close will give me something practical to do to help her, and since hearing the children's disclosures, my queasy anxiety about them has eased as well. What they've gone through is horrific, but now it's out in the open they'll never have to go through anything like it again.

I had emailed a detailed report after Bartley and Caitlin's surprise visit, and with an EPO secured in court, Ethan and little Louis were driven straight to me. In a hurried conversation at teatime on Zoom, Robert told me that when social workers and a police officer arrived at Julie's and demanded immediate entry they'd found Louis trussed to his potty with rope.

I tried not to let my eyes dwell on the welts on his pudgy limbs as I got him ready for bed. It was too enraging. I gave him an extra tight hug as I gave him some warm milk instead. Sitting beside his cot and stroking his hair as he dropped off to sleep, I began cooking up plans to help the relationship between Bartley and Caitlin fully heal.

I'm itching to tuck all four of them up on the sofa on a Sunday afternoon after a long walk by the river, and to generally make a fuss of them so they realise how special they are. 'Robert said –' I begin, but right on cue my phone buzzes again. I give Des an apologetic look. 'It's him, their social worker.'

'Take it. Honestly, don't worry. I'll order another beer.'

I rush outside. 'Sorry to call you again so soon,' Robert says, sounding slightly harassed. The media often represents social workers in a negative light but I've found most, even those I've fundamentally disagreed with, are totally dedicated to the children they're assigned. I know that over a quarter of the caseworkers in our local authority are currently on long-term sick leave. Those remaining are under even more pressure because they have to pick up the slack. That often means working late into the evening. It's not unusual to receive phone calls and emails from social workers past ten or sometimes eleven o'clock at night. 'Julie's been arrested. I thought you'd want to know.'

'Goodness. Right, yes, thanks.'

'How are they?'

'They're with my daughter at the moment,' I tell him a little guiltily. 'She is an official back-up carer.'

'It's fine, Rosie. You have my full confidence.' There's a pause and then he adds, 'Look, I'm sorry about disregarding your concerns.' He hesitates and then adds, 'I appear to have been somewhat taken in.'

'I was too, at first. She's quite the actress.'

'She had me blindsided, if I'm honest. I thought she was lovely, a thoroughly nice, decent woman. You must be very tempted to say I told you so.'

'Not at all.' I would have loved to have been wrong about the pain and suffering the children went through, but being validated is not unpleasant, I have to admit.

'Well, that's very magnanimous of you, thank you.' There's another pause and then he gives me some news that I know Caitlin will love. 'Bonnie's psychiatrist has been in touch. She'd like contact as soon as possible. They've suggested tomorrow. I know the children have their child protection medical and interview in the morning, so I wasn't sure how you'd feel about them having contact in the afternoon. Will it all be a bit too much?'

'I think it'll be lovely after what they've got to endure in the morning.'

'How do you think they'll cope?'

'With the interview? I think they'll be okay.' I'm pleased that Robert is finally interested in my opinion. 'I suspect we've barely scratched the surface in terms of disclosures, though.'

'I think you're right, I'm sorry to say. I suspect there's a whole lot more to come out. I just hope Ryan isn't implicated. Has there been any indication of that, from what you've heard?'

'None at all,' I say, turning away from diners leaving the restaurant, so as not to be overheard. 'He seems to have been a protective influence, as far as I can tell.'

'If that's the case,' Robert says, 'they may not be with you for too long. Ryan is keen to care for them, and Linzi, of course. As long as everything checks out, we'll restore them to his care at the earliest opportunity.'

I heave a sigh as I make my way back into the restaurant, not really knowing what to feel. Part of me is sad that they won't be staying longer, but in my heart of hearts I know that it won't be easy to care for my mum and dedicate the time and attention to them that they'll need. Besides, it's usually in a child's best interests to stay with their family if they possibly can.

'What I can't understand is why someone would offer to take care of children, only to be cruel to them,' I say without preamble, when I join Des again. 'Why not refuse and give them the chance of going to people who want to take good care of them?' As a social worker and my back-up carer, I feel able to discuss some aspects of fostering with Des, without going into specific details that he doesn't need to know.

Des considers me carefully. 'I know you can't bear to accept it, but some people enjoy being cruel. The sense of power sends a rush to their head. And of course, the crueller they are, the more the children withdraw and the less they react, so the punishments get more sadistic to elicit the same reaction.'

I shake my head. 'You're right, I suppose. I don't want to believe it. You know what, though. I never thought I'd say it, but I think physical abuse might actually be less traumatic than emotional. At least Bartley has something tangible to focus his heartbreak on. I worry about Caitlin most of all.'

'Parental alienation is every bit as damaging as physical abuse,' Des agrees. 'But even though the others may have got off lighter than Caitlin, they'll have suffered secondary trauma, simply from being bystanders. And from what I know about Bartley's involvement, he'll be suffering all sorts of guilt and shame. They'll all need referrals to CAMHS.'

I sigh again. The waiting list for an initial consultation with Child and Adolescent Mental Health Services stands at around 18 months in our area. A child has to be suicidal to receive immediate mental health support.

'I just wish I could make it all better for them.'

'Ach, there's nothing you can do to take their pain away. I guess all you can do is be there for them and let them know they're not alone.' He takes another swig of beer and then smiles at me. 'Which is exactly what I plan to do for you in the coming months.'

My phone buzzes on the table again. Our time together is often interrupted by the needs of fostering and family. Des has always understood and agreed that the children come first, no matter what, but sometimes I feel bad about it. I'm not sure he realises how important he is to me. I grimace and shake my head. Des laughs. 'Take it, I don't mind.'

I check the screen. It's an 0800 number I'm happy to ignore. 'I don't know why you put up with me sometimes,' I say, turning the handset over to hide the flashing light. 'You must be potty.'

'Rosie.' He reaches out, takes my hand in his and meets my gaze. 'I really don't know either.'

I giggle and take a sip of my drink. He grins and squeezes my hand. 'I think I must be crazy then, because I still really want to marry you.'

Chapter Thirty-Seven

My hands grip the steering wheel tightly the next morning, Thursday 25 April, as I drive Caitlin and Bartley towards the police interview suite. Sadly, it's a place I've taken a number of children to over the years, when their injuries have been consistent with abuse.

The most difficult child protection medicals are those carried out when sexual abuse is indicated. With the potential of re-traumatising the child all over again, internal examinations are avoided if at all possible. Often, by the time the child arrives in foster care, it's too late for forensic evidence to be secured and, thankfully, I've only supported a few children through that particular experience over the years.

Some medicals are carried out in the paediatric department of our local hospital, but today we've been booked in to have an interview and examination all in one place.

After breakfast I'd explained to Caitlin and Bartley that they wouldn't be going to school because a special interviewer wanted to talk to them about what it was like living with Julie, and that a doctor would also like to take some photographs of Bartley's injury. They'd greeted the news of a day off school with enthusiasm at first, but had grown increasingly withdrawn after we got back from dropping Megan off.

Before setting off on the 30-minute drive to the interview suite, I'd asked Caitlin if she wanted to bring the bear she'd been taking to bed. She'd glanced warily in Bartley's direction before dashing upstairs to fetch it. I found myself tensing as she came back down, waiting for him to look her up and down with smug amusement on his face. I think we were both equally surprised when it didn't happen, and even more shocked by his next words. 'Got any more of those knocking around?'

Only too happy to oblige, I let him have a rummage through the bear suitcase. He chose one small enough to fit in the palm of his hand. 'Ready then?'

He'd nodded. 'Built for battle, me.'

But when we reach our destination and park up, he looks close to tears. 'We're definitely getting McDonald's after, yeah?' He chews on his lip as he waits for an answer and my heart goes out to him.

I remember reading somewhere that a child's concept of time makes it hard for them to tolerate difficult experiences, because they're less able to visualise an ending to their discomfort or pain. When caring for younger children, I often make use of sand timers. If, for example, a child with sensory issues finds cleaning their teeth unbearable, I'll either set a timer so they can 'see' how much brushing time is left, or pull a nursery rhyme up on YouTube and ask them to keep going for the duration of the song.

Bartley, bless him, is working hard to self-soothe; giving his mind something to focus on to get him through whatever the next couple of hours will bring.

'We most definitely are, honey.' On the whole I try to stick to home-cooked healthy foods but I'd promised them a treat for lunch, something to look forward to. I know they're excited to see their mum, but there's some anxiety there as well. Studies have shown that salty foods limit the production of stress hormones like cortisol, and if ever there's a time for comfort food, it's today.

The interview suite is housed in a detached bungalow on an ordinary suburban street. We're greeted in reception by a smiling young police officer dressed casually in T-shirt, leggings and flip-flops. 'Hi, guys, I'm Ciara, I'll take you through to meet Jess and Mark.'

She leads us down a bright hallway, past several closed doors. Having been given a tour of the place several years ago, I know that some rooms are reserved for interviewing while others are fitted with sound and video equipment, all discreetly tucked out of the way so that children aren't intimidated by the sight.

Ciara shows us into a room at the back of the house. Cleverly presented as a classic living room with two sofas facing each other and a coffee table between them with books and a pack of cards on, it's a warm and cosy space. My eyes settle on a large smoked-glass mirror on the wall down one end, behind which lies the room with the recording equipment. The two sets of doors opposite open onto a large garden with neat lawns. There's a swing and slide and a basketball net and football goal on the other side.

'Can we go out there?'

The male officer waiting in the room smiles at Bartley. Older than Ciara but also dressed casually in a hoodie and tracksuit bottoms, there's nothing to hint at his official role, something I'm sure is intentional. 'I'll give you a knockabout later, mate, if you like. I'm Mark, and this is Jess.'

'Hi, Bartley, hi, Caitlin.' Around the same age and in jeans and a rugby top, Jess smiles warmly. 'We need to get through some stuff first.' She pauses and looks from one to the other. 'You both understand why you're here today?'

Caitlin nods politely.

'Let's get it out the way, yeah,' Mark suggests, 'then we'll go outside.' Bartley shrugs. 'Good lad. Right, feel free to grab yourself some squash and biscuits,' he says, tilting his head towards a sideboard. 'Ciara and I will take you to see the doc, Bartley, just for a quick check-over, and Jess here will have a chat with Caitlin. Cool?'

Uncertain, Bartley looks at me. 'It's okay,' Mark assures him. 'We can show Rosie where you'll be if you'd like?'

Mark takes a few steps towards the door but Bartley doesn't move. 'Come on, love.' I slip my arm around him, guiding him towards the officer.

'Rosie will wait for you in the room next to this one, okay,' Mark tells him when we reach the paediatric consultant's office. 'You'll be fine, I promise. It's just a few photos.'

I give Bartley's shoulder what I hope is a reassuring squeeze. 'I'll see you soon, sweetheart.' He gives me a mournful look over his shoulder as he follows Mark and Ciara into the room. I notice his fists closed tight around

Mum's bear. I hope it works as a talisman and gives him strength.

Mark emerges a few seconds later. 'Would you like to join me in here?' he says in a hushed voice. He shows me into the office adjoining the living room where Caitlin is being interviewed and gestures for me to take a seat on the swivel chair next to his.

I can see Caitlin through the two-way mirror, but also on a flat screen monitor on the desk in front of us. Looking tense, she nods as Jess makes small talk next to her on the sofa. For several minutes she doesn't say a word. It's only when the officer hands her a pot of putty that the muscles in her face soften. 'See how many marbles you can find in there,' Jess says. 'It won't be easy though, I'm telling you.'

The effect of the distraction is instant. 'It's so stiff!' Caitlin grins, her shoulders dropping as she digs her fingers into the pot.

'I know! I love this stuff!' Jess takes a pot for herself. She's clearly skilled at getting children to open up, focusing her gaze on the putty instead of on Caitlin. 'So, what are your favourite subjects at school?'

'It's a tricky balancing act,' Mark tells me quietly. 'Dressing the interview up like a casual conversation while making sure all the proper procedures are followed at the same time. She's good, though, Jess is. I've never seen her fail yet.'

Sure enough, Caitlin glances at her and says, 'Science.'

'Oh, I used to love science!'

Caitlin smiles. 'Physics is my favourite. Miss Jackson does some extra stuff, astrophysics and all that, because she knows I love astronomy.'

'She sounds like a cool teacher.'

Caitlin nods.

'So you enjoy school?'

She shrugs. 'Mostly.'

'And what about home?'

Caitlin shakes her head. 'Not since Mum's been gone.'

'You've been staying with your grandparents?'

She nods again. 'We stayed there a lot anyway, or Nan stayed with us at our house because Mum gets sick a lot.'

'I'm sorry to hear that. Can you tell me a bit about what it's like, staying with your grandparents?'

'It's not bad for the others, mostly, but it's hard for me.'

'In what way hard?'

I hold myself stiff as I listen, willing Caitlin to open up.

'Nan doesn't like me,' she says, flushing a deep red. 'And she makes the others hate me too.'

'What sort of thing does she do?' Jess asks gently while studiously pulling marbles from her pot of putty.

Caitlin looks down at the pot resting on her own lap. 'On good days she just ignores me. I'm not allowed to talk, or sit at the table with everyone else, or have dinner, or watch TV, that sort of thing.' I swallow over the lump rising in my throat and will her to say more.

Jess's expression remains neutral, as if what Caitlin has told her is no big deal. 'And on bad days?'

'She gets Bartley to hurt me.'

'Tell me more about that.'

My heart thumps as my gaze flicks from the two-way mirror to the screen, waiting for her to reply. 'He holds me under the water so I can't breathe,' she says eventually. 'Nan puts ice in the bath. It prickles when I lay on it. It hurts all over.' Her matter-of-fact tone makes my heart break even more. 'But I actually don't mind that too much now, I've kind of got used to it. My head goes all fuzzy after a bit, then I start seeing these fluffy white clouds and the pain stops, and then I don't feel anything at all.'

Chapter Thirty-Eight

I look at Mark, horrified. No wonder the poor child had been petrified at my suggestion of a bath. It sounded as if she'd been close to passing out under the water. Mark merely shakes his head. Perhaps it's nothing he hasn't heard before.

'How does Nan get Bartley to do these things?' Jess presses on in a neutral voice.

'She gives him stuff, mostly. She bought him a new phone and gets him whatever he wants. The more horrible he is to me, the nicer she is to everyone else. He said no a few times, but then she took it out on him.'

Jess makes a noise of acknowledgement, encouraging Caitlin to continue, but she still doesn't look at her. 'I hate that most of all,' Caitlin continues. 'I'd rather she did stuff to me. The worst is when she's mean to Louis, though.'

'What does she do to Louis?' Jess asks carefully, trying to establish the facts so that there's no ambiguity, no wriggle room for Julie's defence to pounce on if the case gets to court.

'Ties him up in his buggy, or to a chair. Stuff like that. And she puts chilli powder on his tongue when he's having a strop. He used to be her favourite but not any more. I try to stop her sometimes, but it just ends up getting worse and worse.'

'And what about Grandad?' Jess asks casually, after a small pause. 'What does Grandad do when this is going on?' My hands wring one over the other, hoping that Ryan isn't part of the abuse.

'Nan only does really bad stuff when he goes away. She's less mean when he's home but she still picks on me. If it gets too bad, he takes me to work with him, then he gets clobbered when he gets back.' Caitlin lifts her head and looks at Jess. 'C-can I see Rosie now?'

'Very soon, sweetheart. So, what is it about space that interests you?'

Caitlin's frown dissolves. 'It kind of makes the bad stuff seem less bad I suppose, I don't know why. When we went on holiday, we did the best stargazing. The sky is darker in Whitby so we saw loads more stars than usual. And I saw planets.'

'That sounds like fun!' Jess smiles. 'What got you hooked?'

'My dad used to take me.'

'He *used* to?'

Caitlin nods. 'I don't get to see him now.'

'How come?'

'Grandad won't let him come round.' I look at Mark and my heart sinks. The police officer leans forward, watching the screen intently.

'Why's that?'

'Because Dad and Nan, you know ...'

'What?'

'They, you know,' she whispers, her voice barely audible through the monitor, 'did gross grown-up stuff with each other.'

My heart leaps into my throat, but Jess manages a neutral tone. 'I see.' She doesn't say any more, letting a silent pause do the work for her. It only takes a few seconds and then Caitlin blurts out, 'Nan told Grandad that Dad attacked her but it's not true,' she sobs, tears streaming down her face. 'It's not true.' She shakes her head. 'I know it's not true.' She sniffs and takes some deep breaths, then gives Jess an agonised look. 'Please can I see Rosie now?'

'I just have a couple more questions, then you can.'

'I'm so tired,' she says. 'I just want to go to Rosie's house.'

'I'm sorry, sweetheart, but it's really important that we understand exactly what happened, okay?'

Caitlin sucks in a shaky breath and nods tearily. I know Jess is a professional and she's trying to secure as much evidence as possible so that Caitlin doesn't have to go through this ordeal again, but all I want to do is charge in there and scoop her up and bring an end to her upset.

'How do you know, sweetie, about the grown-up stuff?'

'Because I saw them doing it,' she mutters. 'They were downstairs, but Nan knew I was there.'

Her disclosure makes me shudder. It seems like Julie was determined to torture Caitlin in whatever way she could. Mark and I exchange glances. 'Not easy to hear,' he says softly. 'But it's fantastic. She's done so well.'

I know he's right. The evidence has been recorded,

hopefully sparing them the upset of having to attend court in person, but I still feel sick to my stomach. Poor Caitlin. She shakes her head when Jess asks about other grown-ups coming into the house and whether she's ever felt threatened by anyone else. Her eyes are glazed over. She's clearly reached her limit.

I dash out the door as soon as Jess brings the interview to an end. When Caitlin emerges and sees me in the hallway, she falls into my arms and sobs.

We play snakes and ladders when she's calmed down and, true to his word, Mark takes them into the garden for a game of football when Bartley's interview is over.

'Bartley corroborated Caitlin's version of events,' Jess tells me in the kitchen after making me a cup of tea. 'It seems his nan plied him with stuff to make him do her bidding. Compliance meant a new phone, more screen time, whatever gadgets he wanted. Non-compliance meant he'd suffer the abuse himself. What 11-year-old could cope with that? He was as powerless to stop it as Caitlin, poor lad. But they were both superb in their testimony.'

I glance out the window and watch the siblings as they pass the ball to each other and try to get past Mark to the goal. 'So what happens now?'

'We'll pass the file to the CPS and await their charging decision. There's plenty to go on. The children's accounts match up so it'll be pretty hard to dismiss. I'm sure that several charges will stick. We'll interview Bonnie, of course, when she's up to it. If this is how the woman treats her grandchildren, can you imagine what their mum went through when she was a child?'

Silenced

I shake my head. I'd been thinking the same. 'Must be hard, having to interview children who've been through horrors like that.'

Jess sighs. 'Part of me hates putting them through it. What keeps me going is the thought of people like their grandmother getting their just deserts.'

It's a relief when we're back in the fresh, cool air.

'Right, McDonald's here we come,' I say lightly, putting my arms around the two of them. 'What do you say?'

They both look exhausted, but Bartley manages a cheeky grin. 'Would be rude not to,' he says, then adds the inevitable, 'Jamie says that.'

Chapter Thirty-Nine

'Are we nearly there, Rosie?' Caitlin asks anxiously from the back of the car. I'm not sure whether it's the prospect of contact with her mum, or the relief of knowing that she doesn't have to endure abuse at the hands of her grandmother any longer, but she's been chatty and animated since the drive-thru at McDonald's, barely stopping to draw breath between sentences. Perhaps it's a mixture of the two.

Her brother, in contrast, has barely said a word. Staring pensively out of the window, it's almost as if he and his sister have swapped personalities.

'Ten minutes away,' I smile, turning onto the single-track road that leads to Sandfields. The bright blue sky disappears behind the canopy of overhanging trees and Caitlin falls silent for the first time since leaving home.

I'm feeling quite nervous about meeting Bonnie myself. It's not easy for parents to accept that their children are being looked after outside of their own family. Emotions often run high, particularly when mental health issues are thrown into the mix. Robert assures me that Bonnie's medication is working well, though, and it will be good for the children to see us together.

Children often find it easier to settle in placement when they know there's no animosity between their foster carer and birth parents. No matter what trauma they've been through at home, most children remain fiercely loyal to their parents. Some even concoct alternative histories for themselves, because the reality of being rejected by some-one so close is simply too painful to acknowledge.

As the black wrought-iron entrance gates of the hospital come into view, I'm hit with a memory of bringing baby Sarah here to see her birth mother years ago. The skyline has changed considerably since then with all the building work of the last decade, classy new apartment buildings standing alongside the main country house.

Part of the extensive plot was sold off to developers some years back. The funds were used to improve the aesthetics of the main hospital building and the luxury flats dotted between treatment hubs give patients the sense that they're still part of the community, rather than feeling removed from it. The whole place is designed to resemble a local town or university campus, and most in-patients are free to mingle with the general public in the grounds and the tree-lined streets. The shops, all run by qualified mental health nurses, are open for business from patients and private residents. Based on an innova-tive Scandinavian model, the set-up is supposed to make reintegration back into the community less of a daunting leap for patients.

It's reassuring to know that progress is being made in the bid to improve fragmented mental health services.

Things have certainly come a long way since vulnerable and traumatised patients were branded lunatics, bound up in straitjackets and fed a cocktail of drugs to make them easier to manage.

Clever planting of tall ornamental grasses and palm trees makes the main hospital building look more like a sprawling beach-front property than a secure psychiatric unit. Aside from the barbed wire stretched across the top of the boundary walls, a discreet sign saying 'Sandfields' and the familiar blue and white logo of the NHS is one of the few clues as to the nature of the facility.

It's a beautifully calming venue and I find my own nerves steadying as we climb out of the car.

Caitlin and I make our way towards the entrance. I turn and wait for Bartley to catch up. 'You all right, sweetheart?'

'Soldier, aren't I, ready for anything,' he blags, but he leans his head docilely against me when I slip an arm around his shoulder.

The large reception area is much brighter than I remember, the old bleakness softened by a makeover in pastel shades. With its fabric couches, fur throws and colourful cushions, the place resembles a swish hotel, albeit one with a rather strong antiseptic scent. The partitioned office to our left looks familiar, although the old wooden hatch of the past has been replaced with a glass screen. Just as I press the buzzer, a young man appears and checks my ID.

Our bags are searched after we sign in. Caitlin grips my hand as we're introduced to the social worker who has the task of supervising contact and then reporting back to Robert. A middle-aged woman with short curly hair, she smiles warmly at the children. 'I'm Karen. I'll be sitting with you today.'

Her kindly, gentle manner seems to have a soothing effect on Caitlin. She releases my hand and follows the social worker along a bright corridor with inspirational quotes on the walls.

Bartley stays rooted to the spot. 'Rosie, can you stay?'

'If that's what you want, of course I will,' I soothe, putting my arm around him again. I'm supposed to join Robert and Ryan for a meeting but I can feel Bartley's whole body shaking. I won't leave him until he's ready to let me go. After all they've been through and the long separation from their mum, a reunion somewhere so outside of their everyday experience is a lot for them to cope with, no matter how comfortable the surroundings. 'Must feel funny, coming to a place like this, and I know it's been weeks since you've seen her, but she's still the same mum, sweetheart.'

He nods bravely and falls into step beside me.

Karen turns her head as we hurry after her. 'Far end of the corridor,' she says over her shoulder. 'She's waiting for you.'

Caitlin starts running. Never one to be beaten, whatever the circumstances, Bartley breaks into a sprint. Their trainers pound the floor until they run out of corridor and come to an abrupt stop.

'It's okay, you can go in,' Karen encourages when we catch them up. She gives a brief tap on the door and goes in. A smell of new paint greets us as the social worker props the door open. The large open space in front of us has the same set-up as our local family centre where contact is usually held. The only difference is that our contact rooms are slightly shabby, whereas this place has obviously been recently refurbished. Tall arched windows throw lots of light into the space, and floor-to-ceiling shelves full of games and huge potted ferns give the room a homely feel.

My eyes settle on the slight, hollow-faced woman biting her nails on one of the sofas. The family resemblance is unmistakable. Bonnie's dark-brown hair is pulled back in a ponytail, giving her a youthful appearance. She's painfully thin and fragile looking. 'Mum!' Caitlin cries.

Bonnie's head jerks up. Almost instantly, she bursts into tears. She gets to her feet and opens her arms. Caitlin rushes over and they fall into a hug.

Rooted to the spot, Bartley watches them with an intense expression. 'Bart?' Bonnie says after a few seconds, lifting an arm towards him. He flies towards her then. The three of them clutch each other and sob.

I don't try too hard to stop my own tears flowing. 'I'm a mess,' I say apologetically, when Karen hands me a tissue.

She gives me a sympathetic, slightly watery smile. 'Occupational hazard for both of us.'

Chapter Forty

Huddled together on the sofa with their mum, Caitlin and Bartley give me an unconcerned nod when I tell them I'm going to a meeting. Karen stays with them to supervise, and a nurse in scrubs and white crocs escorts me along a maze of corridors to an outdoor seating area. It's a lovely space, bird boxes fixed at intervals along an ivy-covered wall, and there's a vegetable patch down one end.

'They'll be out shortly,' the woman tells me with an efficient bob of her head, before disappearing inside. Robert emerges a minute or so later, dressed in his usual colourful jacket and cravat. Ryan follows him, his head bent low. A leggy, bearded gentleman in a smart suit is last out. Around 50 or so, he shakes our hands in turn, introducing himself as Professor Copthorne, consultant psychiatrist, then takes a seat at the head of a small table.

Ryan sits between the psychiatrist and Robert, and I take one of the metal chairs directly opposite the grandfather. After a minute or so of small talk, Robert confirms that Julie is still in police custody. 'Ryan is keen to take care of the children,' he explains, looking at the professor, 'but obviously we need to know how Bonnie feels about the arrangement.'

Ryan keeps his gaze lowered. However abusive Julie has been, she is still the mother of his child. It can't be easy, knowing that life will never be the same again.

'For confidentiality reasons I can't go into great detail,' Professor Copthorne says, 'but I can tell you that I've shared the children's disclosures with their mother. While she's extremely upset to hear what's been going on, there's a lot she's come to realise about her mother's potential to inflict harm.

'As you probably know, children acclimatise themselves to their surroundings exceptionally well. While this may help them survive their immediate situation, it sadly prevents them from recognising how dysfunctional it is. I know Bonnie won't object to me saying that she used drugs and alcohol –' he breaks off as a thin, track-suited young woman in Nike trainers shuffles past our table. When she's out of earshot, he clears his throat and continues, 'She depended on substances to cope with her mother's ongoing abuse. Not that she recognised it as such. Sadly, her addiction offered her mother yet another stick to beat her with, metaphorically speaking, because in some ways Julie was right. After years of being controlled and undermined, Bonnie did struggle to cope.

'Her self-esteem is in tatters. She desperately wants to see the children, but she's fearful about how she'll cope. I've asked Karen, the social worker supervising their contact today, to give us a quick update as to how the session is progressing. She'll be along soon, when someone's free to relieve her.'

Robert leans forward and gives the professor a questioning look. 'Does Bonnie support Ryan in his application to take care of the children?'

'Most certainly.' Professor Copthorne inclines his head and addresses Ryan directly. 'Bonnie tells me that you have been a protective influence in all of their lives. She's more than happy for the children to return to your care.'

Ryan covers his eyes with his hands, wiping them roughly.

'I got your report, Robert, following the children's interviews,' Professor Copthorne continues in a steady tone. 'I know that one child was singled out for the worst abuse, but the others will have suffered secondary trauma from witnessing it, as well as seeing the domestic violence against their grandfather. I'm therefore recommending that the older children take part in family therapy with their mother. You too, Ryan, and your daughter. Linzi, isn't it? I don't feel it would be appropriate for Ethan to join in. We'll offer play therapy for him, hopefully as part of a pastoral package through school.

'We also host a weekly group for men who've lived through experiences similar to yours, Ryan. I recommend that you take up a place. Past participants have found it invaluable.'

Ryan nods and wipes his sleeve roughly over his face again. He hasn't raised his eyes once. Humiliated, he looks utterly broken.

When it's my turn to speak, I tell them about Caitlin's growing confidence and Bartley's progress in managing his emotions. 'He even forgot to bring his phone out with him this morning.'

'Ah, all to the good.' Professor Copthorne smiles. 'It sounds like they'll do very nicely with you, for the time being.'

'She's an absolute diamond,' Ryan says gruffly, taking me completely by surprise.

Robert nods in agreement. 'The children will stay with Rosie while we carry out a few more checks. Then they can hopefully be restored to your care, Ryan.' He turns to me. 'Rosie, Ryan will need support for the foreseeable, if you still have room in your hub?'

'Absolutely,' I say, smiling at Ryan. 'I'll check with the fostering team manager, but I think it will be fine.' The grandfather flicks a quick glance at me, gives a curt nod, then stares back at the ground.

'Looking long term,' Robert continues, 'do you have any idea how long until their mother will be fit for discharge?'

'Bonnie has made significant progress in the last week or so. In fact, she began to improve a couple of days after I suspended visits from her mother.'

Robert lifts an eyebrow. The professor nods. 'The nursing staff had noticed a change in Bonnie's mood after her mother's visits. That sometimes happens because family members remind the patient of what they're missing at home. But when we got the heads-up from the foster carer,' he says, with a nod in my direction, 'it clicked with us that Julie was a detrimental influence. It turns out she was using the visits to continue feeding her daughter a diet of toxic emotional abuse.

'Within days, Bonnie started to recognise how she'd been manipulated.' He looks at Robert. 'The incident that brought the children into care, for example, when Bonnie apparently left them in the house alone, was entirely staged by Julie. She'd insisted on giving Bonnie a night off and offered to babysit, then walked out after the children went to bed. Bonnie suspects she then called social services to report her.'

Robert pinches the bridge of his nose and winces. Ryan shakes his head.

'It's difficult to put an exact time frame on her release,' the professor continues. 'Moving forward, once she does get home, we'll assign her a volunteer with lived experience who'll be popping in for daily visits.'

'She'll need it,' another voice adds. We turn as Karen strides across the courtyard. Taking the seat next to mine, she reveals that ten minutes into the contact session Bartley reverted to his old ways. 'Bonnie tried her best but he was walking all over her, and lashing out at his sister. I ended the session early,' the social worker explains with a regretful look, then she looks at me. 'I've separated them. They're with my play therapists at the moment.'

'Oh dear,' Robert grimaces. 'That doesn't sound hopeful.'

'She'll cope,' Ryan snaps. 'The kids love her. We'll manage.'

The social worker looks unconvinced. 'I have some strategies that work well for Bartley, Robert,' I interject. 'Sometimes it takes a while for children to understand that newly established rules follow them wherever they go, and whoever they're with, so I'm not surprised Bartley reverted back to the way he used to behave towards his mum.'

I'm pleased to see the professor nodding his agreement. It breaks my heart to think that, after all they'd been through, the family might never get the chance to reunite. 'I could work through the strategies with Ryan, and then Bonnie, when she comes home. They don't work for every child, but as I say, Bartley responded well.'

Robert, perhaps hoping to make up for his laxity with Julie by taking a tough stance, still looks sceptical.

'Sounds like an excellent plan,' Professor Copthorne jumps in helpfully. The social worker, having been given little space to object, reddens and fumbles with his cravat. 'As I'm sure you've seen many times, Mrs Lewis, children have an astonishing ability to heal rapidly, when the right conditions are put in place. We mustn't forget the impact that coercive control has on the whole family. Happily,' the psychiatrist finishes, turning from me to Robert, 'the most effective way to move on from the abuse is by keeping the rest of the family intact, so they can all support each other.'

'Well, absolutely, I agree that often –'

'We humans are remarkably easy to manipulate,' Professor Copthorne smoothly interrupts Robert again. 'Consequently, someone with a narcissistic personality doesn't have to work very hard to press their agenda on those around them. One study we did recently illustrated the point to such great effect that we were all surprised, even though we'd anticipated the results. What we did,' he says, glancing from one to the other of us, 'was interview a group of individuals with a small screen behind our backs. For the first part of the interview the screen showed a row of shops, one of which was a funeral parlour.

'For the second set of questions the scene was changed, the undertakers replaced by a gift shop. What happened was astonishing. The sombre mood of the participants changed dramatically halfway through the interview, their answers suddenly scoring high on optimism and all the other wellbeing markers. When we spoke to them afterwards, not one had consciously noticed the screen, or what was being displayed on it. In effect, the shot of the funeral directors reminded their subconscious of their mortality and affected the way they viewed the world in that moment. Without them even realising.

'There are so many signals being fired at us from all directions every day. When those signals are consistently negative, we can be depressed without having any idea why. *Doctor, I have everything a person could wish for, a lovely home, good job, well-behaved children, and yet I just don't want to live any more.* I can't tell you how many times I've heard this from patients.'

'That's fascinating,' I say, looking between the doctor and Karen, who is nodding wholeheartedly.

'That's one of the reasons I love my job so much,' she says. 'You meet so many people with such different life circumstances, and at first you can't for the life of you work out what's brought them here. But they all have a story, and it never fails to surprise.'

The professor nods in agreement. We all fall silent.

'She never wanted any more children,' Ryan mumbles, just as we're pushing out our chairs, preparing to leave. Surprised by his sudden participation, there's half a second's pause before we settle back in our seats. 'She was adamant about it, when we got married. Which was fine with me. But then Bon got pregnant and Julie couldn't stand her hogging the limelight, not that the poor girl ever tried to.

'There was no discussion, nothing. With Jules it was always her way or the highway. And I knew what was coming. Sure enough, a few months later she announced she fell pregnant with Linzi.' He keeps his eyes focused on the ground and shakes his head. 'If the blokes I'd served with knew what had gone on in the last ten years, they'd never get their heads around it.

'They all loved Jules. Thought I was punching way above my weight. Which I was, of course. But when she turns, my God, it's rough. What she put Bonnie through,' he shakes his head again, looking slightly nauseous, 'I just didn't know how to stop it. It was so subtle sometimes, you know. I'd tell myself it was just complex mother–daughter stuff I had no business messing with.

'I thought about leaving, course I did. Many times. I was on the verge of doing it, but I couldn't leave the kids. Who knows what would've happened to them.' He scratches his head, as if he still can't work out what actually happened. 'Sometimes things were really good. Once she'd vented, she could go weeks before she'd tense up again. We'd be so happy, all of us, that I knew I had to stick with it.'

'You're a victim as well as the children, Mr Chambers,' Karen says gently. 'It's going to take time to process what you've all been through.'

She invites him to spend some time with Caitlin and Bartley, so I pop to the hospital cafeteria for a cup of tea.

Side by side an hour later, the children walk ahead of me into the afternoon sunshine. We've barely left the building when Bartley starts bumping into his sister. I find myself tensing for a second, but then Caitlin playfully bumps back into him. They giggle and jostle each other all the way back to the car.

Chapter Forty-One

A month later, on Friday 30 May, Des and I finally tie the knot. It's a low-key event at our local registry office with Jamie as best man and Emily and my mum as witnesses. Caitlin and of course our little Megan are enthusiastic flower girls, and Bartley, Ethan and Louis are page boys. I thought I'd have a job on my hands getting Bartley into a suit, but he was chuffed to bits when he first tried it on and insisted on wearing it to play darts with Jamie.

Consequently, his younger brothers are thrilled with theirs too. Throughout the service I'm distracted by Louis, who keeps looking down at his shiny new shoes with an admiring grin on his face.

'Only took us a decade,' Des smiles, as we make our way out onto the lane, where the children spray us with rice. Mum, ever the rebel, throws traditional, non-biodegradable confetti at us from her newly acquired wheelchair, much to Emily's chagrin.

We had planned to take everyone out for a meal afterwards, as long as my mum felt up to it, but Emily insists on us returning home. I walk into the kitchen in my glad rags ready to pull some pizzas out of the freezer, something easy to give myself an evening off from cooking, but my eye is caught by shifting light in the garden. A shadow flits across the patio doors, and then Emily throws them open. 'As if I was going to let you cook, Mum, on your wedding day.'

She links her arm through mine and leads me out onto the patio. Several tables have been draped with silk and large white bows, and they're all laden with food and bowls filled with colourful drinks and floating fruits. The glow from dozens of lanterns strung across the space in loose zig-zags lights up the whole garden. 'Jeez, you've outdone yourself, girl,' Des shakes his head as he follows us outside.

'Emily, I don't know what to say.' Choked, I give her a hug. I'd been so worried about how she might take the news that I'd almost turned Des down again. Both she and Jamie had been happy when I'd told them. Megan, over the moon, had immediately asked whether our marriage meant she could call Des 'Daddy'. He'd been chuffed to bits when I told him that. 'Thank you, darling. Were you in on this too?' I ask Jamie as he wheels his grandmother out to join us.

'Who d'you think did all the cooking, Ma?'

Emily grabs a celery stick and slaps him with it. 'You absolute liar, Jamie!' Caitlin and Megan giggle as Bartley joins in, and Mungo jumps up and snaps at the air, trying to grab their makeshift swords. Ethan passes Mungo a carrot to gnaw on instead.

'So much food! I won't have to cook for a month!'

'Ah well yes, about that …' Emily gives me a mysterious smile. 'There might not be much left by the end of the evening.'

Des and I exchange puzzled glances, and Mum looks at a loss as well. When the doorbell goes, it becomes clear that the beautifully decorated garden and the unexpected feast aren't the only surprises Emily has been keeping up her sleeve.

'I don't believe it.' I put my hands on my cheeks at the sight of the smiling nine-year-old coming into the hall. My eyes prick with tears. 'Come here, you.' I open my arms and Sarah grins, rushing forward to give me a hug. I wrote about Sarah's struggle with neonatal abstinence syndrome in *Helpless*. She was just a little dot when I picked her up from the maternity unit, and though she only spent her first six weeks of life with us before being adopted she still feels like one of the family. It's always a joy to see her.

Kate and Paul, Sarah's adopters, usher their growing brood into the house, closely followed by other family and friends, all of them secretly invited by Emily in the last few weeks.

By 8.30 p.m., our garden is bustling with people, some of whom I haven't seen for years. 'Look who's over there, Mum.' I lean over the back of her wheelchair and point to the far corner of the garden, where a young woman with light-brown plaits is rocking gently on the swing. Phoebe. The last decade falls away as I look at her. Memories of her disclosures on that very swing are softened by the knowledge that she's enjoyed nine happy and secure years since then, with her adoptive mother, Maxine.

Preferring to make an understated entrance via the side gate, Phoebe made an immediate beeline for the swing on arrival, and has barely spoken a word to anyone since planting herself there. Knowing that her autism makes large gatherings a challenge for her, the fact that she made the effort to come at all means all the more to me.

Mum's jaw drops. 'Well, blow me, is that Phoebe?! Look how big she's got. She's a grown woman now!'

Emily narrows her eyes and peers across the darkening space. 'Is she wearing headphones?'

'Yep, a vital accessory for every social occasion,' Jamie says, grinning. 'Classic Phoebe.'

Emily smiles fondly. 'What an absolute legend.'

Des kisses the top of my head as we stand together at the patio doors a while later, as the light shimmers over our unexpected guests.

Emily drapes a blanket lovingly over her grandmother's knees and pulls a chair up beside her, so she can hold her hand. My throat tightens at the sight, but I won't let my mind stray to the future and what the next few weeks might bring.

I'm not sure how we'll cope with the loss looming on the horizon, but I'm so pleased that at least we managed to have one final holiday as a three-generational, fostering family.

With Des's arm around my shoulder, I focus on the fragrant smoky air, Mungo's excited barks and the sight of Megan and Caitlin as they spin round and round in the middle of the lawn, hands joined together, their heads thrown back in carefree laughter.

I take a breath and savour the moment, taking in every detail so I'll remember it always.

Epilogue

I pay my last official Mockingbird visit to the Powell family a month later, on the fourth Thursday in June.

Caitlin greets me at the door with a bunch of flowers. 'From Mum and Grandad,' she says as she presses the bouquet into my arms. Her grin is slightly self-conscious, but she's a world away from the girl I met five months ago. Back in February she was so shy she could barely lift her head, let alone look me in the eye.

'From all of us really,' Bonnie says with a smile as she walks up the hall. Free from the clasp of addiction and the slow drip, drip of abuse, she's managed to gain a few pounds over the last two months. She's still slight and pale, but her cheeks are less hollowed out and her eyes are bright.

I've been visiting the family on alternate days since the children returned home three weeks ago. They made me feel so welcome that it was almost home from home. But today is different. Goodbyes are never easy, and there's a tension in the air that wasn't there before.

I decide to keep the visit brief as I follow Bonnie and Caitlin down the hall.

A light breeze from the open bi-fold doors greets me as I walk into the living area. Ethan and Bartley wave to me from the garden, where they're playing football, and Louis toddles over and puts his arms up to me for a carry. I scoop him up and watch as Caitlin and Linzi pick up where they left off, stencilling temporary glitter tattoos on each other's arms. The contrast with the tense, agitated children I'd met in late winter is like night and day and the sight warms my heart.

I'd gifted the family a fully stocked 'calm box' when they moved back to their grandfather's house. Armed with that and the three baskets technique, Ryan and then Bonnie, once she was released from hospital, quickly managed to lengthen Bartley's short fuse. Ryan found the regulating strategies useful in forging a new, healthier relationship with his daughter as well.

It took Linzi almost a week to accept that her father was in charge. She flounced around for several days giving me daggers and making repeated threats to call Childline, before finally conceding defeat.

'Julie's been charged with two counts of assault occasioning actual bodily harm,' Ryan tells me quietly in the kitchen, when we get a moment to ourselves. 'She's out on bail, but she's not allowed to contact us.' He sighs and looks at me from a lowered brow. 'Linzi wants to see her. Robert says he'll organise a supervised session. The rest of them don't want anything to do with her.' He pauses and adds gruffly, 'To be honest, neither do I.'

He doesn't mention that the CPS also filed a charge of engaging in sexual activity in the presence of a child against Julie, as well as Caitlin's father. According to Robert,

Trevor Penrose is adamant that he was coerced on the understanding that if he acquiesced Julie would allow him access to his daughter. Trevor strongly insists that he believed his daughter to be in school on the day in question. I hope, for Caitlin's sake, that there's a way of proving his case.

I spent ages puzzling over Julie's motivations for getting involved with Trevor, but then I remembered that Ryan had allowed Billy Harcourt to collect Bartley from school, against her wishes. Manipulating Trevor must have been Julie's way of taking control away from her husband, while simultaneously striking yet another a painful blow against Caitlin.

As Ryan, Bonnie and I exchange small talk over a cup of tea, my thoughts drift to Millie. The teenager has FaceTimed me a couple of times in the last month. Thankfully, the move into supported living has worked out well for her. The manager of the care home seems to have built a great rapport with the teenager, and apparently doesn't mind when Millie jokingly refers to her as 'Mum'.

I'm relieved that she'll have someone to support her through the coming months. Luke, her mother's partner, is awaiting trial after being charged with the rape of a child under 16, according to Joan. Millie will need to dig deep to find the strength to follow her disclosure through and give evidence against him. It beggars belief that, despite the charge, her mother has decided to stand by him, ostracising her daughter instead.

When I've finished my tea, Bonnie calls the boys in from the garden. Ethan charges over and throws his arms around my middle, but Bartley hovers by the door, his head hung low.

I'd accompanied Bonnie on a visit to the SENCo at Millfield a few days ago. Out of the grip of her mother's influence, Bonnie fully supported an application to the local authority for an EHCP. The process is likely to take months, but the SENCo is hopeful that Bartley will get the support he needs.

'Tell Jamie bye from me,' he mutters, his eyes fixed on the floor. The sight of the scar on his forearm triggers a memory of his disclosure the day he and Caitlin absconded from school. I've wondered many times whether he might have been spared the assault if I'd seen through Julie's glossy veneer sooner.

Having helped out on many domestic violence courses over the years and listened to women's experiences first-hand, my immediate assumption that Julie was the victim of abuse, instead of Ryan, is perhaps understandable.

Switch on the news any random day of the week and it quickly becomes apparent that violence against women and girls is rife, both in the UK and globally.

The majority of domestic abuse victims are women, and the perpetrators are overwhelmingly male. Female victims are more likely to experience repeated, sustained and severe abuse, and are also at far greater risk of being seriously injured or killed.

The Chambers' case is a reminder that while female violence against men is much rarer, it's a crime that impacts heavily on the children in the family, devastating their ability to stay calm and regulate their own emotions as well as their self-esteem and capacity to trust.

'That reminds me, Jamie and his bandmates are off to the recording studios next week,' I tell Bartley with a smile. 'He wondered if you'd like to join them one day?'

I'd already squared the invite with Bonnie, so I know he'll be allowed, if he wants to go. His head jerks up. 'Seriously?' he cries, his cheeks flushing with pleasure. 'Yeah! Course! I'd love to!'

I ruffle his hair then crouch down and give Louis a final cuddle. When I get to my feet, I'm surprised by an unexpected hug from Linzi. Once she'd forgiven me for helping to recalibrate the balance of power in the house, we got on like a house on fire. One afternoon, she'd even painted my nails.

When I turn to say goodbye to Caitlin, she bursts into tears. After I give her a hug, I'm pleased to see that she cuddles into her mum for comfort. With her arms around her daughter, Bonnie mouths a silent thank you over the top of her head. I smile and pat her arm.

It's a job to stop the tears forming in my own eyes as Ryan leads me down the hall.

'Thanks for everything,' he says at the door, sounding a bit choked. He clasps one of my hands between his. 'I mean it. Christ knows where we'd be if it weren't for you. I know they've called a stop to your visits, but don't be a stranger, please.'

The fostering team have already filled the Powells' slot in my hub, but I'm more than happy to support the family unofficially. I assure Ryan that I'll be there for them as long as they need me. It might well be that when they fully find their feet, our contact dwindles to the odd postcard here and there, and perhaps a card at Christmas. I'm comfortable with that.

When I first began fostering, I used to worry about how I'd cope with the inevitable 'letting go'. Over the years I've learned to appreciate that while many of the children who come into our home may not stay long, and we may never see them again, they always leave a trace. Not one of our placements has ended without us learning something new about ourselves, or each other.

The Powells may not even remember us when they're older, but I hope that in some small way we've made a difference in their lives. That's more than enough for me.

Acknowledgements

Lots of love and a big thank-you to my family. Also a massive thank-you to Andrew for his support, as well as lovely Ajda and the team at HarperCollins; your hard work is very much appreciated. Finally, thank you to my readers and a cyber-hug to the wonderfully warm and supportive community on my Facebook page, some of whom are now friends. You regularly make me smile – and sometimes laugh out loud.